DESIGNED FOR:

Fat Restricted Diets
Weight Loss Diets
Diabetic Diets

SAMPLE MENUS
INCLUDED

CONVENIENCE FOODS
CAKE MIXES
MUFFIN MIXES
SKILLET MEALS
RICE AND NOODLE MIXES
CONVERTED TO LOW FAT

THE
LOW - FAT
DOWN HOME
COOKBOOK
BY
MARY STANGL

OVER 450 KITCHEN TESTED RECIPES FOR
GREAT TASTING FOOD WITH REDUCED FAT

This book has been designed for people on a variety of diets such as fat-restricted diets, weight-loss diets and diabetic diets. Its purpose is to teach people how to prepare foods in a more healthful manner and to stimulate an awareness of the importance of good nutrition. Its end goal is to make low-fat cooking easy and fun.

Editor Patrick O. Stangl

Copyright 1994
Stangl Publishing Company
808 West Second Street
Ottumwa, IA 52501

FIRST EDITION
First Printing - September 1994
Second Printing - September 1999

Library of Congress Catalog Number 94-093870
International Standard Book Number 0-9631854-2-X

Printed by
Jumbo Jack's Cookbooks
Audubon, IA 50025

The Low-Fat
Down Home Cookbook

is dedicated to:

My husband, Pat, who had a massive stroke in
June of 1994. Through sheer determination and
unwavering positive thinking he has fought
his way back.
I am very proud of him.

It is also dedicated to:

Our support team who was there for us during
this difficult period and during the weeks
when I was recovering from surgery.
Pat's sister and her husband,
Marykay and Bud Mendez
my siblings,
Patty Hagerman, Donna Sheehan and Donald Jones
my cousin, Mary Long
and last, but not least, our neighbor and friend
Linda Degrofft

A special "thank you" is also extended to
Dr. Scott King.

Notes

Table of Contents

FAVORITE RECIPES

FROM MY COOKBOOK

Recipe Name	Page Number

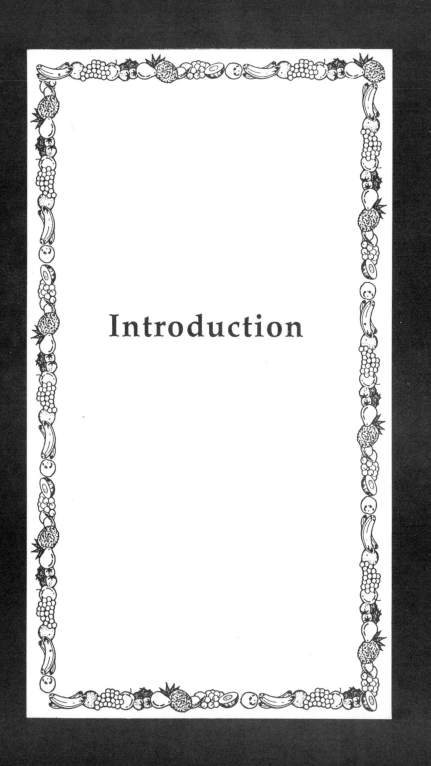

Introduction

Introduction

❖ ❖ ❖

The "Low-Fat Down Home Cookbook" has been designed to provide foods that taste great to people on a variety of diets—fat-restricted diets, weight-loss diets and diabetic diets.

The key to all of these diets is fat reduction. It's easy to understand why fat is the culprit in most diets. A gram of fat contains 9 calories while a gram of carbohydrates or protein contains only 4 calories.

I can recall the time when I would not even consider pasta, potatoes or bread on a diet. Years ago we were taught that carbohydrates were the downfall to successful dieting.

Now we are learning that carbohydrates and protein are what we should be eating and fat is what must be cut down in the diet.

We are very fortunate that manufacturers are recognizing the need for food lower in fat and are answering the call. More and more low-fat foods are appearing on the market.

In the early years of fat-restricted diets, many manufacturers got cute with their labeling. They would declare a food product "cholesterol-free" leading the consumer to believe that it was a good product when in truth it was loaded with fat.

The FDA has now stepped in and called for more honest labeling and complete labeling on products. However, this has not turned out as well as I had hoped and the consumer must still beware of the labeling. Read the section included in the book on the new labeling. You'll be surprised by what you find.

Whatever type of food you are preparing, the name of the game is convenience. For this reason I have tested some "box" convenient foods. I have had to change many of them a little to make them acceptable on a fat-restricted diet, but have done so successfully.

When starting on a fat-restricted diet you should be aware of the nutrients the body needs to function properly.

The body needs a balance of nutrients and it is important to understand just what nutrients are. The following outlines the nutrients we need on a daily basis and how they work in the body.

Carbohydrates are much needed nutrients. It is the function of the carbohydrate to provide the main supply of fuel to the body. In the perfect diet, carbohydrates would account for fifty % of the body's daily nutrients. On the diabetic diet a range of 40 to 60 grams of carbohydrates is allowed.

There are two types of carbohydrates—complex and simple. Simple carbohydrates include the sugar, honey and syrup based foods—foods the sweet tooth craves.

Simple carbohydrates contain next to no nutrients and are usually discouraged because of their lack of nutrition. It is for this reason that they are often referred to as "empty food". Too many simple carbohydrates are not believed to be beneficial and should be limited by everyone. It's best to stick, mostly, to complex carbohydrates.

Fat is another nutrient everyone needs on a daily basis. However, only 1 tablespoon of fat per day will supply more than the amount of fat the body needs.

Anything beyond this small amount of fat per day must be stored somewhere in (or on) the body. It's this storage system that accounts for artery blockage and subsequent heart attacks.

The American public has been carrying on a love affair with fat for years and most people consume more like a half of cup of fat per day than one tablespoon.

Saturated fat is the real culprit. This is the fat found in animals and animal by-products as well as in coconut, coconut oils and palm kernel oil.

The guideline for the diabetic is 20 % fat per day. Not a bad guideline for everyone.

Protein is the third essential nutrient. You might say that protein is in charge of the upkeep and maintenance of every tissue in the body.

Protein not only builds muscles, but it is in charge of determining the condition of the hair, enzymes, hemoglobin, hormones and even insulin.

For the average diet 20 % protein is recommended. The diabetic is allowed a range of 12 to 20 % of the daily diet.

Vitamins and Minerals are also important nutrients. Everyone needs calcium and iron to keep their bones and blood strong. However, other vitamins and minerals are needed by the body in varying amounts.

One of the best ways to insure you are feeding your body proper amounts of vitamins and minerals is to consume a balanced diet that includes the five major food groups.

It is recommended that people consume 2 to 4 servings of fruit; 3 to 5 servings of vegetables (include all types); 6 to 11 servings of bread, cereal and other grains; 5 to 7 ounces of meat; and 2 servings of milk, cheese or yogurt. A chart is included in the book showing the amount that constitutes a serving.

In the book, a serving is referred to as an exchange. Using the exchange system, as diabetics do, it is possible to plan meals and include all food groups and nutrients easily and simply.

Special attention should be paid to the bread food group. The National Cancer Institute recommends that people consume 10 to 35 grams of fiber per day and that it come from a variety of sources. It is believed that high-fiber diets may prevent or help to lower the rates of colon cancer.

Water is the most forgotten nutrient. Many people do not even consider water to be a nutrient since it is such an everyday thing to drink water and due to the fact that it contains no calories.

It is really not that difficult to maintain a healthy diet. The most difficult part is in developing the good habit of eating properly.

The ideal healthy diet is considered to consist of 50 % carbohydrates, 20 % protein and 30 % fat.

The recipes in this book, for the most part, are kept well below the 30 % mark. When fat is decreased in the diet, the percentages of carbohydrates and protein go up—and this is all right.

The dessert recipes call for artificial sweetener, however, the amount of sugar it is replacing is listed and sugar can be used if desired. Desserts should be kept at a minimum and fruits should be used as desserts in most cases.

Salt has been used in the recipes in moderate amounts. In some recipes a sodium-free seasoned salt is used. More people than not are still using salt and prefer it be used in recipe books. However, if you eliminate or cut down on the salt, it is easy to change the sodium breakdown. Salt contains 2,132 milligrams of sodium per teaspoon. Simply recalculate the sodium using this figure. A good rule of thumb when using sodium is to use it at the stove, in moderate amounts, and not use it at the table. I season foods lightly with salt at the stove, but we never salt at the table.

I have also tested some convenience foods to allow the reader to use them without the "high-fat" guilt trip. We live in a busy world and cooking needs to be made as easy as possible.

The secret to a low-fat diet, is to prepare foods lower in fat and to become an ingredient label reader. Also, keep the foods balanced in the diet.

Balance is important. If you consume a high-fat food at noon, the evening meal should be low in fat to offset the high-fat meal.

After you have been on a low-fat diet for a few weeks, you will be surprised by how much high-fat foods turn you off. At least give low-fat foods an honest try. You will be glad you did. Bon appetit!

❖ ❖ ❖

How Much Fat and Cholesterol Should Be Consumed Daily?

A great deal of research has been done in an attempt to determine the amount of fat and cholesterol to be consumed on a daily basis. Most experts accept the guidelines put out by the American Heart Association as being a reliable dietary guideline. The American Heart Association advises that no more than 30 % of a person's daily caloric consumption come in the form of fat. Saturated fats, which are found in animal meats and animal by-products, coconut oils, cocoa butter and many hydrogenated shortenings should not exceed 10 % of the daily caloric intake.

One of the best ways to cut saturated fat in the diet is to consume less red meat and eat more poultry, fish and dried beans and peas.

The recommended allowance of fat per day should not exceed 40 grams for women and 60 grams for men. As for cholesterol, it is recommended that no more than 300 milligrams of cholesterol be consumed daily based on no more than 100 milligrams per 1,000 calories.

The following chart shows the amount of fat and cholesterol allowed for the number of calories consumed.

❖ ❖ ❖

Daily Calories Consumed	30% Daily Calories	Grams of Fat	20% Daily Calories	Grams Of Fat	10% Daily Calories	Grams Of Fat	Daily Mg Cholest. Allowed
1,000	300	33.3	200	22.2	100	11.1	100
1,100	330	36.7	220	24.4	110	12.2	110
1,200	360	40.0*	240	26.7	120	13.3	120
1,300	390	42.2	260	28.9	130	14.4	130
1,400	420	46.7	280	31.1	140	15.6	140
1,500	450	50.0	300	33.3	150	16.7	150
1,600	480	53.3	320	35.6	160	17.8	160
1,700	510	56.7	340	37.8	170	18.9	170
1,800	540	60.0*	360	40.0*	180	20.0	180
1,900	570	63.3	380	42.2	190	21.1	190
2,000	600	66.7	400	44.4	200	22.2	200
2,100	630	70.0	420	46.7	210	23.3	210
2,200	660	73.3	440	48.9	220	24.4	220
2,300	690	76.7	460	51.1	230	25.6	230
2,400	720	80.0	480	53.3	240	26.7	240
2,500	750	83.3	500	55.6	250	27.8	250
2,600	780	86.7	520	57.8	260	28.9	260
2,700	810	90.0	540	60.0*	270	30.0	270
2,800	340	93.3	560	62.2	280	31.1	280
2,900	870	96.7	580	64.4	290	32.2	290
3,000	900	100.0	600	66.7	300	33.3	300

According to the American Heart Association guidelines, no more than 30% of total calories consumed should be fat calories. In instances where there is a health condition involved, a physician may recommend an even lower percentage of calories consumed be made up of fat. The chart shows the amount of calories consumed daily and the grams of fat and the milligrams of cholesterol allowed for calories consumed. Cholesterol is given for 10% of caloires consumed. Fat is given for 10%, 20% and 30% of calories consumed.
*NOTE: It is further recommended that women consume no more than 40 grams of fat per day and men consume no more than 60 grams of fat per day.

Fat Content of Foods

Food Group	Very Low Fat 9% of calories or less	Low Fat 10-29% of calories	Moderate Fat 30-49% of calories	High Fat 50% of calories or more
BEVERAGES	Alcoholic beverages Coffee Fruit drinks Lemonade Tea			
DAIRY PRODUCTS	Cheese (1% butterfat) Dry cottage cheese Egg substitute Egg whites Milk (skim, skim evaporated) Yogurt (home recipe)	Buttermilk Cheese (2-3% butterfat) Cottage cheese (low-fat) Milk (1%) Milk shake (with ice milk & 1% milk) Pudding (tapioca or vanilla, made with 1% milk) Sherbet Yogurt, commercial	Cheese (4-8% butterfat) Cottage cheese (cream style) Chocolate pudding Ice cream Milk (2%) Milk (whole)	Cheese (10% and over) Eggnog Evaporated milk Half & Half cream Non-dairy whipped topping Powdered non-dairy creamer Premium ice cream Sour cream
FATS and OILS				Butter and margarine Lard Oil (safflower, corn, olive sunflower, etc.) Salad dressing Vegetable shortening

Fat Content of Foods

Food Group	Very Low Fat 9% of calories or less	Low Fat 10-29% of calories	Moderate Fat 30-49% of calories	High Fat 50% of calories or more
FRUITS	Apple Apricot Banana Berries Candied fruit plus citron and ginger Cherry Date Fig Fruit cocktail Fruit juices Grapefruit Grapes Kiwi Lemon Mandarin orange Melons Nectarine Orange Peach Pear Pineapple Plum Raisins Rhubarb Tangerine			

Fat Content of Foods

Food Group	Very Low Fat 9% of calories or less	Low Fat 10-29% of calories	Moderate Fat 30-49% of calories	High Fat 50% of calories or more
GRAIN PRODUCTS	Air popped popcorn Angel food cake Bagel Cereal (cooked cream of rice, farina, wheat) Cereal (ready-to-eat) Cornflakes Bran Flakes Grapenuts Rice Krispies Puffed Rice Shredded Wheat Total Wheaties Wheat Chex	Animal crackers Bread (Rye, raisin white, whole wheat) Buns (hamburger or hot dog) Cereal, cooked (oatmeal) Cereal (ready-to-eat) Cheerios, Raisin Bran Dinner rolls Fig bars Graham crackers Melba toast Soda crackers Tortilla (flour) Zwieback	Biscuits Brownies Cakes Cookies (oatmeal, sandwich) Croissant Croutons (home recipe) Fried snack pie Granola Muffin Oil popped popcorn Pancake Sweet rolls Vanilla wafers Waffle	Cheesecake Cookies (chocolate chip, peanut butter) Corn chips Doughnuts Pie crust
LEGUMES, NUTS and SEEDS	Cooked dried beans Carob Lentils Split peas Water chestnuts	Pork and beans	Cooked soybeans	Almonds Cashews Coconut Macadamia nuts Peanuts, dry roasted oil roasted Peanut butter Pecans

Fat Content of Foods

Food Group	Very Low Fat 9% of calories or less	Low Fat 10-29% of calories	Moderate Fat 30-49% of calories	High Fat 50% of calories or more
LEGUMES, NUTS and SEEDS (Continued)				Pistachio nuts Pumpkin seeds Sesame seeds Sunflower seeds Tofu Walnuts (black, California)
MEAT, EGGS, FISH and POULTRY	Egg substitute Egg white Lobster Shrimp, boiled Tuna, water packed	Beef, lean only Flank steak Round steak Clams Corned beef Crab, canned or fresh Fish, baked, broiled or poached Egg substitute, my recipe Oysters, canned or fresh Salmon, fresh Scallops, steamed Turkey, baked or broiled	Beef, lean only Chuck roast Filet mignon Ground round New York strip Porterhouse T-Bone Tenderloin Rump roast Round roast Sirloin Fish, fried Fish sandwich Fish sticks Ham, lean only Hamburger Lamb chop, lean only Liver Macaroni & cheese Pork, lean only, 10% fat Ham, picnic ham	Bacon Bologna Beef, lean & fat Brisket Chuck steak Club steak Ground beef Ground chuck Pot roast Ribeye roast Ribeye steak Standing rib roast Spareribs Pot pies (beef, chicken, tuna) Cheeseburger Deviled ham Eggs, however prepared Hot dogs Lamb chops, lean and fat

Fat Content of Foods

Food Group	Very Low Fat 9% of calories or less	Low Fat 10-29% of calories	Moderate Fat 30-49% of calories	High Fat 50% of calories or more
MEAT, EGGS, FISH and POULTRY (Continued)			Fresh pork, lean only, 13-20% fat Boston butt Roast Chop or loin Shoulder Shrimp, fried Salmon, canned, pink or red Spaghetti & meatballs Trout (Brook) Tuna, oil packed Veal	Pork, lean and fat Fresh 23-30% fat Boston butt Ground Ham, loin picnic Shoulder Spareribs Sausages Luncheon meats Taco Trout (Rainbow)
SOUPS, SAUCES and GRAVIES	Apple butter Apple sauce Barbecue sauce Butterscotch topping Caramel topping Catsup Chili sauce Cranberry sauce Horseradish Marshmallow topping Mustard Soy sauce	Bouillon Gravy (mix) Soups made with water -- Tomato Vegetable beef	Gravy (home recipe) Soups made with milk--skim or 1% White sauce (mix)	Cocoa Mayonnaise Soups made with whole milk All creamed soups Soups made with water -- Cream of chicken Cream of mushroom Cheese sauce Hollandaise Tartar sauce White sauce

Fat Content of Foods

Food Group	Very Low Fat 9% of calories or less	Low Fat 10-29% of calories	Moderate Fat 30-49% of calories	High Fat 50% of calories or more
SOUPS, SAUCES and GRAVIES (Continued)	Strawberry topping Tomato paste Tomato sauce Worcestershire sauce			
SWEETS	Gelatin dessert Gumdrops Honey Jam Jelly Jelly beans Marmalade Marshmallows Mints Popsicle Molasses Syrup	Butterscotch Caramels Fudge 3 Musketeers Tootsie Roll	Malted milk balls Mars candy bar M & M's Raisins, chocolate covered Peanut brittle Snickers	Chocolate bars Chocolate chips Chocolate-coated peanuts Chocolate kisses Mr. Goodbar Nestle's Crunch Peanut Butter Cups
VEGETABLES	Artichoke Beans, green, Italian, kidney, snap & wax Bean sprouts Beets Brussels Sprouts Broccoli Cabbage	Asparagus Spinach	French fries Hash browns Potatoes au gratin Potatoes (scalloped)	French fried onion rings Potato salad Potato chips Olives

Fat Content of Foods

Food Group	Very Low Fat 9% of calories or less	Low Fat 10-29% of calories	Moderate Fat 30-49% of calories	High Fat 50% of calories or more

VEGETABLES (Continued)	Carrot
	Cauliflower
	Celery
	Corn
	Cucumber
	Eggplant
	Lettuce
	Mushroom
	Onion
	Parsley
	Peas
	Pepper
	Pickles
	Potatoes
	  Baked
	  Boiled
	  Mashed
	Pumpkin
	Radishes
	Squash
	Sweet Potatoes
	Tomatoes
	Turnips
	Tnip greens
	Watercrest
	Yams			

What You Should Know About Manufacturer Labeling
Is The American Public Once Again Being Deceived?

We have been reading about the labeling guidelines the Food and Drug Administration is requiring of manufacturers. Myself, I was excited at the thought of the nutritional breakdown being right there with no little quirks that would fool me.

At first glance the new labeling appeared to be laid out plain and simple in easy to understand terms. Following the "Amount per Serving" caption, I found the calories listed along with the calories from fat. It was given in two columns—"As Packaged" and "Prepared".

Just from the total calories and total calories from fat, I could tell at a glance if the product was low in fat.

However, I soon discovered that once I passed this point it became a game of **buyer beware**. The next figure shown—a little below the total calories and calories from fat, was the "Total Fat".

Now, when I think of total fat in a product, I think of the total fat in the prepared product. But what about the little asterisk beside this figure? Reading the fine print below I discover that the total fat given was for the total fat in the mix. It did not include the fat contained in the margarine and milk to be added during preparation.

From this point on the numbers I am going to show are from an actual box of convenience food.

I glanced at the total fat and saw that the prepared mix was shown as 19 %. This would be acceptable. But, wait a minute. I had just read that the total calories for a prepared serving was 320 and the calories from fat were 90. Something was wrong. When I calculate these figures, I discover that the total fat is 28 % instead of 19 %.

Checking the label closer I spot some fine writing that shows that column to be "Daily Values***". Reading the fine print below, I discover that ***"Percent Daily Values are based on a 2,000 calorie diet. Your daily values may be higher or lower depending on your calorie needs."

Most people on a low-fat diet do not consume 2,000 calories a day. And why are the total percentage figures not based on the calories in a serving instead of the total daily calories?

Let's face it. We all know the answer to this. This little deceptive move is to make the product look lower in fat to the consumer than it really is. How many of us actually read the fine print at the bottom of the labeling when we check for fat percentages.

More people than not are glancing at the total fat and the percentage figures and assuming they represent a serving of the product.

IT IS, THEREFORE, VERY IMPORTANT THAT YOU NOT ALLOW THE MANUFACTURERS TO TRICK YOU INTO PURCHASING THEIR PRODUCT. USE ONLY THE FIGURES SHOWING "TOTAL CALORIES FOR PREPARED SERVING" AND "TOTAL CALORIES FROM FAT". THIS WILL GIVE YOU BASICALLY WHAT YOU NEED TO KNOW. AS FOR THE REMAINING INFORMATION IN THE LABELING SECTION READ THEM CAREFULLY AND MAKE VERY SURE YOU ARE AWARE OF WHAT THEY REPRESENT. MORE THAN LIKELY THEY WILL BE BASED ON 2,000 CALORIES PER DAY INSTEAD OF A SERVING OF THE PRODUCT.

I must confess that I am very disappointed with the new labeling and how it is designed to deceive the public. We can only hope that someday the manufacturers will be honest and above board enough to put figures on their packages to assist the consumer in controlling their fat intake instead of tricking them into buying their product.

❖ ❖ ❖

The Exchange Diet

When people hear the word "diet" it often causes a negative bell to go off in their head. Unfortunately most people don't think of being on a diet as a pleasant adventure.

For many years the American public has carried on a love affair with foods high in fat as well as foods that can be harmful to them in the long run.

Today, however, people are connecting diet with good nutrition. And good nutrition is becoming more and more popular as its importance becomes evident with quality living.

Once again, the word nutrition leads us to the "diet" word. Therefore, for starters it is important to develop a good attitude about nutrition and diets. This begins with the forming of good eating habits so a good nutritious diet is the norm.

It all boils down to forming a good lifestyle; one that will develop a healthy you as the years pass by.

There was a time when the exchange system in the diet was used only by the diabetic. Today, however, it is used by many and is a very acceptable way to keep good nutrition on track.

In this book, I have tried to make following the exchange system as easy as possible. However, it does not mean that you can only use recipes contained in the pages of this book. On the following pages you will find a list of the exchanges that can be moved around to fit your own family.

The secret to successfully using the exchange system is balance. You must consume foods from each food group daily.

For the fat-restricted diet it will mean keeping fat consumption at the level recommended by your physician. The American Heart Association recommends that fat consumption be kept to under 30 % of the total calories consumed.

For weight-reduction diets it will mean keeping fat in the 10 to 15 % range of total calories consumed. The number of calories consumed each day should be recommended by your physician. It is always wise when going on a weight-reduction diet to consult a physician.

For the diabetic it will mean keeping fat in the 20 % range. Once again, the number of calories consumed should be determined by the physician or a dietitian.

Using the exchange system may seem complicated in the beginning. To better understand how to use it, consult the sample menus in the book. In no time you will be planning your own menus to fit your lifestyle. The key to success is to plan ahead. A week of pre-planned menus is best, but if this doesn't work for you, plan at least a day ahead.

When using the exchange system, I recommend that you count your calories and grams of fat. If you select foods from all of the food groups, there should be no problems with consuming the proper amount of nutrients. Always try to make cooking and nutrition as simple as possible.

You'll be surprised by how quickly this type of eating becomes the norm for you and by how little sacrifice you are really making. There are very few foods that you can't have. They just must be prepared with less fat and with nutrition in mind. Good luck!

❖ ❖ ❖

The Milk Exchange

One exchange of milk contains 12 grams of carbohydrates, 8 grams of protein, just a trace of fat and approximately 80 calories.

You should have 2 servings of milk per day—teens should have 4 servings.

Skim milk	1 cup
Non-fat dry milk granules (or powder)	1/3 cup (dry)
Evaporated skim milk (canned)	1/2 cup
Buttermilk made from skim milk	1 cup
Yogurt, plain unflavored made from skim milk	1 cup

Skim milk products have improved drastically over the years and are not difficult to adapt to. Using skim milk products is an easy way to cut a great deal of fat from the diet.

❖ ❖ ❖

Vegetable Exchanges

One vegetable exchange contains about 5 grams of carbohydrates, 2 grams of protein, only a trace of fat and 25 calories.

You should have 3 to 5 servings of vegetables each day and should include all types of vegetables—dark green, deep yellow, starchy (in bread exchange), legumes (in bread exchange) and other.

Dark Green

Broccoli	1/2 cup
GREENS	
Beet	1/2 cup
Chards	1/2 cup
Collards	1/2 cup
Dandelion	1/2 cup
Kale	1/2 cup
Mustard	1/2 cup
Spinach	1/2 cup
Turnip	1/2 cup

Vegetable Exchanges

Romaine Lettuce	1/2 cup
Spinach	1/2 cup

Deep Yellow

Carrots	1/2 cup
Pumpkin	1/2 cup
Sweet Potatoes	1/2 cup
Winter Squash	1/2 cup

Starchy
These will be found in the bread exchange.

Dry Beans and Peas (Legumes)
These will be found in the bread exchange.

Other Vegetables

Artichokes	1/2 cup
Asparagus	1/2 cup
Bean and Alfalfa Sprouts	1/2 cup
Beets	1/2 cup
Brussels Sprouts	1/2 cup
Cabbage	1/2 cup
Cauliflower	1/2 cup
Celery	1/2 cup
Eggplant	1/2 cup
Green Beans	1/2 cup
Green Peppers	1/2 cup
Mushrooms	1/2 cup
Okra	1/2 cup
Onions (mature and green)	1/2 cup
Rhubarb	1/2 cup
Sauerkraut	1/2 cup
String Beans	1/2 cup
Summer Squash	1/2 cup
Tomatoes	1/2 cup
Turnips	1/2 cup
Vegetable Juices	1/2 cup
Zucchini	1/2 cup

Raw Vegetables that can be used as a Free Food
Chicory
Chinese Cabbage

Vegetable Exchanges

Cucumbers
Endive
Escarole
Lettuce
Parsley
Pickles, Dill
Radishes
Watercrest

❖ ❖ ❖

Fruit Exchanges

One exchange of fruit contains about 10 grams of carbohydrates and 40 calories.

You should have 2 to 4 servings of fruit per day.

Apple	1 small
Apple Juice	1/3 cup
Applesauce (unsweetened)	1/2 cup
Apricots, Fresh	2 medium
Apricots, Dried	4 halves
Banana	1/2 small
Blackberries (fresh or canned)	1/2 cup
Blueberries (fresh or canned)	1/2 cup
Cantaloupe	1 cup diced pieces
Cherries (fresh or canned)	10 large
Cider	1/3 cup
Cranberries, cooked	1/2 cup
Dates	2
Figs, Fresh	1
Figs, Dried	1
Grapefruit	1/2
Grapefruit Juice	1/2 cup
Grapes	12
Grape Juice	1/4 cup
Mango	1/2 small
Honeydew Melon	1/8 medium
Kiwi	1 small
Nectarine	1 small
Orange	1 small

Fruit Exchanges

Orange Juice	1 small
Papaya	3/4 cup
Peach	1 medium
Pear	1 small
Persimmon, Native	1 medium
Pineapple	1/2 cup
Pineapple Juice	1/3 cup
Plums	2 medium
Prunes	2 medium
Prune Juice	1/4 cup
Raisins	2 Tablespoons
Raspberries (fresh or canned)	1/2 cup
Strawberries (fresh)	1/2 cup
Tangerine	1 small

❖ ❖ ❖

Bread Exchanges

One exchange of bread contains about 15 grams of carbohydrates, 2 grams of protein, trace of fat and 70 calories.

You should have 6 to 11 servings from the bread exchange each day.

Bread

Bagel, 1 small	1/2
Bread, reduced calorie, wheat or white	2 slices
Bread, whole wheat or white	1 slice
Bread, French	1 slice
Bread, Italian	1 slice
Bread, Rye	1 slice
Bread, Pumpernickle	1 slice
Bread, Raisin	1 slice
Dried Bread Crumbs	3 Tablespoons
English Muffin, small	1/2
Frankfurter Bun	1/2
Frankfurter Bun, reduced calorie	1
Hamburger Bun	1/2
Hamburger Bun, reduced calorie	1

Bread Exchanges

Roll, Dinner	1
Tortilla, 6 inch	1

Cereal

Bran Flakes	1/2 cup
Other Low Sugar Cereals	3/4 cup
Puffed Cereal (unfrosted)	1 cup
Cooked Cereal	1/2 cup

Pasta, Rice and Grains

Barley, cooked	1/2 cup
Cornmeal, dry	2 Tablespoons
Flour, dry	2 1/2 Tablespoons
Grits, cooked	1/2 cup
Macaroni, cooked	1/2 cup
Noodles, cooked	1/2 cup
Popcorn (dry popped, no-fat added—large kernels)	3 cups
Rice, cooked	1/2 cup
Spaghetti, cooked	1/2 cup
Wheat Germ, dry	1/4 cup

Crackers

Arrowroot	3
Graham, 2 1/2-inch square	2
Oyster	20
Pretzels, 3 1/3 x 1/8-inch	25
Rye Wafers, 2 x 3 1/2-inch	3
Saltines	6
Soda, 2 1/2-inch square	4

Dried Beans, Peas and Lentils

Black Beans, cooked	1/2 cup
Black-Eyed Peas, cooked	1/2 cup
Chickpeas (Garbanzos), cooked	1/2 cup
Kidney Beans, cooked or canned	1/2 cup
Lentils, cooked	1/2 cup
Mung Beans, cooked	1/2 cup
Navy Beans, cooked	1/2 cup
Pinto Beans, cooked	1/2 cup
Split Peas, cooked	1/2 cup

❖ ❖ ❖

Starchy Vegetables

Corn	1/3 cup
Corn on the cob	1 small
Hominy	1/3 cup
Lima Beans	1/2 cup
Parsnips	2/3 cup
Peas, Green, canned or frozen	1/2 cup
Potatoes, White or Red	1 small
Potatoes, Mashed	1/2 cup
Pumpkin, cooked	3/4 cup
Sweet Potato, cooked	1/4 cup
Winter Squash (Acorn or Butternut), cooked	1/2 cup
Yams, cooked	1/4 cup

❖ ❖ ❖

Meat Exchanges

One exchange of lean meat (1 ounce) contains about 7 grams of protein, 3 grams of fat and 55 calories.

You should have 5 to 7 ounces of meat daily.

Beef

Chipped Beef (this is usually high in sodium)	1 ounce
Chuck Steak, all visible fat removed	1 ounce
Chuck Roast, all visible fat removed	1 ounce
Flank Steak, all visible fat removed	1 ounce
Ground Round (or diet lean)	1 ounce
Round Steak (bottom or top) lean only	1 ounce
Rump Roast, lean only	1 ounce
Thin Sliced Packaged Beef	1 ounce

Cheese

Cottage cheese, cream-style less than 5 % butterfat	1/4 cup

Meat Exchanges

Cottage cheese, dry	1/4 cup
"Free" No-Fat Shredded Cheddar	2 ounces
"Free" No-Fat Shredded Mozzarella	2 ounces
"Free" No-Fat American	1 slice
Any cheese containing less than	
5 % butterfat	1 ounce

Fish

Any Fresh or Frozen (unbreaded)	
Fish	1 ounce
Clams	5
Crab, canned	1/4 cup
Lobster, canned	1/4 cup
Mackerel, canned	1/4 cup
Oysters	5 or 1 ounce
Salmon (skin discarded)	1/4 cup
Scallops	5 or 1 ounce
Shrimp	5 or 1 ounce
Tuna, water packed	1/4 cup

Lamb

Leg, lean only	1 ounce
Rib, lean only	1 ounce
Sirloin, lean only	1 ounce
Loin—Roast or Chops	1 ounce
Shank, lean only	1 ounce
Shoulder, lean only	1 ounce

Pork

Canadian Bacon, all visible	
fat removed	1 ounce
Ham, Smoked—center slices only,	
all visible fat removed	1 ounce
Tenderloin, all visible fat removed	1 ounce

Poultry

Chicken Breast, no skin, no-fat	1 ounce
Chicken, thin sliced breast,	
packaged	1 ounce
Turkey Breast, no skin, no-fat	1 ounce
Turkey Breast, ground	1 ounce
Turkey Breast Sausage	1 ounce

Meat Exchanges

Turkey, thin sliced, packaged	1 ounce
Cornish Hen, no skin	1 ounce

Veal

Cutlets	1 ounce
Leg, all visible fat removed	1 ounce
Loin, all visible fat removed	1 ounce
Rib, all visible fat removed	1 ounce
Shank, all visible fat removed	1 ounce
Shoulder, all visible fat removed	1 ounce

❖ ❖ ❖

Fat Exchanges

One fat exchange contains 5 grams of fat and 45 calories.

Fats should be avoided as much as possible. Less than one tablespoon of fat is needed daily.

Avocado (4-inches in diameter)	1/8
Margarine, no more than 6 grams of fat per tablespoon	1 teaspoon
Nuts:	
Almonds	5 small
Pecans	10 whole
Spanish Peanuts	20 whole
Virginia Peanuts	10 whole
Walnuts	6 small
Other Nuts	6 small
Oil—Canola, Corn, Cottonseed, Olive, Safflower, Soy, Sunflower	1 teaspoon
Olives	5 small

❖ ❖ ❖

Planning Menus Using the Exchange System

Menu planning is really not that difficult. Study the lists under the different exchange listings. You will be surprised by the variety of foods to choose from.

Also, every recipe in this book can be used in menu planning. For the convenience of the reader, I have tested some convenience foods and also included them. They must be altered to remove some of the fat, but they really do taste good and are easy to prepare.

The main thing to remember when planning menus is to include foods from every food group. It's best if you can do that at each meal, but this is not always possible—for example, breakfast is not the best place for vegetables every day.

When planning, don't overlook the fact that the starchy vegetables are listed with the bread exchange.

And don't pig out on desserts. Desserts containing sugar can take up too many of your precious exchanges. The simple fact is that sugar is an empty food and contains next to no nutrition, so avoid it as much as possible.

On the following pages you will find some sample menus. I have listed only the calories and the fat along with the food exchanges. Keep things as simple as possible when planning menus.

If you try to balance out the carbohydrates and protein, you will go crazy. The truth is, that if your meals are balanced and you choose from all of the food groups, the protein and carbohydrates will take care of themselves.

It should be noted at this point that we all need five to seven ounces of meat each day. Do be sure your meal planning includes the proper protein.

Try the sample menus or make some of your own. Not only will you find it fun to plan nutritious meals for your family, but you will discover that it is really not all that difficult.

❖ ❖ ❖

Menus

1200 Calories—Day One
(Approximately 12 % fat for day)

Breakfast
2 slices whole wheat bread
1 teaspoon no-fat tub margarine (optional)
2 teaspoons unsweetened all-fruit jam
1 (8 ounce) glass skim milk

Calories: 255   **Fat:** 2.8 grams
Exchanges: 2 bread, 1 milk, 1 fruit

Lunch
Chicken Strip Sandwich (see index)
8 ounces skim milk
1 small peach

Calories: 401   **Fat:** 5.8 grams
Exchange: 3 meats, 1 bread, 1 milk, 2 vegetable, 1 fruit

Dinner
Vegetable Meatloaf with Vegetables (see index)
2 slices Dill bread (see index)
1 tablespoon no-fat margarine (optional)
Strawberries with Strawberries (see index)

Calories: 478   **Fat:** 8.1 grams
Exchanges: 2 meat, 2 bread, 3 vegetable, 1 milk, 2 fruit

Evening Snack
3 cups air-popped corn—no butter added

Calories: 70   **Fat:** trace
Exchange: 1 bread

Daily Totals
Calories: 1,204   **Fat:** 16.7 grams
Exchanges: 5 meat, 6 bread, 3 milk, 5 vegetable, 4 fruit

❖ ❖ ❖

1200 Calories—Day Two
(Approximately 11 % fat for the day)

Breakfast
1 Bagel (see index)
2 tablespoons "Free" no-fat cream cheese
1/3 cup unsweetened apple juice
1 banana

Calories: 271   **Fat:** 0.7 grams
Exchanges: 2 bread, 1/4 milk, 3 fruit

Lunch
Turkey Club Sandwich (see index)
Relishes (see index)
8 ounces skim milk

Calories: 366   **Fat:** 5.1 grams
Exchanges: 2 meat, 2 bread, 1 milk, 1 1/2 vegetable

Dinner
Salmon Balls with Carrots and Potatoes (see index)
Deluxe Tossed Salad (see index)
2 slices reduced-calorie whole wheat bread
1 tablespoon no-fat margarine (optional)
Sea Foam Salad (see index)

Calories: 496   **Fat:** 8.6 grams
Exchanges: 3 meat, 2 bread, 2 vegetable, 1 milk, 1 1/2 fruit

Evening Snack
1/2 cup seedless grapes

Calories: 48   **Fat:** trace
Exchange: 1 fruit

Daily Totals
Calories: 1,181   **Fat:** 14.4 grams
Exchanges: 5 meat, 6 bread, 2 1/4 milk, 5 1/2 fruit, 3 1/2 vegetable

❖ ❖ ❖

1200 Calories—Day Three
(Approximately 12 % fat for day)

Breakfast
1/4 cup egg substitute, scrambled (see index)
2 slices reduced-calorie whole wheat toast
1 tablespoon "Free" no-fat margarine (optional)
1 tablespoon unsweetened all-fruit jam
8 ounces skim milk

Calories: 251   **Fat:** 2.6 grams
Exchange: 1 meat, 1 bread, 1 milk, 1 fruit

Lunch
Flounder on a Bun (see index)
New Potato, Potato Salad (see index)
8 ounces skim milk
Simple Fruit Salad (see index)

Calories: 407   **Fat:** 4.6 grams
Exchanges: 2 meat, 2 bread, 1 milk, 1/2 vegetable, 1 fruit, 1/2 fat

Dinner
Easy Beef Skillet (see index)
Deluxe Tossed Salad (see index)
1 Sour Cream Roll (see index)
1 tablespoon "Free" no-fat margarine (optional)
Six-Cup Salad (see index)

Calories: 496   **Fat:** 8.4 grams
Exchanges: 3 meat, 2 bread, 1 milk, 2 vegetable, 1 1/2 fruit

Evening Snack
Small apple

Calories: 40   **Fat:** trace
Exchange: 1 fruit

Daily Totals
Calories: 1,194   **Fat:** 15.6 grams
Exchanges: 6 meat, 5 bread, 3 milk, 2 1/2 vegetable*, 3 1/2 fruits, 1 1/2 fat

*It appears that this menu is short of vegetables for the day; however, there is a starchy vegetable (potato) listed in the bread exchanges making the vegetable exchanges sufficient. Keep this in mind when planning menus yourself—the starchy vegetables are listed in the bread exchange, but should be counted as a vegetable also when accounting for the vegetables for the day.

❖ ❖ ❖

1200 Calories—Day Four
(Approximately 10 % fat for the day)

Breakfast
1/2 cup cooked oatmeal
2 to 3 packages artificial sweetener of choice
4 ounces skim milk
2 slices reduced-calorie whole wheat toast
1 tablespoon unsweetened all-fruit jam
1/2 banana

Calories: 268   **Fat:** 2.4 grams
Exchanges: 2 bread, 1 milk, 1 fruit

Lunch
Tuna Salad Sandwich (see index)
Relishes (seed index)
8 ounces skim milk
Small apple

Calories: 371   **Fat:** 4.1 grams
Exchanges: 2 meat, 1 1/2 bread, 1 milk, 1 1/2 vegetable, 1 fruit

Dinner
Tortilla Pie (see index)
Tossed Salad (see index)
2 Mini Hot Muffins (see index)
Melon Gelatin (see index)

Calories: 525   **Fat:** 7.3 grams
Exchanges: 3 meat, 3 bread, 3 vegetable, 1 fruit, 1 fat

Evening Snack
1 small peach

Calories: 51   **Fat:** trace
Exchanges: 1 fruit

Daily Totals:
Calories: 1,215   **Fat:** 13.8 grams
Exchanges: 5 meat, 6 1/2 bread, 2 milk, 4 1/2 vegetable, 4 fruit, 1 fat

❖ ❖ ❖

1200 Calories—Day Five
(Approximately 12 % Fat)

Breakfast
Egg substitute to = 1 egg, scrambled
1/2 English muffin
1 tablespoon no-fat margarine (optional)
1 tablespoon unsweetened all-fruit jam
4 ounces unsweetened orange juice

Calories: 265   **Fat:** 2.5 grams
Exchanges: 1 meat, 1 bread, 1 milk 1 1/2 fruit

Lunch
Pita Pizza (see index)
Tossed Salad (see index)
8 ounces skim milk
Small orange

Calories: 400   **Fat:** 3.7 grams
Exchanges: 1 meat, 2 bread, 1 milk, 2 vegetable, 1 fruit 3/4 fat

Dinner
Zucchini-Chicken and Pasta (see index)
Sour Cream Roll (see index)
1 tablespoon no-fat margarine (optional)
Poached Pears with Orange Sauce (see index)

Calories: 450   **Fat:** 9.3 grams
Exchanges: 3 meat, 1 1/2 bread, 1 vegetable, 3 fruit, 1 fat

Evening Snack
3 cups air-popped corn, no fat added

Calories: 70   **Fat:** trace
Exchanges: 1 bread

Daily Totals:
Calories: 1,185   **Fat:** 15.5 grams
Exchanges: 5 meat, 4 1/2 bread, 2 milk, 5 1/2 vegetable, 5 1/2 fruit, 1 1/2 fat

1200 Calories—Day Six
(Approximately 14 % fat)

Breakfast
2/3 cup Cheerios cereal
2 to 3 packages artificial sweetener of choice
8 ounces skim milk
1 slice whole wheat toast
1 tablespoon no-fat tub margarine (optional)
1 tablespoon all-fruit jam
4 ounces unsweetened orange juice

Calories: 297   **Fat:** 2.5 grams
Exchanges: 2 bread, 1 milk, 2 fruit

Lunch
Creamy Salmon Salad Sandwich (see index)
Green Pea and Potato Soup (see index)
4 saltine crackers
1 small apple

Calories: 401   **Fat:** 7.7 grams
Exchanges: 2 meat, 3 bread, 1/2 milk, 1 fruit

Dinner
Iowa Hash (see index)
Deluxe Tossed Salad (see index)
1 slice reduced-calorie whole wheat bread
1 tablespoon no-fat tub margarine (optional)
Raspberry Fluff (see index)

Calories: 507   **Fat:** 9.1 grams
Exchanges: 3 meat, 2 bread, 1/2 milk, 3 vegetable, 1 fruit, 1 fat

Evening Snack
Relishes (see index)

Calories: 25   **Fat:** trace
Exchanges: 1 vegetable

Daily Totals:
Calories: 1,230   **Fat:** 19.3 grams
Exchanges: 5 meat, 7 bread, 2 milk, 4 vegetable, 4 fruit, 1 fat

❖ ❖ ❖

1200 Calories—Day Seven
(Approximately 12 % fat for the day)

Breakfast
Denver Omelet (see index)
1 slice reduced-calorie whole wheat toast
1 teaspoon no-fat reduced-calorie tub margarine (optional)
1 tablespoon unsweetened all-fruit jam
4 ounces skim milk

Calories: 281   **Fat:** 4.6 grams
Exchanges: 2 meat, 1 bread, 1/2 milk, 1 vegetable, 1/2 fruit, 1/4 fat

Lunch
Open Face Vegetable Sandwich (see index)
Taco Pasta Salad (see index)
8 ounces skim milk
Mmmmmm Good Salad (see index)

Calories: 403   **Fat:** 3.7 grams
Exchanges: 2 milk, 2 bread, 2 vegetable, 1 fruit, 1/2 fat

Dinner
Chinese Chicken Rolls with Carrots and Rice (see index)
Sour Cream Roll (see index)
Baked Banana Pudding (see index)

Calories: 464   **Fat:** 7.5 grams
Exchanges: 3 meat, 3 bread, 1 vegetable, 1 1/2 fruit

Evening Snack
1 small apple

Calories: 40   **Fat:** trace
Exchanges: 1 fruit

Daily Totals:
Calories: 1,188   **Fat:** 15.8 grams
Exchanges: 5 meat, 6 bread, 2 1/2 milk, 4 vegetable, 4 fruit, 3/4 fat

❖ ❖ ❖

1500 Calories—Day One
(Approximately 8 % fat for day)

Breakfast
Wheat 'N Date Waffles (see index)
1 tablespoon no-fat tub margarine (optional)
2 tablespoons "Light" maple syrup
4 ounces unsweetened orange juice
8 ounces skim milk

Calories: 405   **Fat:** 1.4 grams
Exchanges: 2 bread, 1 3/4 milk, 2 fruit, 1 fat

Lunch
Toasted Ham and Cheese on Bun (see index)
Easy Corn Chowder (see index)
Relishes (see index)
8 ounces skim milk
Easy Apple Salad (see index)

Calories: 495   **Fat:** 4.0 grams
Exchanges: 2 meat, 2 bread, 1 3/4 milk, 1 vegetable, 2 fruit

Dinner
Salmon, Potato and Corn Scallop (see index)
Tossed Salad (see index)
1 Cornmeal Roll (see index)

1 teaspoon no-fat tub margarine (optional)
Applesauce Salad (see index)

Calories: 569   **Fat:** 8.8 grams
Exchanges: 3 meat, 3 1/2 bread, 1/2 milk, 1 1/2 vegetable, 1 fruit,
3/4 fat

Evening Snack
1/2 cup seedless grapes

Calories: 48   **Fat:** trace
Exchanges: 1 fruit

Daily Totals:
Calories: 1,517   **Fat:** 14.2 grams
Exchanges: 5 meat, 8 bread, 4 1/2 milk, 2 1/2 vegetable, 4 1/2 fruit,
1 3/4 fat

❖ ❖ ❖

1500 Calories—Day Two
(Approximately 10 % fat for day)

Breakfast
Applesauce Filled Pancakes (see index)
8 ounces skim milk
8 ounces unsweetened orange juice

Calories: 351   **Fat:** 1.9 grams
Exchanges: 1 1/2 bread, 1 1/2 milk, 3 fruit

Lunch
Potato and Onion Omelet (see index)
2 slices whole wheat toast
1 tablespoon no-fat tub margarine (optional)
1 tablespoon unsweetened all-fruit jam
8 ounces skim milk
Melon Gelatin (see index)

Calories: 484   **Fat:** 5.1 grams
Exchanges: 2 meat, 3 bread, 1 milk, 1 vegetable, 1 1/2 fruit

Dinner
Swiss Steak and Mashed Potatoes (see index)
Deluxe Tossed Salad (see index)
1/3 cup corn (see index)
Potato Biscuit (see index)
2 teaspoons no-fat tub margarine
1 tablespoon unsweetened all-fruit jam
Fresh Fruit Medley (see index)

Calories: 630   **Fat:** 9.5 grams
Exchanges: 3 meat, 3 bread, 1 milk, 3 vegetable, 2 1/2 fruit

Evening Snack
1/2 cup water-packed fruit cocktail

Calories: 46   **Fat:** trace
Exchanges: 1 fruit

Daily Totals:
Calories: 1,511   **Fat:** 16.5 grams
Exchanges: 5 meat, 7 1/2 bread, 3 1/2 milk, 4 vegetable, 8 fruit

❖ ❖ ❖

1500 Calories—Day Three
(Approximately 11 % fat for day)

Breakfast
Egg substitute to = 2 eggs, scrambled
2 slices whole wheat toast
1 tablespoon no-fat tub margarine (optional)
1 tablespoon unsweetened all-fruit jam
8 ounces skim milk
4 ounces unsweetened orange juice

Calories: 404   **Fat:** 5.0 grams
Exchanges: 2 meat, 2 bread, 1 milk, 2 fruit

Lunch
Deluxe Cheeseburger (see index)
Mandarin Orange Salad (see index)
8 ounces skim milk

Calories: 445   **Fat:** 5.7 grams
Exchanges: 3 1/2 meat, 1 1/2 bread, 1 milk, 1 vegetable, 1 fruit

Dinner
Vegetable Manicotti (see index)
Deluxe Tossed Salad (see index)
Cornmeal Roll (see index)
Baked Banana Pudding (see index)
3 Oatmeal Crispies (see index)

Calories: 572   **Fat:** 7.5 grams
Exchanges: 3 1/2 bread, 1/2 milk, 4 vegetable, 3 fruit, 1 1/2 fat

Evening Snack
1 cup air-popped corn, no fat added

Calories: 70   **Fat:** trace
Exchanges: 1 bread

Daily Totals:
Calories: 1,491   **Fat:** 18.2 grams
Exchanges: 5 1/2 meat, 8 bread, 2 1/2 milk, 6 fruit, 5 vegetable, 1 1/2 fat

❖ ❖ ❖

1500 Calories—Day Four
(Approximately 11 % fat for day)

Breakfast
Vegetable Omelet (see index)
2 slices whole wheat toast
1 tablespoon no-fat tub margarine
1 tablespoon unsweetened all-fruit jam
4 ounces unsweetened orange juice

Calories: 392   **Fat:** 4.5 grams
Exchanges: 2 meat, 2 bread, 3/4 milk, 1 vegetable, 1 1/2 fruit

Lunch
Salmon and Cream Cheese on Bagel (see index)
New Potato, Potato Salad (see index)

8 ounces skim milk
Mini Cheesecake (see index)
Small apple

Calories: 479   **Fat:** 7.0 grams
Exchanges: 1 meat, 2 bread, 2 1/2 milk, 1 1/2 fruit, 1/2 fat

Dinner
3 ounces chicken breast filet, grilled or broiled in oven
Deluxe Tossed Salad (see index)
Baked New Potato Rosettes (see index)
Oatmeal Muffin (see index)
1 tablespoon no-fat margarine (optional)
Baked Carrot Sticks (see index)
Strawberry Cream Pie (see index)

Calories: 602   **Fat:** 7.3 grams
Exchanges: 3 meat, 3 1/4 bread, 1 milk, 3 vegetable, 1 fruit, 1/2 fat

Evening Snack:
Relishes (see index)

Calories: 25   **Fat:** trace
Exchanges: 1 vegetable

Daily Totals:
Calories: 1,498   **Fat:** 18.8 grams
Exchanges: 6 meat, 7 1/4 bread, 4 1/2 milk, 4 vegetable, 4 fruit, 1 fat

❖ ❖ ❖

1500 Calories—Day Five
(Approximately 13 % fat for day)

Breakfast
2 Seasoned Yogurt Waffles (see index)
2 tablespoons "Free" no-fat cream cheese
8 ounces skim milk

Calories: 375   **Fat:** 2.0 grams
Exchanges: 4 bread, 1 1/4 milk

Lunch
Creamy Broccoli Tuna Helper (see index)
Deluxe Tossed Salad (see index)
1 slice reduced-calorie whole wheat bread
8 ounces skim milk
1/2 cup Thompson seedless grapes

Calories: 508   **Fat:** 6.9 grams
Exchanges: 1 meat, 2 1/2 bread, 1 1/2 milk, 3 vegetable, 1 fruit, 1 fat

Dinner
4 ounces ground round, grilled or broiled
Fried Rice-A-Roni (see index)
Scalloped Tomato (see index)
Easy Gelatin Salad (see index)
Banana Cream Pie (see index)

Calories: 545   **Fat:** 12.1 grams
Exchanges: 4 meat, 2 bread, 2 vegetable, 2 fruit, 1 fat

Evening Snack:
1 large apple

Calories: 80   **Fat:** trace
Exchanges: 2 fruit

Daily Totals:
Calories: 1,508   **Fat:** 21.0 grams
Exchanges: 5 meat, 8 1/2 bread, 2 3/4 milk, 5 vegetable, 5 fruit, 2 fat

❖ ❖ ❖

1500 Calories—Day Six
(Approximately 11 % fat for day)

Breakfast
Egg substitute to = 2 eggs, scrambled
1 Bagel (see index)
2 tablespoons "Free" no-fat cream cheese
1 cup diced, chilled cantaloupe

Calories: 355   **Fat:** 2.8 grams

Exchanges: 2 meat, 2 bread, 1 fruit, 1/2 milk, 1/2 fat

Lunch
Fajita Sandwich (see index)
Relishes (see index)
Easy Apple Salad (see index)
8 ounces skim milk
2 Sugarless Fruit Cookies (see index)

Calories: 519   **Fat:** 8.7 grams
Exchanges: 1 1/2 meat, 2 bread, 2 milk, 1 vegetable, 2 fruit, 1/2 fat

Dinner
Skillet Macaroni and Tuna (see index)
Sautéed Mushrooms (see index)
Sour Dough Bran Biscuit (see index)
Mmmmmm Good Salad (see index)
3 Oatmeal Crispies (see index)

Calories: 552   **Fat:** 6.8 grams
Exchanges: 2 meat, 3 bread, 1 1/2 milk, 2 vegetable, 1 fruit, 1 fat

Evening Snack
1 banana

Calories: 80   **Fat:** trace
Exchanges: 2 fruit

Daily Totals:
Calories: 1,506   **Fat:** 18.3 grams
Exchange: 5 1/2 meat, 7 bread, 4 milk, 3 vegetable, 6 fruit, 2 fat

NOTE: Cookies are included for both lunch and dinner on this daily menu. This type of menu planning can be done to satisfy the sweet tooth. However, if you include two desserts per day be sure the other required exchanges are met first. It is also best to include only low-sugar or sugar-free desserts. Sugar, which is a simple carbohydrate, is an empty food and contains next to no nutrition.

❖ ❖ ❖

1500 Calories—Day Seven
(Approximately 12 % fat for day)

Breakfast
2 Oatmeal Muffins (see index)
2 tablespoons "Free" no-fat cream cheese
8 ounces skim milk
1/2 banana

Calories: 355   **Fat:** 2.2 grams
Exchanges: 3 bread, 1 1/4 milk, 1 fruit

Lunch
Zucchini Lasagna (see index)
Deluxe Tossed Salad (see index)
2 slices whole wheat bread
Pistachio Dessert (see index)

Calories: 499   **Fat:** 7.8 grams
Exchanges: 2 meat, 2 1/2 bread, 1 milk, 4 vegetable, 1 fruit

Dinner
4 ounces strip steak, all visible fat removed, grilled or broiled
1 large baked potato
1 tablespoon no-fat tub margarine (optional)
1/4 teaspoon sour cream granules, sprinkled over potato
    (more if desired)
Deluxe Tossed Salad (see index)
1 slice French bread
1 tablespoon no-fat margarine (optional)
Apricot Salad Deluxe (see index)

Calories: 617   **Fat:** 9.7 grams
Exchanges: 4 meat, 3 bread, 3/4 milk, 2 vegetable, 2 fruit

Evening Snack:
1 small apple

Calories: 40   **Fat:** trace
Exchange: 1 fruit

Daily Totals:
Calories: 1,511 **Fat:** 19.7 grams
Exchanges: 6 meat, 8 1/2 bread, 3 milk, 6 vegetable, 5 fruit

❖ ❖ ❖

1800 Calories—Day One
(Approximately 10 % fat for day)

Breakfast
Oven Omelet (see index)
English muffin
1 tablespoon no-fat tub margarine (optional)
1 tablespoon unsweetened all-fruit jam
8 ounces skim milk
1 banana

Calories: 518 **Fat:** 5.2 grams
Exchanges: 1 meat, 2 bread, 1 1/2 milk, 4 fruit, 1 vegetable

Lunch
Taco Deluxe (see index)
8 ounces skim milk
Raspberry Fluff (see index)

Calories: 582 **Fat:** 7.0 grams
Exchanges: 3 meat, 3 bread, 1 milk, 2 vegetable, 1 fruit, 1 fat

Dinner
Chicken and Rice with Orange Sauce (see index)
Sour Dough Hard Roll (see index)
Summer Squash Treat (see index)
Fresh Peach Pie (see index)

Calories: 655 **Fat:** 8.2 grams
Exchanges: 3 meat, 3 1/4 bread, 3 vegetable, 3 fruit, 1 1/2 fat

Evening Snack:
1 medium apple

Calories: 40 **Fat:** trace
Exchanges: 1 fruit

Daily Totals:
Calories: 1,795   **Fat:** 20.4 grams
Exchanges: 7 meat, 8 1/4 bread, 2 1/2 milk, 6 vegetable, 9 fruit, 2 1/2 fat

❖ ❖ ❖

1800 Calories—Day Two
(Approximately 11 % fat for day)

Breakfast
3 Blueberry Pancakes Deluxe (see index)
1 tablespoon "Free" no-fat margarine (optional)
2 tablespoons "Light" or sugar-free syrup
8 ounces skim milk
8 ounces orange juice
1/2 grapefruit

Calories: 483   **Fat:** 5.9 grams
Exchanges: 2 bread, 1 milk, 5 1/2 fruit, 1 fat

Lunch
Puréed Vegetable Soup (see index)
Deluxe Hamburger (see index)
8 ounces skim milk
1 small apple

Calories: 508   **Fat:** 6.0 g
Exchanges: 3 meat, 2 1/2 bread, 1 milk, 2 vegetable, 1 fruit

Dinner
Salmon, Potato and Corn Scallop (see index)
Deluxe Tossed Salad (see index)
Green Bean Sauté (see index)
Italian, Italian Bread Slice (see index)
Chocolate Shortcake with Strawberries (see index)

Calories: 738   **Fat:** 9.8 grams
Exchanges: 3 meat, 4 bread, 2 1/4 milk, 2 vegetable, 1 fruit, 1 fat

Evening Snack:
3 cups air-popped corn, no butter added

Calories: 70   **Fat:** trace
Exchanges: 1 bread

Daily Totals:
Calories: 1,799   **Fat:** 21.7 grams
Exchanges: 6 meat, 9 1/2 bread, 4 milk, 4 vegetable, 7 1/2 fruit, 2 fat

❖ ❖ ❖

1800 Calories—Day Three
(Approximately 10 % fat for day)

Breakfast
1 cup corn flakes
8 ounces skim milk
2 to 3 packages artificial sweetener
1 banana
1 English muffin
1 tablespoon tub margarine (not to exceed 5 grams of fat)
1 tablespoon unsweetened all-fruit jam

Calories: 470   **Fat:** 9.8 grams
Exchanges: 3 1/2 bread, 1 milk, 2 1/2 fruit, 1 fat

Lunch
Turkey Burger (see index)
Low-fat French Fries (see index)
Relishes (see index)
8 ounces skim milk
Fresh Fruit Medley (see index)

Calories: 459   **Fat:** 4.2 grams
Exchanges: 2 meat, 2 bread, 1 milk, 2 vegetable, 2 fruit

Dinner
1 (4 ounce) Flounder filet, poached
Cheddar and Sour Cream Potatoes (see index)
Bread Knot (see index)
Marinated Vegetables (see index)
Canned Beets (see index)
Lovin' Lite White Cake (see index)
Mandarin Orange Topping (for cake) (see index)

Calories: 780   **Fat:** 6.7 grams
Exchanges: 4 meat, 5 1/2 bread, 1 milk, 3 vegetable, 1/2 fruit

Evening Snack
3 cups air-popped corn

Calories: 70   **Fat:** trace
Exchange: 1 bread

Daily Totals
Calories: 1,779   **Fat:** 20.7 grams
Exchanges: 6 meat, 12 bread, 3 milk, 5 vegetable, 5 fruit, 1 fat

❖ ❖ ❖

1800 Calories—Day Four
(Approximately 15 % fat)

Breakfast
Egg substitute to = 1 egg (see index)
2 ounces Turkey Sausage (see index)
2 slices reduced calorie whole wheat toast
1 tablespoon unsweetened all-fruit jam
8 ounces skim milk
4 ounces unsweetened orange juice

Calories: 396   **Fat:** 5.8 grams
Exchanges: 3 meat, 1 bread, 1 milk,1 1/2 fruit, 1/2 fat

Lunch
Pita Pizza (see index)
Deluxe Tossed Salad (see index)
8 ounces skim milk
Sea Foam Salad (see index)
Large apple

Calories: 559   **Fat:** 4.9 grams
Exchanges: 1 meat, 1 bread, 3 milk, 2 vegetable, 2 1/2 fruit, 1 fat

Dinner
Chicken Spaghetti Casserole (see index)
Tossed Salad (see index)

2 slices Italian, Italian Bread Slices (see index)
Deluxe Neapolitan Pie (see index)

Calories: 781   **Fat:** 18.5 grams
Exchanges: 3 meat, 5 bread, 2 milk, 2 vegetable, 1 fat

Evening Snack
3 cups air-popped corn, no fat added
Calories: 70   **Fat:** trace
Exchanges: 1 bread

Daily Totals:
Calories: 1,806   **Fat:** 29.2 grams
Exchanges: 7 meat, 8 bread, 6 milk, 4 vegetable, 4 fruit, 2 1/2 fat

1800 Calories—Day Five
(Approximately 12 % fat for day)

Breakfast
Egg substitute to = 1 egg, scrambled
Sour Dough Apple Muffin (see index)
1 tablespoon no-fat margarine (optional)
1 tablespoon unsweetened all-fruit jam
8 ounces skim milk
8 ounces unsweetened orange juice
1/2 cup chilled fruit cocktail, canned in own juice

Calories: 395   **Fat:** 2.9 grams
Exchanges: 1 meat, 1 1/2 bread, 1 milk, 4 fruit

Lunch
Chef's Salad (see index)
1 slice Dill Bread (see index)
2 tablespoons no-fat cream cheese
8 ounces skim milk
Fresh Fruit Medley (see index)

Calories: 588   **Fat:** 6.2 grams
Exchanges: 3 meat, 2 bread, 1 milk, 3 vegetable, 2 fruit, 1 fat

Dinner
Beef Burgundy with Rice (see index)
Deluxe Tossed Salad (see index)
Mushrooms and Brussels Sprouts (see index)
Pin Wheel Roll (see index)
1 tablespoon tub margarine, not to exceed 5 grams fat
Fresh Strawberry Pie (see index)

Calories: 753   **Fat:** 15.6 grams
Exchanges: 3 meat, 5 bread, 4 vegetable, 1 fruit, 2 fat

Evening Snack
3 cups air-popped corn, no-fat added

Calories: 70   **Fat:** Tr.
Exchanges: 1 bread

Daily Totals:
Calories: 1,806   **Fat:** 24.7 grams
Exchanges: 7 meat, 10 bread, 2 milk, 7 vegetable, 6 1/2 fruit, 3 fat

❖ ❖ ❖

1800 Calories—Day Six
(Approximately 14 % fat for day)

Breakfast
2 Chocolate Waffles (see index)
1 tablespoon tub margarine, not to exceed 5 grams fat
2 tablespoon unsweetened all-fruit jam
8 ounces skim milk
8 ounces unsweetened orange juice

Calories: 422   **Fat:** 7.6 grams
Exchanges: 2 1/2 bread, 1 milk, 3 fruit, 1 fat

Lunch
Taco Deluxe (see index)
Apricot Salad Deluxe (see index)
8 ounces skim milk

Calories: 538   **Fat:** 5.3 grams

Exchanges: 3 meat, 2 bread, 1 1/2 milk, 1 vegetable, 1 fruit, 1 fat

Dinner
Baked Flounder with Vegetables (see index)
Fettuccini Pasta (see index)
Deluxe Tossed Salad (see index)
Lemon Cottage Cheese (see index)
Sourdough Hard Roll (see index)
Mandarin Orange Cream Pie (see index)

Calories: 816   **Fat:** 15.4 grams
Exchanges: 3 meat, 4 bread, 1 milk, 6 vegetable, 2 fruit, 1 fat

Evening Snack
Small apple

Calories: 40   **Fat:** trace
Exchange: 1 fruit

Daily Totals:
Calories: 1,816   **Fat:** 28.3 grams
Exchanges: 6 meat, 8 1/2 bread, 3 1/2 milk, 7 vegetable, 7 fruit, 3 1/2 fat

❖ ❖ ❖

1800 Calories—Day Seven
(Approximately 14 % fat for day)

Breakfast
Broccoli, Red Pepper and Cheese Omelet (see index)
English muffin
1 tablespoon no-fat tub margarine
1 tablespoon unsweetened all-fruit jam
8 ounces skim milk
1/2 grapefruit

Calories: 465   **Fat:** 6.3 grams
Exchanges: 2 meat, 2 bread, 1 milk, 1 vegetable, 1 1/2 fruit, 1 fat

Lunch
Broiled Crab Meat Open Sandwich (see index)
Herbed Potatoes (see index)
Buttered Carrots (see index)
8 ounces skim milk
Fried Apples (see index)

Calories: 463   **Fat:** 5.1 grams
Exchanges: 2 meat, 2 bread, 1 milk, 3 vegetable, 1 1/2 fruit

Dinner
Pork Chops and Rice in a Skillet (see index)
Quick Dinner Roll (see index)
Baked Fresh Green Beans (see index)
Carrot-Pineapple Gelatin (see index)
2 Mini Cheesecakes (see index)

Calories: 831   **Fat:** 16.5 grams
Exchanges: 3 meat, 4 1/2 bread, 1 milk, 4 vegetable, 2 fruit, 2 fat

Evening Snack
Small peach

Calories: 40   **Fat:** trace
Exchange: 1 fruit

Daily Totals:
Calories: 1,799   **Fat:** 27.9 grams
Exchanges: 7 meat, 8 1/2 bread, 3 milk, 8 vegetable, 6 fruit, 3 fat

Notes & Recipes

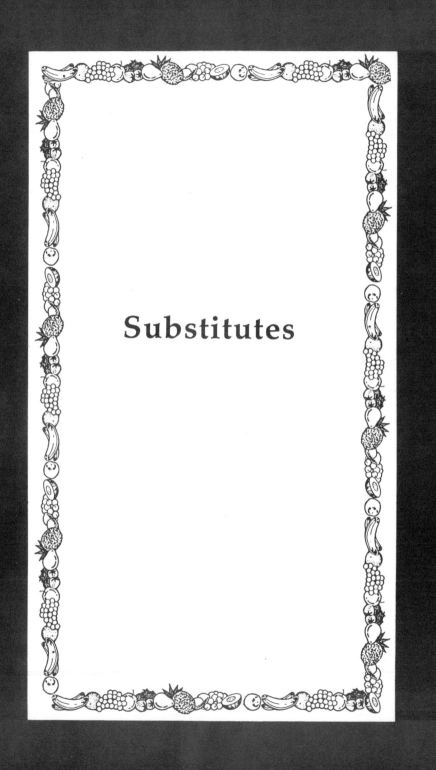

Substitutes

Substitutes

Within the pages of this chapter, lies the key to successfully cooking food that is lower in fat content. In my first two books, I used more substitutes than I use in this book. The reason for this is that manufacturers are trying very hard to produce products lower in fat content. Some of these are now acceptable in low-fat cooking.

Many people cannot spend a great deal of time in the kitchen, and for this reason, I have swayed toward low-fat products instead of substitutes.

Convenience is the name of the game. Most people are looking for the quick and easy route when it comes to cooking. Using as many convenience foods as possible, I have tried to make low-fat cooking simple.

It is, however, very important that you stroll through the substitute chapter before embarking on low-fat cooking. As you go through the chapter, make a list of the ingredients needed to set you up in low-fat cooking. Whip up the substitutes you'll be using and keep them handy. Only when substitutes are on the shelf, ready for use, will they be used.

Butter Taste Substitutes

In the recipes of this book, I refer to an ingredient I call "butter granules". It is granules that give food the taste of butter without the fat. I used the Molly McButter brand in the recipes in this book. However there are several different brands—Butter Buds-Butter Sprinkles, etc. Select the one you like best and use when a recipe calls for butter granules.

Cheese Substitutes

For the most part, cheese is high in fat content and should be avoided. However, there are now some no-fat cheese available that work very well in cooking. The nice part about many of these no-fat cheeses, is that they taste good and the texture is good. Of course there is some sacrifice in these areas. Any time fat is cut out or reduced, there is sacrifice.

Cream Cheese

In my first two books, I strictly used a cream cheese substitute. It is now possible, however, to buy a no-fat cream cheese. In the recipes in the book, I used the "Free" no-fat Philadelphia Cream Cheese. Alpine Lace also makes a no-fat cream cheese that works well. I'm sure there are other brands available, but I did not take the time to research. For those who prefer to use the cream cheese substitutes, here they are:

Cream Cheese Substitute
for Cold Dishes

(With home recipe yogurt, recipe contains only a trace of fat; With commercial low-fat yogurt,
recipes contains approximately 25% fat)

1 (8 oz.) ctn. plain low-fat yogurt

Secure a piece of cheesecloth or a coffee filter over a glass allowing pouch to extend down into the glass. Pour yogurt into pouch, cover top with plastic wrap and put in the refrigerator for several hours. During the setting time, the whey will drain from the yogurt; it will be found in liquid form in the bottom of the glass. The yogurt will now be a more solid product that will perform well in recipes calling for cream cheese. Plain "yogurt cheese" works well in cold dishes.

Yield: 1 cup or 16 tablespoons

Approximate Per Tablespoon:
(if using home-recipe yogurt):

Calories: 10	**Carbohydrates:** 1 g
Fat: tr.	**Protein:** 1 g
Cholesterol: 0.3 mg	**Sodium:** 11 mg

Approximate Per Tablespoon:
(if using commercial yogurt):

Calories: 13	**Carbohydrates:** 1 g
Fat: 0.3 g	**Protein:** 1 g
Cholesterol: 1.3 mg	**Sodium:** 10 mg

Exchange: Free food when used in limited amounts

Cream Cheese Substitute
for Hot Dishes

(With home-recipe yogurt, recipe contains only a trace of fat; With commercial low-fat yogurt, recipe contains approximately 21% fat)

1 (8 oz.) ctn. plain low-fat yogurt	1 scant tsp. cornstarch

Secure a piece of cheesecloth or a coffee filter over a glass allowing a pouch to extend down into the glass. Pour yogurt into the pouch and cover top with plastic wrap. Put in refrigerator for several hours. During this time, the whey will drain from the yogurt; it will be found in liquid form in the bottom of the glass. The yogurt will now be in a more solid form that will perform well in recipes calling for cream cheese. Just before using "yogurt cheese", stir in cornstarch and blend well. This works very well in hot dishes. **Yield: 1 cup or 16 tablespoons.**

Approximate Per Tablespoon:
(if using home-recipe yogurt):

Calories: 12	**Carbohydrates:** 1 g
Fat: tr.	**Protein:** 1 g
Cholesterol: 0.3 mg	**Sodium:** 11 mg

Approximate Per Tablespoon:
(if using commercial yogurt):

Calories: 13	**Carbohydrates:** 1 g
Fat: 0.3 g	**Protein:** 1 g
Cholesterol: 1.3 mg	**Sodium:** 10 mg

Exchange: Free food when used in limited amounts

American Cheese Substitute

There is now a "Free" no-fat American cheese available that tastes good and melts good. This is the "Kraft-Free" brand. It comes in packages of individual slices. If you want the American cheese taste in a shredded cheese, simply dice up the slices. Be sure to check out the other brands—there are many. Perhaps you will like one of the other "no-fat" American sliced cheeses better.

Cheddar Cheese Substitute

As with many other cheeses, there is a fat-free shredded Cheddar cheese as well as a fat-free block cheese. I have chosen to use the "Healthy Choice" brand of shredded Cheddar and have not used the block no-fat cheese. However, there are other brands available—for instance, Alpine Lace also has a fat-free shredded and block cheese. Try them and use the one you like best.

Cheese Granules

Cheese granules lend a good cheese taste to foods, but add no fat to the recipe. In the book, in recipes calling for cheese granules, I have used the "Molly McButter" brand. There are other brands that I am sure are just as good. Try them and stick to the one you like.

Mozzarella Cheese

Yes, there is also a no-fat shredded mozzarella cheese that melts nice and tastes good. I use the "Healthy Choice" brand. If you like another brand better, by all means use it.

When baking put the ingredients needed to the left of the mixing bowl. As you use the ingredient put it to the right of the mixing bowl. If interrupted you will know which ingredients you have already used.

Cheese
No-Fat Cheeses

	Cal	Fat	Cho	Car	Pro	Sod	% of Fat
Block Cheese							
Alpine Lace Cheddar							
1 oz.	45	0.0	5.0*	2.0	8.0	280	0%
Alpine Lace Mozzarella							
1 oz.	45	0.0	5.0*	2.0	8.0	280	0%
Cream Cheese							
Healthy Choice							
Cream Cheese; 2 T.	25	0.0	15	0.0	4.0	200	0%
Cream Cheese with							
Strawberries; 2 T.	36	0.0	15	0.0	4.0	200	0%
Kraft							
Philadelphia Cream							
Cheese; 2 T.	30	0.0	Tr.	2.0	5.0	160	0%
Sliced Cheese							
Borden Fat-Free							
1 slice	30	0.	5.0*	2.0	5.0	310	0%
Kraft "Free" American							
1 slice	30	0.0	5.0*	3.0	5.0	320	0%

Cheese (continued)

No-Fat Cheeses

	Cal	Fat	Cho	Car	Pro	Sod	% of Fat
Sliced Cheese (continued)							
Weight Watcher's sharp Cheddar; 1 slice	30	0.0	5.0*	2.0	5.0	320	0%
Weight Watcher's American; 1 slice	25	0.0	5.0*	2.0	5.0	300	0%
Shredded Cheese							
Healthy Choice, Cheddar 1/4 c.	45	0.0	5.0*	2.0	9.0	200	0%
Healthy Choice, Mozzarella 1/4 c.	45	0.0	5.0*	2.0	9.0	200	0%
Alpine Lace, Cheddar 1/4 c.	40	0.0	5.0*	2.0	8.0	290	0%
Alpine Lace, Mozzarella 1/4 c.	45	0.0	5.0*	2.0	8.0	280	0%

Reduced Fat Cheeses

	Cal	Fat	Cho	Car	Pro	Sod	% of Fat
Block Cheese							
Kraft Reduced Fat Cheddar, 1 oz.	80	5.0	20	0.0	9.0	220	56%

Cheese (continued)

Reduced Fat Cheese (continued)

	Cal	Fat	Cho	Car	Pro	Sod	% of Fat
Block Cheese (continued)							
Kraft Reduced Fat Mild Cheddar, 1 oz.	80	5.0	20	0.0	9.0	230	56%
Kraft Reduced-Fat Sharp Cheddar; 1 oz.	80	5.0	20	0.0	90	220	56%
Cream Cheese							
Kraft Philadelphia Cream Cheese--1/3 less fat--1 oz.	60	6.0	20	Tr.	3.0	120	90%

Note: It appears that the only reduction here is the calories. The percentage of fat is still 90%--the same as the regular cream cheese. Because the calories are less, the fat grams are less, but the total product is still 90% fat!!!

Sliced Cheese							
Alpine Lace 1 slice	50	2.0	10	1.0	4.0	260	36%
Kraft 1/3 less fat American; 1 slice	50	3.0	10	2.0	5.0	330	54%
Kraft 1/3 less fat, Sharp Cheddar; 1 slice	70	4.0	15	2.0	6.0	390	51%

Cheese (continued)
Reduced Fat Cheese (continued)

	Cal	Fat	Cho	Car	Pro	Sod	% of Fat
Sliced Cheese (continued)							
Kraft 1/3 less fat Swiss; 1 slice	50	2.5	10	2.0	5.0	270	45%
Shredded Cheese							
Kraft 1/3 less fat 1/4 c.	90	6.0	20	Tr.	10	230	60%
Kraft part skim Mozzarella 1/4 c.	80	5.0	20	Tr.	8	190	56%
Sargento part skim Mozzarella; 1/4 c.	80	6.0	15	1.0	7.0	150	68%
Regular Cheese							
Block Cheese							
Cracker Barrel Nat. Cheddar; 1 oz.	110	9.0	30	Tr.	7	180	74%
Cracker Barrel Extra Sharp; 1 oz.	110	9.0	30	Tr.	7	180	74%
Kraft Colby--Monterey Jack; 1 oz.	110	9.0	30	Tr.	7	190	74%
Kraft Cheddar 1 oz.	110	9.0	30	Tr.	7	180	74%

Cheese (continued)
Regular Cheese Continued

	Cal	Fat	Cho	Car	Pro	Sod	% of Fat
Block Cheese (continued)							
Kraft Mozzarella							
1 oz.	80	5.0	15	Tr.	8	200	56%
Sliced Cheese							
Kraft Deluxe							
1 slice	80	7.0	20	1.0	4.0	340	79%
Kraft Old English							
1 slice	110	9.0	30	Tr.	6.0	460	74%
Kraft Sharp							
1 slice	70	6.0	20	Tr.	4.0	300	77%
Kraft Singles							
1 slice	60	5.0	15	2.0	4.0	250	75%
Kraft Swiss							
1 slice	70	5.0	15	1.0	4.0	320	64%
Velveeta							
1 slice	70	5.0	15	2.0	4.0	310	64%
Regular Shredded							
Kraft Sharp Cheddar							
1/4 c.	110	9.0	25	1.0	7.0	170	74%

Cheese (continued)
Regular Cheese (continued)

	Cal	Fat	Cho	Car	Pro	Sod	% of Fat
Regular Shredded (continued)							
Kraft Mild Cheddar; 1/4 c.	110	9.0	25	Tr.	7.0	170	74%
Kraft Parmesan; 1 T.	20	1.5	Tr.	0.0	2.0	75	68%
Kraft Taco; 1/4 c.	100	8.0	25	Tr.	6.0	180	72%
Kraft Pizza; 1/4 c.	90	7.0	20	Tr.	6.0	210	70%
Kraft Pizza Four Cheese, 1/4 c.	90	7.0	20	Tr.	7.0	230	70%
Kraft Swiss 1/4 c.	110	8.0	25	Tr.	8.0	45	65%
Sargento Colby Jack 1/4 c.	110	9.0	25	1.0	6.0	190	74%
Sargento Nachos and Tacos 1/4 c.	110	9.0	25	1.0	6.0	240	74%
Sargento Pizza Double 1/4 c.	90	6.0	20	1.0	7.0	150	60%

On the above chart, you have been given no-fat cheese, reduced fat cheese and regular cheese. The cheeses used were the cheeses available to me in my area. There are many, many more cheeses. Check out the ones in your area; make a list and figure the fat. The grams of fat per serving multiplied by nine and divided into the calories per serving will give you the percent of fat in a serving. Cheeses can be a real pitfall. Choose your cheeses carefully. In the book the no-fat cheeses are used.

Casserole Cream Soup Substitute

Even with the "light" and "low-sodium" cream soups, they still contain too much fat and sodium. The Casserole Cream Soup Mix contains less than a gram of fat for the equivalent of one can of cream soup, however, the sodium is still too high. If you wish to reduce the sodium even lower, use the low sodium bouillon.

Mix it up and keep it on hand. It's easy to prepare and simple to use in casseroles or any recipe calling for a can of cream soup. Use it as you would any cream soup. If the recipe calls for Cream of Mushroom soup you might want to add a few chopped mushrooms, but it really is not necessary.

Once you get used to using the substitute you will like it. And it's a lot less expensive than canned soups.

Casserole Cream Soup Mix
(Recipe contains approximately 5% fat)

2 c. instant nonfat dry
    milk
3/4 c. cornstarch
1/4 c. instant chicken
    bouillon, low-sodium

2 T. dried onion flakes
1/2 tsp. pepper
1 tsp. dried thyme
1 tsp. dried basil
1 tsp. celery salt

Combine all ingredients, mixing very well. Store in airtight container. Makes 3 cups of mix that is equivalent to 6 (10 1/2-ounce) cans of condensed cream soup.

To use a substitute for 1 can creamed soup:

1/2 c. dry soup mix (should
    be scant 1/2 c.)

1 1/4 c. water

Put soup mix and water in a saucepan and cook over medium heat until thickened. Equivalent to one can condensed cream soup.

This cream soup substitute contains only about 1/4 the fat of regular canned cream soups and will season recipes just as well.

Approximate Per Can:
Calories: 160
Fat: 0.9 g
Cholesterol: 0.0 mg

Carbohydrates: 27 g
Protein: 11 g
Sodium: 1173 mg

Exchanges: 1 milk, 2 fruit

Substitute for Heavy or Light Cream

(Recipe contains approximately 3% fat)

Evaporated skim milk

Use cup for cup in recipes calling for heavy or light cream

Approximate Per Cup:

Calories: 200

Fat: 0.6 g

Cholesterol: 10 mg

Carbohydrates: 2 g

Protein: 1 g

Sodium: 124 mg

Exchange: 2 milk

Seasoned Crouton Substitutes

Don't fall prey to the commercial seasoned croutons that are in abundance on the grocery shelves. Most are loaded with saturated fats and are not good for you. Besides that, why pay a lot for croutons when they are so easy to prepare yourself? Making your own croutons also gives you the advantage of seasoning them just as your family likes.

Make them when you have a little extra time. Make up a big batch and store them in freezer bags or airtight tins. You'll be surprised at the many uses you'll find for them.

Before sifting flour onto waxed paper, always crease the paper down the center. This creates a handy pouring spout.

Seasoned Croutons

(Recipe contains approximately 22% fat)

40 slices reduced-calorie
   bread, cut in 1/4" to 1/2"
   cubes
Low-fat cooking spray
1/4 c. parsley flakes
2 tsp. garlic powder (opt.)
2 tsp. sweet basil

1 T. poultry seasoning or
   1 tsp. sage
1/4 c. celery flakes
1/4 c. minced onion
1/4 c. green pepper flakes
1 T. sodium-free seasoned salt
   (opt.)
1 T. onion powder

Cut bread into cubes of desired size and spread out on two baking sheets that have been lined with foil and sprayed with cooking spray. Spray bread cubes as you toss with a fork to allow coating of all sides. Blend remaining ingredients and sprinkle over bread cubes, tossing to coat all sides. Spray lightly one more time, then bake at 250° for at least one hour, stirring frequently. Allow to stand a couple of hours before storing in bags. Store in airtight containers or in freezer bags in the freezer. Use as you would any other croutons. Keep on hand at all times.
Yield: 22 cups

Approximate Per Cup:
Calories: 85
Fat: 2.1 g
Cholesterol: 0.0 mg

Carbohydrates: 22 g
Protein: 4 g
Sodium: 234 mg

Exchanges: 1 bread

To make hot roll mix or bread rise quickly, set the bowl of dough on a heating pad turned to low. Dough rises in no time.

Egg Substitute

The undisputed "miracle worker" in the kitchen is the ever ready egg. It thickens puddings, sets custards, stabilizes cakes, binds meatballs and provides mountains of meringue. As a breakfast or brunch food item, it can be fried, boiled, poached, scrambled, stuffed or whipped into a fluffy omelet or a towering soufflé.

Eggs are choked full of vitamins and minerals and they contain a high quality of complete protein. But, lurking behind that innocent looking hard shell is an over-abundance of fat. And in that fat is a substance known as cholesterol—enough to cause many physicians to warn their patients of its hazards.

After extensive research, the egg has become more and more suspect of being a heavy contributor to a variety of health problems, including heart attacks. Because of the growing dangers posed by high cholesterol levels, the American Heart Association has even revised its dietary guidelines. They are now advising the American public to eat less fat—less than 30% of the daily caloric consumption should come in the form of fat.

Saturated fats, which are found in animal flesh, coconut oils, cocoa butter and palm kernel oils, should not exceed 10% of the daily caloric intake. People are further advised to eat less of cholesterol-rich foods. Daily intake should not exceed 100 milligrams of cholesterol per 1,000 calories, not to exceed 300 milligrams per day.

Neither my husband or myself have been advised to eliminate eggs from our diets, however, we have chosen to use an egg substitute instead of eggs. The egg substitutes in this book were developed by me and will work very well in the recipes in this book. When out of egg substitute, use two egg whites instead of an egg. It will also work.

Be forewarned that it will not be easy in the beginning to discard the egg yolk. At first, when I threw away the yolks, I could hardly stand to watch them slide out of sight. That all changes, however, and after a while the regard for them will be no more than the regard of an egg shell.

The recipes in this book have been kitchen tested with egg substitute and no eggs are necessary for any recipe in this book. Once again, the secret to success will be to keep egg substitute on the shelf or in the freezer at all times. If you begin to think fondly of the egg, remember this: one egg yolk has 270 milligrams of cholesterol—more cholesterol than most people are allowed in a day.

Egg Substitute on the Shelf

(Recipe contains approximately 18% fat)

2 c. non-fat dry milk
  granules - use good grade
2 tsp. baking powder
2 T. cornstarch
1 tsp. cream of tartar

1/4 tsp. yellow food coloring
  (must have an oil base
  such as the kind used for
  candy melts)

Grind dry milk to a fine powder in a mortar with a pestle, or in a mixing bowl with the back of a heavy tablespoon. Pour powdered milk into a medium bowl and blend in baking powder, cornstarch and cream of tartar. In a cup, mix oil and food coloring. Slowly add milk granules to oil mixture until you have a rather dry mixture. Pour this mixture into remaining milk granules. Grind with a tablespoon until mixture is even in color and fluffy. Store in airtight container. Egg substitute need not be refrigerated, but it will remain fresh longer if refrigerated, if you don't use much of it.

To Use: Mix one tablespoon egg substitute with two tablespoons cool water and blend until smooth. Add two egg whites and mix until smooth and even in color. When prepared as directed above, it is equal to one egg and can be used in most recipes calling for eggs. Egg substitute is great scrambled or used in omelets. For salads, simply scramble and chop up.

Yield: Enough for equivalent of 36 eggs

Approximate Per Egg Equivalent:
(1 T. egg substitue equals 2 egg whites):
Calories: 60
Fat: 1.2 g
Cholesterol: 0.7 mg

Carbohydrates: 4 g
Protein: 7 g
Sodium: 124 mg

Exchanges: 1 vegetable; 1 meat

Like your oatmeal piping hot on cold mornings? Don't add cold milk. Instead stir in 1/3 cup instant dry milk per serving and add a little extra water as you cook it. Makes it creamy, smooth and piping hot..

Egg Substitute in the Freezer
(Recipe contains approximately 29% fat)

1 dozen egg whites
2 T. canola oil
1 to 2 drops yellow food
  coloring (oil based like
  used for candy melts)

1/2 tsp. baking powder
1/2 c. powdered milk

Put egg whites, oil and food coloring in blender and process until smooth. Slowly add baking powder and powdered milk. One-fourth cup equals 1 egg.
Yield: 2 cups (equivalent to 8 eggs)

Approximate Per 1/4 Cup:
Calories: 56
Fat: 1.8 g
Cholesterol: 0.8 mg

Carbohydrates: 3 g
Protein: 6 g
Sodium: 102 mg

Exchanges: 1 vegetable; 1/2 meat

Master Baking Mix Substitute

We all like having a premixed baking or biscuit mix on hand. It has so many uses that it is nice to always have on the shelf. The problem is that commercial master baking mixes have far too much fat in them to be acceptable on a fat restricted diet.

However, the home-style baking mixes can be used at will because the fat is held to 30%. It means you don't have to give up the convenience of baking with it. Make a batch and store it in the refrigerator in an airtight can. It will keep up to 3 months.

Use a 1-inch paint brush when icing cookies.

Master Baking Mix
(Recipe contains approximately 30% fat)

12 1/2 c. flour (whole wheat,
   unbleached or enriched
   all-purpose)
1/2 c. baking powder*

2 c. non-fat dry milk
   granules
2 tsp. salt (opt.)
1 1/2 c. tub margarine

Blend dry ingredients and cut in margarine. Store in airtight container for 2 to 3 months in the refrigerator.

*If using whole wheat flour, blend flour or half whole wheat and half unbleached, increase baking powder to 3/4 cup.

Approximate Per Cup:
Calories: 573
Fat: 19.4 g
Cholesterol: 1.6 mg

Carbohydrates: 79 g
Protein: 13 g
Sodium: 613 mg

Exchanges: 5 bread, 4 fat

Olive Oil Substitute

Most people enjoy the taste olive oil lends foods. Especially in Italian food or a good tossed salad. However, since it contains over one hundred calories per tablespoon and 14 grams of fat, it must be used very sparingly, if at all.

One of the best ways to introduce the olive oil taste to foods without calories and fat is to use the canned olive oil spray. A single serving of olive oil spray (the amount it takes to cover 1/3 of a 10-inch skillet) contains only 2 calories and 1 gram of fat.

For pasta, cook and drain, then spray and toss before putting on serving plate. Use the spray very sparingly. It doesn't take a lot to accomplish the taste. For a salad, try spraying each salad bowl, or the main serving salad bowl, with olive oil before tossing the salad. If not happy with the taste, spray the salad greenery before adding the dressing.

When sautéing with a frozen stock cube, spray the skillet first with the olive oil and then melt the cube. This works great and keeps the fat down.

Minute Rice and Noodle Substitute
Minute Rice
(Approximately 4% fat)

Not only does Minute Rice not have the taste of brown rice or long-grain rice, it does not have the nutrition. However, you can make your own Minute Rice which is ready to serve in just minutes. It's easy to do and easy to prepare.

Cook desired amount of rice you wish to convert to "Minute Rice". When cooked, put rice in a seive and run hot water through the rice for about a minute to remove some of the starch. Then run under cold water until rice has cooled to room temperature. Spray rice lightly with cooking spray to prevent sticking together.

SINGLE SERVINGS: For individual servings, put 1/2 cup cooked rice in a 6 ounce custard cup, sprayed with cooking spray; cover very tightly with plastic wrap and freeze for several hours. When frozen solid, remove from custard cup and slip into a freezer bag. To serve, simply remove from freezer and slip back into custard cups. Cover with wax paper and zap in microwave on 100% POWER. DO NOT ADD WATER. Microwave 1 1/2 to 2 minutes for 1 custard cup; 2 to 2 1/2 minutes for 2 custard cups; and 4 to 4 1/2 minutes for 4 custard cups.

FAMILY SERVINGS: Prepare rice the same as for single servings. Instead of custard cups, put 2 cups of rice in freezer bags or freezer containers and freeze. To serve, simply remove from the bag or container and put into microwave-safe bowl. Add 2 tablespoons of water; cover with wax paper and microwave on 100% POWER for about 5 minutes, or until heated through. For larger amounts, put the frozen product in a seive and drop into boiling water until heated through.

Approximate Per 1/2 Cup Serving:
Calories: 115   **Carbohydrates:** 25.0 g
Fat: 0.5 g   **Protein:** 2.5 g
Cholesterol: 0.0 mg   **Sodium:** 3 mg

Exchanges: 1 1/2 Bread

Use a piece of uncooked spaghetti to test a cake.

Minute Noodles

(Approximately 11% fat)

Cook noodles and rinse the same as with the rice. Freeze and reheat the same as you do for rice. Works great.

Approximate Per 1/2 Cup Serving:
Calories: 100
Fat: 1.2 g
Cholesterol: 0.0 mg

Carbohydrates: 20.0 g
Protein: 5.0 g
Sodium: 10 mg

Exchanges: 1 1/2 Bread

Sausage Substitute

(Approximately 19% fat)

3 pounds ground turkey
   breast
1 pound ground round
1 teaspoon cumin
1 tsp. marjoram
1 teaspoon seasoned salt
1 teaspoon black pepper
1 teaspoon oregano

2 teaspoons basil
2 teaspoons thyme
2 teaspoons sage
1 teaspoon garlic powder
1/2 teaspoon nutmeg
1/2 cup whole wheat,
   reduced-calorie bread
   crumbs

Combine all ingredients, mixing well. Cover and refrigerate several hours to allow flavors to mingle. Freeze in 1 pound portions or form into 32 (2-ounce) sausage patties and freeze.
Yield: 4 pounds or 32 (2 ounce) patties.

Approximate Per Pound:
Calories: 770
Fat: 16.6 g
Cholesterol: 344 mg

Carbohydrates: 1.9 g
Protein: 145.9 g
Sodium: 900 mg

Approximate Per Patty:
Calories: 96
Fat: 2.1 g
Cholesterol: 43 mg

Carbohydrates: 0.2 g
Protein: 18.2 g
Sodium: 113 mg

Exchanges Per Patty: 2 meat

Sautéing without the Fat

Far too much margarine and oil are used when sautéing. Most cooks think the ingredients being sautéed must swim in butter, margarine or oil in order to come out tasty.

This is not true. Margarine, butter or oil are not even necessary for sautéing. You can sauté in plain water if you wish. True, the skillet will not get as hot, but water will work.

What is being accomplished when food is sautéed, is to encourage the food to release its flavor. The food will release its flavor in a water based sauté just as it will in an oil based sauté.

I prefer to use water with butter granules in it, or stock, to sauté. There is a secret when using these ingredients to sauté. It is important to cook until all liquid is absorbed.

Sautéing with a Butter Taste

To sauté with a butter taste, simply use water and butter granules. Each recipe in the book states how much of each to use. The amount of water and butter granules used depends upon the amount of ingredients being sautéed.

Sautéing with Stock

When you sauté with stock, you can use whatever stock flavor you wish according to what food is being prepared. Depending on how much time you have, you can make your own stock or buy the canned broth and defat it.

If necessary, you can also prepare bouillon cube for sautéing. Just remember that bouillon cubes are very high in sodium.

I like to make my own stock, pour it into ice cube trays, freeze it and transfer it to freezer bags for convenient use. If it works better, keep a small container of stock in your refrigerator for sautéing.

For your convenience, I am including recipes for stock. Be sure to simmer the stock down so the end result is a very hearty stock. This makes a very good sautéing frozen stock cube that will add flavor to the food. Homemade adds the best taste to foods, however, canned broth or even bouillon cubes will work.

Stock

(Recipe contains less than 6% fat)

2 to 3 lb. leftover or fresh
   bones
2 1/2 qt. water
2 tsp. seasoned salt (opt.)
3 or 4 c. vegetables—
   whatever you have
   leftover or in your crisper

1 lg. onion, coarsely
   chopped
Bouquet garni (tie 2 tsp.
   parsley flakes, 1/2 tsp.
   dried basil & 1 bay leaf in
   a piece of cheesecloth)

Break or saw bones into the smallest pieces possible and place into a heavy bottomed pan with a tight-fitting lid. Add water and salt. Bring to a boil and simmer 8 to 10 hours. If using fresh bones, brown first. Chop vegetables into small pieces along with the onion. After bones have boiled 4 hours, add vegetables and bouquet garni. Boil slowly several hours. Remove from heat and leave covered. Allow to stand 1 hour. Strain through cloth. Refrigerate and allow fat to solidify. Defat and use stock immediately, or freeze for later use.

This stock makes a wonderful base for many soups with the addition of noodles, rice, vegetables, etc. With the use of a little imagination, you can create your own low-fat soups.

Yield: 1 quart

Approximate Per Cup:
Calories: 10
Fat: 0.1 g
Cholesterol: tr. mg

Carbohydrates: 0 g
Protein: 0 g
Sodium: 0 mg

Exchange: Free food in limited amounts

*When baking French bread, shape some into buns
for individual submarine sandwiches.*

Brown Bone Stock

(Recipe contains only a trace of fat—less than 5%)

3 lb. beef bones
3 sm. onions, quartered
2 carrots, chunked
1 stalk celery, chunked
Bouquet garni (4 sprigs parsley,
    pinch dried thyme, pinch
    basil & 2 bay leaves tied
    in a cheesecloth pouch)

5 peppercorns
3 qt. water
1 1/2 tsp. salt (opt.)

Wipe bones with paper towel. Don't wash unless a must. Put bones in a large, heavy-bottomed pan over medium heat and fry bones for 10 minutes, or until browned. DO NOT ADD FAT. Stir bones around in pan frequently. DO NOT ALLOW TO BURN. Add vegetables and brown with bones, cooking another 10 to 15 minutes, and stirring very frequently. Add water, bouquet garni, peppercorns and salt. If water level isn't about 2/3 above ingredients, change pans and add a little more water.

Bring to a slow boil. Put lid on pan, covering only half of pan (this allows liquid to reduce) and simmer for 4 to 5 hours. Stock should be strong with a good taste at end of cooking time. If not, allow to continue to simmer. At end of cooking time, this should be a hearty stock, great for sauces and casseroles. If you want a stock for soups, dilute stock with water using 1 cup water to 2 cups stock. Or, if you prefer, re-boil bones with fresh vegetables for soup stock.

Strain stock through cheesecloth. You should have about 6 cups of strong brown bone stock. Re-use bones for soup stock if you so desire. Place stock in the refrigerator until any fat that might be present has solidified. Remove fat, then use stock or freeze in ice cube trays and drop a cube or two in casseroles and soups at time of preparation.

Drop in casseroles or soup at will, as it will not affect the fat contained in the recipe. Great way to add extra taste to a recipe without adding countable calories, fat or cholesterol.

Yield: approximately 6 cups stock times 16 tablespoons equals 96 tablespoons or 48 (2 tablespoon) cubes.

Approximate Per 2 tablespoon Cube:
Calories: 1   **Fat:** tr.
Cholesterol: tr.

Exchange: Free food

Fish Fumet

*(Recipe contains less than 6% fat per cup when diluted soup stock;
recipe contains only a trace of fat per cube
for 2 tablespoon cubes)*

2 1/2 to 3 lb. fish bones—I
use bones after fish have
been filleted. Most fish
lovers include heads, but
I've never been inclined
to do so.
12 c. water
6 stalks celery & leaves,
chopped

2 lg. onions, chopped
1 clove garlic, chopped
1 lg. carrot, cut in chunks
Bouquet garni (tie 1/2 tsp.
dried thyme, 1 bay leaf,
4 sprigs parsley, 1/2 tsp.
basil & 10 peppercorns in
in cheesecloth)
3 T. lemon juice

Tie the fish bones and scrap meat in a cheesecloth so it will be
easy to discard. Put all ingredients, except lemon juice, in a large
heavy-bottomed pot and bring to a boil. Lower heat and simmer for
30 minutes. Put pot in sink and tie cheesecloth containing fish
around water spigot. Allow juices to drip into pan for 30 minutes.
Squeeze cheesecloth gently before discarding, to further strengthen
stock.

Strain stock into a smaller saucepan and discard vegetables and
bouquet garni; return to stove. Simmer, uncovered, until reduced
by half. Great for sauces and casseroles. For stocks, add 2 cups
water for 3 cups stock. Stock must be chilled and defatted before
use. Use at will.

Yield: about 6 cups full strength; 9 cups diluted for soup stock

Approximate Per 1 cup Diluted Soup Stock:
Calories: 16   **Fat:** 0.1 g
Cholesterol: tr. mg

Exchange: Free food

Approximate Per 2 tablespoon Cube:
Calories: 2   **Fat:** tr. g
Cholesterol: tr. mg

Exchange: Free food

Mixed Stock

(Recipe contains less than 6% fat as soup base;
recipe contains a trace of fat as a 2 tablespoon cube)

2 to 3 lb. leftover bones—
chicken, steak, roast, ham
along with any leftover
meat trimmed of visible
fat (don't be afraid to mix
bones)

6 to 8 c. root vegetables—
carrots, celery, onions, or
scrubbed potato peels (it
doesn't matter if they look
shriveled, the flavor is
still there)

Bouquet garni (3 parsley
stalks, pinch of thyme,
pinch of basil & 1 bay
leaf tied in a cheesecloth
bag)

1 tsp. salt (opt.)

3 qt. water

Break or saw bones in small pieces—the more bone exposure, the
better the stock. Chop all vegetables coarsely for cut vegetable
exposure. Put bones and vegetables in heavy-bottomed kettle and
add water and bouquet garni; add salt. Water level should cover
vegetables and bones and extend about 2/3 above ingredients. If it
doesn't, change pans or add additional water. Half cover pan and
simmer 2 hours, or until stock has a strong, good taste. Stock should
reduce by 1/3. Strain, cool, chill and then defat. Use in sauces and
casseroles. For soups, dilute with water—1 cup water for 2 cups
stock.
Yield: 2 quarts

Approximate Per One Cup Soup Base:
Calories: 16 **Fat:** 0.1 g
Cholesterol: tr. mg

Exchange: Free food

Approximate Per Each 2 Tablespoon cube:
Calories: 2 **Fat:** tr. g
Cholesterol: tr. mg

Exchange: Free food

Sour Cream Substitute

I have used some commercial "light" sour cream in some of the recipes in this book. This was done to make the recipes more simple to make. Let's face it, many people do not have a lot of time to spend in the kitchen and will only use low-fat recipes if they are made simple. For those of you who have the time or are willing to spend the time to make the substitute, I have included the Sour Cream Substitute.

Mock Sour Cream

(Recipe contains approximately 22% fat)

1 c. "yogurt cheese" (see index)

If using in hot dish, use 1 scant teaspoon cornstarch. Stir in cornstarch just before using.
Yield: 1 cup or 16 tablespoons

Approximate Per Tablespoon:
Calories: 11   **Carbohydrates:** 1 g
Fat: 0.3 g   **Protein:** 1 g
Cholesterol: 0.9 mg.   **Sodium:** 10 mg

Exchange: Free

Approximate Per Cup:
Calories: 180   **Carbohydrates:** 16 g
Fat: 4.4 g   **Protein:** 12 g
Cholesterol: 14.0 mg   **Sodium:** 159 mg

Exchange Per Cup: 2 milk

Sour Cream Granules

It is now possible to buy sour cream granules. I use the Molly McButter brand, but there are several on the market. These granules, when mixed in or sprinkled on food, lend a nice sour cream taste. Give them a try. You'll be surprised how good they taste.

White Sauce, Thin

(Recipe contains approximately 30% fat)

1 tsp. tub margarine	Pinch of pepper
1 T. flour	1 c. skim milk
1/4 tsp. salt (opt.)	

Put margarine in the top of a double boiler and, over boiling water, allow margarine to melt. Add flour, salt and pepper, cooking for 2 minute and stirring constantly. Remove from stove and very gradually add milk. Return to stove and cook until mixture thickens.

Yield: 1 cup

Approximate Per Tablespoon:

Calories: 9	**Carbohydrates:** 1 g
Fat: 0.3 g	**Protein:** tr. g
Cholesterol: tr. g	**Sodium:** 44 mg

Exchange Per 2 Tablespoons: 1/4 milk

Whipped Topping Substitute

In my last two books, I used a whipped topping substitute in my recipes. In this book, I used the "light" Cool Whip. Once again my reasoning was encouraging people to use the low-fat recipes by making them simpler to prepare. In talking to people the biggest complaint is the extra work it takes to prepare low-fat food. It is for this reason that I have used the "light" Cool Whip.

For those of you with the time and dedication to even lower fat, I am including a Whipped Topping Substitute.

Put corn in a French fry basket before boiling,
for simple removal from pan.

Whipped Topping Substitute II

(Recipe contains approximately 3% fat)

1 (8 oz.) pkg. fat-free
    cream cheese
1 can evaporated skim
    milk, very cold

2 tsp. vanilla
12 pkt. Equal sweetener,
    or sweetener of choice to
    equal 1/2 c. sugar

In a large mixing bowl, beat cream cheese until fluffy—this takes about 5 minutes. In a second mixing bowl, beat evaporated skim milk until it forms peaks. Gradually add sweetener to whipped milk. Beat whipped milk into cream cheese. Put in a container and store in refrigerator.

Yield: About 5 cups

Approximate Per Tablespoon:
Calories: 9
Fat: tr. g
Cholesterol: 1 mg

Carbohydrates:1 g
Protein: 1 g
Sodium: 46 mg

Exchange: 1 to 2 tablespoons free food

Yogurt

Making Your Own Yogurt

There is nothing difficult about making yogurt. The main thing to remember is that the temperature must be right for the milk to yog. Homemade yogurt is lower in fat than any you can buy, and costs only pennies a cup. It takes very little time to mix up, and yogs while you're taking care of other chores, or even while you're at work.

When yogurt doesn't yog, it usually means that your heat was not at the proper temperature or that the containers were not properly washed and rinsed. Any kind of milk can be used for yogurt. Experiment and see which flavor you like best. You can also experiment and discover how long you like your yogurt to yog.

Time determines the tartness the yogurt takes on. Once you have learned to make your own yogurt and discovered its many uses, you'll have it on hand in your refrigerator at all times.

Low-Fat Yogurt

(With cool water, recipe contains approximately 7% fat;
with skin milk, recipe contains approximately 6% fat)

2 1/2 c. low-fat dry milk
    granules
4 c. cool water

2 T. yogurt (use a good
    grade of yogurt from a
    previous batch)

OR:

2 c. low-fat dry milk
    granules

4 c. skim milk (for a
    richer yogurt)
2 T. plain yogurt

In a large heavy-bottomed saucepan, blend water (or milk) with dry milk granules. Stir until granules have dissolved. Cook over medium heat to scalding point. Do not boil. Remove from heat and allow to cool until temperature reaches 110° to 115°. Use a candy thermometer to determine proper temperature.

Stir in yogurt, blending until smooth. Pour into containers that have been thoroughly washed and rinsed with boiling water. Use incubation method you prefer.

Incubation: To incubate yogurt, it's necessary to keep the temperature between 90° to 120°. Anything above 120° will kill the yogurt culture. Anything below 90° will more than likely turn into no more than soured milk. For the best yogurt, the temperature should be kept as close to 115° as possible.

If you have a commercial yogurt maker, simply follow the manufacturer's directions for incubation. If you don't have a yogurt maker you will have to improvise the method best for you. This can only be done by experimenting with water and a thermometer until you find a place that will keep yogurt formula at an even temperature as near 115° as possible.

One of the following incubation methods might work for you:

1. Set a pan of water over the pilot light of your stove (if you cook with gas). Put a candy or meat thermometer into the water and leave it for three hours. After three hours, check to see what the temperature is. If the water is over 115°, try placing the pan on a trivet to adjust temperature and run another 3 hour test.

Continued on following page.

Continued on preceding page.

2. Place a pan of water on a trivet over the small burner of an electric stove and set the burner at lowest setting. Insert thermometer and check after three hours. If temperature is within incubation range, this method may be used.

3. Float a casserole dish in a pan of water and set on pilot light or small burner of stove at low setting. Follow described testing procedure above.

4. Place a pan of water on a heating pad and follow testing procedure.

5. Set a pan of water on an electric warming tray, set at low setting (or higher, if necessary) and follow testing procedure.

6. Fill a chafing dish with water and follow testing procedure.

Almost any kind of milk can be used for yogurt as long as it is low in fat. If you don't care for the recipes I use, try using evaporated skim milk or combine it with fresh skim milk or low-fat dry milk. Experiment until you get the taste you like best.

Yogurt should yog within 5 hours. The nearer the temperature is to 115°, the faster the formula will yog. If you don't have yogurt within 5 hours, your temperature is probably below 90° and you'll never have anything more than soured milk.

Yield: each recipe makes 1 quart

Approximate Per 1/2 Cup:
(if cool water is used):

Calories: 77

Carbohydrates: 12 g

Fat: 0.6 g

Protein: 8 g

Cholesterol: 4 mg

Sodium: 126 mg

Approximate Per 1/2 Cup:
(if using skim milk):

Calories: 120

Carbohydrates: 12 g

Fat: 0.8 g

Protein: 8 g

Cholesterol: 6 mg

Sodium: 127 mg

Exchange: 1 1/2 milk

Yogurt Cheese

(Recipe contains approximately 22% fat)

1 c. plain low-fat yogurt   **1 coffee filter**

Put coffee filter over glass and fasten securely with a rubber band. Cheesecloth works even better. Put yogurt into coffee filter and cover with plastic wrap. Put in refrigerator for several hours to allow whey to drip out of yogurt. This makes a more solid product that will not separate as easily when used in a salad or casserole. If you wish, put whey in a soup, stew or casserole for extra nutrition.

Note: When using "yogurt cheese" in a recipe, measure yogurt before removing whey and use amount of "yogurt cheese" remaining after whey has dripped out. When using "yogurt cheese" in hot dishes, always blend one scant teaspoon of cornstarch into yogurt. This gives the yogurt the courage to stand up in most recipes and not break down.

Approximate Per Tablespoon:
Calories: 9   **Cabohydrates:** 1 g
Fat: 0.2 g   **Protein:** 1 g
Cholesterol: 0.9 mg   **Sodium:** 10 mg

Exchange: Free food

Approximate Per Cup:
Calories: 144   **Carbohydrates:** 16 g
Fat: 3.5 g   **Protein:** 12 g
Cholesterol: 14 mg   **Sodium:** 159 mg

Exchange: 1 milk

Soups & Tidbits

Soups and Tidbits

In most families, as the dinner hour approaches, family members begin to gather in the kitchen to announce their hunger and oversee the final preparation of dinner.

This kitchen congestion can be a problem for large family gatherings as the kitchen begins to fill with wall to wall people.

There is, however, a very simple solution. Before the final preparation of dinner, simply serve the soup course in another room. This may sound like there should be a problem with its consumption, however, it can be done very simply.

First, serve a puréed soup and if a formal sit-down dinner is being served, serve the soup in a nice stemmed wine glass. For a less formal dinner serve the soup in a nice tea or coffee cup. If it is a picnic or very informal affair, serve soup in a paper or plastic cup. Cold soups are nice for picnics on hot days.

With the soup, serve some simple tidbits. Just remember that the soup course should only dull the appetite and not satisfy it. Fill the glasses or cups in the kitchen and serve them on a tray with some tidbits.

What you are doing here is serving the first course before your family or guests come to the table. Keep the serving small, no more than six to eight ounces. As for the tidbits, allow for not more than two or three small tidbits per person.

This works great, keeps your family and guests happy and keeps the traffic out of the kitchen.

The soups in this chapter are puréed and the tidbits are simple and small. Bon Appetit!

When you can't get anymore dressing from the bottle add 2 tablespoons vinegar and shake--creates a new dressing and lets you use all the dressing in the bottle.

Hot Soups

Cauliflower Soup

(Recipe contains approximately 3% fat)

1/4 c. water
1 tsp. butter granules
1/2 c. minced onions
1 med. head cauliflower, cut
   in 1" pieces
1 1/2 c. canned chicken broth
   (can use bouillon)

1 c. evaporated skim milk
1/4 tsp. garlic powder
1/4 tsp. seasoned salt
1/4 tsp. white pepper
Dash of nutmeg

Put water and butter granules in a saucepan and bring to boil. Add onions and sauté until soft. Add cauliflower; cover and cook 5 minutes, stirring several times to prevent burning (add a bit of water, if needed). Pour in enough stock just to cover vegetables, cover and bring to boil. Reduce heat and simmer 10 minutes, or until cauliflower is tender. Purée vegetables in a blender (do in several batches) and return to pan. Add evaporated skim milk, remaining stock and seasoning. Return to stove and heat through. DO NOT BOIL. Serve in stemmed glasses or in cups.
Yield: 5 servings

Approximate Per Serving:
Calories: 70
Fat: 0.2 g
Cholesterol: 1.5 mg

Carbohydrates: 9.9 g
Protein: 4.5 g
Sodium: 350 mg

Exchanges: 1/2 milk; 1 vegetable

Notch your bread board in inches, so when you roll dough you'll know exactly when you have the dough the right size.

Cream of Broccoli Soup

(Recipe contains approximately 4% fat)

1/2 c. water	1/4 tsp. salt (opt.)
1 tsp. butter granules	1/4 tsp. pepper
1 med. onion, chopped	2 (10 1/2 oz.) pkg. chopped
1 lg. potato, diced	broccoli
2 cans chicken broth	1 c. evaporated skim milk

Put water and butter granules in a saucepan and bring to boil. Add onions and sauté until soft. Add potato, broth, salt, pepper and chopped broccoli. Bring to boil, lower heat and simmer until potato is tender (about 15 minutes). Remove from heat and purée mixture in blender, in batches. Return to pan and add skim milk. Heat through—DO NOT BOIL! Serve immediately.
Yield: 6 servings

Approximate Per Serving:

Calories: 113	**Carbohydrates: 18.2 g**
Fat: 0.5 g	**Protein: 9.2 g**
Cholesterol: 1.5 mg	**Sodium: 429 mg**

Exchanges: 1 bread; 2 vegetable

Glue rubber fruit-jar rings under each corner of your pastry board so it won't slide around when you roll out biscuits or knead dough.

Easy Corn Chowder

(Recipe contains approximately 4% fat)

1 med. red potato, peeled
   & diced
1 onion, chopped
1 c. water
1 chicken bouillon cube
1 (16 oz.) can cream-style
   corn

2 c. skim milk
2 tsp. butter granules
1/4 tsp. salt
1/4 tsp. pepper
Egg substitute to = 1 egg
1 green onion, chopped

Put potatoes, onion, water and bouillon cube in saucepan and bring to a boil. Simmer for 15 to 20 minutes, or until potato is tender. Add corn, skim milk, butter granules, salt and pepper. Bring to boil. Remove from heat and add a little of hot mixture to egg substitute. Add egg substitute to corn mixture. Blend, then return to stove until hot. Remove from stove and purée in blender, in batches. Add chopped green onion. Serve in stemmed glasses or cups.
Yield: 4 servings

Approximate Per Serving:
Calories: 125
Fat: 0.6 g
Cholesterol: 1.0 mg

Carbohydrates: 24.1 g
Protein: 5.0 g
Sodium: 212 mg

Exchanges: 1 bread; 3/4 milk

If you don't have herbs, substitute with dried herbs.
Use only half the dried herbs.

Good for You Potato Soup

(Recipe contains only a trace of fat)

1 onion, chopped	3 c. water
1/4 c. water	3 c. chicken stock
1 tsp. butter granules	1/2 bay leaf
10 cloves garlic, peeled	1/4 tsp. seasoned salt
Skins from 4 lb. scrubbed	1/4 tsp. pepper
potatoes	1/4 c. fresh, minced parsley

In a heavy-bottomed pan, put water and butter granules and bring to a boil. Add onion and sauté about 10 minutes, or until soft—stir often. Add garlic and cook 2 to 3 minutes, stirring. Stir in potato skins, water, stock, bay leaf, seasoned salt and pepper. Bring to a boil, then simmer for 45 minutes. Discard bay leaf and process in blender, in batches. Add parsley. Return to stove and heat through, stirring until hot. DO NOT BOIL. Remove from stove and cool. Chill, covered, overnight to allow flavors to blend. Reheat and serve in stemmed glasses or cups.
Yield: 6 servings

Approximate Per Serving:

Calories: 79	**Carbohydrates: 10.9 g**
Fat: Trace	**Protein: 3.3 g**
Cholesterol: 0.0 mg	**Sodium: 124 mg**

Exchanges: 1 bread; 1/4 vegetable

Use kitchen shears to cut pizza quick and easy.

Green Pea and Potato Soup

(Recipe contains approximately 4% fat)

1 lg. onion, chopped
1/4 c. water
1 tsp. butter granules
6 med. potatoes, peeled &
    sliced
3 c. fresh (or frozen) peas
6 c. canned chicken broth

1 bay leaf
1/4 tsp. garlic powder
1/4 tsp. sodium-free seasoned
    salt
1/2 c. evaporated skim milk
1/2 tsp. butter granules

Put water and butter granules in a saucepan and bring to boil. Add onions and sauté until soft. Add remaining ingredients, except milk and 1/2 teaspoon butter granules. Simmer 20 minutes, or until potatoes are tender. Discard bay leaf. Purée in blender, in several batches. Stir in evaporated milk and butter granules. Return to stove and heat through. DO NOT BOIL. Serve in stemmed glasses or cups.

Yield: 10 servings

Approximate Per Serving:
Calories: 101
Fat: 0.4 g
Cholesterol: 1.0 mg

Carbohydrates: 18.9 g
Protein: 5.2 g
**Sodium: 701 mg (for lower
    sodium use low-sodium broth)**

Exchanges: 1 1/2 bread

*When box instructs "press here" use the pointed side of
a beverage can opener. Saves the fingernails.*

Hot Apple Soup

(Recipe contains approximately 10% fat)

1/4 c. water	1 T. tub margarine
1 tsp. butter granules	2 T. water
1 lg. onion, chopped	1/2 tsp. chicken bouillon
4 c. chicken stock	granules
2 lg. Granny Smith apples,	1/4 c. enriched all-purpose
peeled, cored & chopped	flour
Juice of half a lemon	1/2 c. evaporated skim milk
1/4 tsp. curry powder	1/2 tsp. butter granules

Put water and butter granules in a saucepan and bring to boil. Add onions and sauté until soft. Add chicken stock, apples, lemon juice and curry. Bring to boil and simmer about 10 minutes. In a second saucepan, melt margarine. Dissolve bouillon in water and add to margarine. Stir in flour, blending. Cook 2 minutes, stirring constantly, to cook flour. Very gradually stir in apple mixture. Bring to boil—DO NOT BOIL. Remove from stove and press through sieve, using back of spoon. Add salt and pepper to taste. Stir in milk and 1/2 teaspoon butter granules. Return to stove and just heat through.

Yield: 8 servings

Approximate Per Serving:

Calories: 95	**Carbohydrates: 14.8 g**
Fat: 1.1 g	**Protein: 4.7 g**
Cholesterol: 0.6 mg	**Sodium: 391 mg**

Exchanges: 1/2 bread; 1 fruit; 1/2 fat

Use a nylon scouring pad to scrub vegetables for cooking.

Puréed Vegetable Soup

(Recipe contains approximately 2% fat)

4 med. potatoes, peeled
   & diced
2 c. shredded cabbage
1 lg. carrot, scraped & sliced
2 lg. ribs celery, chopped
2 med. onions, peeled &
   chopped

3 1/2 c. chicken stock
1/4 tsp. garlic powder
1/2 tsp. sodium-free seasoned
   salt (opt.)
1/4 tsp. pepper
Fresh parsley, chopped

Put all ingredients in a saucepan, except parsley; bring to boil and simmer 25 minutes, or until vegetables are tender. Remove from stove and purée in a blender, in batches. Serve in stemmed glasses or in cups. Sprinkle chopped parsley over top.
Yield: 6 servings

Approximate Per Serving:
Calories: 95
Fat: 0.2 g
Cholesterol: 0.0 mg

Carbohydrates: 20.3 g
Protein: 5.2 g
Sodium: 423 mg

Exchanges: 1 bread; 1 vegetable

*If you run out of confectioners' sugar in the midst of a recipe,
substitute with granulated sugar that has been run through the blender.*

Chilled Soups

Chilled Cantaloupe Soup
(Recipe contains approximately 3% fat)

1 (4 lb.) cantaloupe
Artificial sweetener of choice,
   to equal 1/4 c. sugar

1/2 c. dry sherry (can use
   orange juice)
1 T. fresh lime juice

Halve and seed cantaloupe. Scoop out flesh and put in blender. Add sweetener, sherry and lime juice. Process until smooth. Put in glass container, cover and refrigerate overnight. Serve very cold. This soup must be refrigerated for 24 hours for best flavor.
Yield: 4 servings

Approximate Per Serving:
Calories: 97
Fat: 0.3 g
Cholesterol: 0.0 mg

Carbohydrates: 19.2 g
Protein: 1.7 g
Sodium: Trace

Exchanges: 2 1/2 fruit

A watering can with a small spout is great for filling ice cube trays.

Chilled Celery and Potato Soup

(Recipe contains approximately 16% fat)

1/4 c. water
1 tsp. butter granules
3 c. chopped celery
1 c. chopped onion
3 c. chicken stock
2 c. water
1 tsp. garlic powder

1/2 tsp. sodium-free seasoned
   salt
1 bay leaf
3 c. peeled, diced potatoes
1/2 c. evaporated skim milk
Chopped parsley

Put water and butter granules in a saucepan and bring to boil. Add celery and onions and sauté until soft, about 10 minutes. Add stock and water. Stir in garlic powder and seasoned salt. Add bay leaf and potatoes and simmer about 20 to 25 minutes, or until potatoes are tender. Remove bay leaf. Purée in blender, in several batches. Strain purée (if desired) and stir in milk. Allow to cool. Chill at least 6 hours (overnight is even better). Serve in stemmed glasses with chopped parsley.
Yield: 8 servings

Approximate Per Serving:
Calories: 63
Fat: 1.1 g
Cholesterol: 0.6 mg

Carbohydrates: 120 g
Protein: 3.0 g
Sodium: 393 mg

Exchanges: 1/2 bread; 1 vegetable

When preparing a covered dish for a co-op dinner, line dish with aluminum foil. Allows you to take your dish home clean.

Chilled Mushroom Soup

(Recipe contains approximately 7% fat)

1 tsp. tub margarine
3 bunches green onions
(whites only)
2 T. green onions (green only)
1 1/2 T. enriched all-purpose
flour
1/2 tsp. curry powder

2 1/2 c. warm water
2 1/2 c. evaporated skim
milk, warm
1 c. finely-chopped
mushrooms
1/2 tsp. garlic powder
1/4 tsp. seasoned salt

Melt margarine and sauté green onions. Add flour and curry powder—cook two minutes, stirring constantly. Remove saucepan from stove and slowly whisk in water and milk. Add remaining ingredients, along with a little pepper, if desired. Partially cover pan and simmer for 30 minutes. Purée in blender, in several batches. Allow to cool, then chill at least 6 hours or overnight. Serve in stemmed glasses. Sprinkle with chopped onion green.
Yield: 6 servings

Approximate Per Serving:
Calories: 132
Fat: 1.0 g
Cholesterol: 3.8 mg

Carbohydrates: 20.3 g
Protein: 9.1 g
Sodium: 152 mg

Exchanges: 1 milk; 1/2 vegetable; 1 fat

Small handpainted tiles make attractive and inexpensive coasters.

Cold Apple Soup

(Recipe contains approximately 4% fat)

1/4 c. water
1 tsp. butter granules
1 med. onion, diced
3 med. apples, peeled, cored
  & sliced
1 carrot, sliced thin
1 green pepper, seeded &
  diced

1 rib celery, diced
2 whole cloves
1 tsp. curry powder
Pinch of ground nutmeg
6 c. chicken stock
1/4 tsp. pepper

Put water and butter granules in a 6-quart saucepan and bring to boil. Add onion and sauté until soft (about 10 minutes). Add apples, carrots, green pepper and celery. Sauté until soft. Add more water, if needed. Add cloves, curry and nutmeg. Stir in chicken stock and add salt and pepper. Cover and simmer 30 to 40 minutes. Remove from stove and purée in blender, in batches. Pour into bowl. Cover and allow to cool. Refrigerate at least 6 hours. Serve in stemmed glasses or cups.
Yield: 8 servings

Approximate Per Serving:
Calories: 43
Fat: 0.2 g
Cholesterol: 0.0 mg

Carbohydrates: 8.9 g
Protein: 1.3 g
Sodium: 728 mg

Exchanges: 1 fruit

Turn strong onions into sweet onions: Slice thin, pour boiling water over them, drain and chill. Will come out crisp and sweet.

Cucumber Vichyssoise

(Recipe contains approximately 2% fat)

1/4 c. water
1 tsp. butter granules
1/4 c. diced onion
1/4 c. diced celery
2 lg. potatoes, peeled & diced
1 can chicken broth

1/4 tsp. seasoned salt
1/4 tsp. pepper
1 c. skim milk
1 tsp. sour cream granules
1/2 c. finely-chopped
   cucumber

Put water and butter granules in saucepan and bring to boil. Add onions and celery. Sauté until soft (about 10 minutes). Add potatoes, broth, seasoned salt and pepper; bring to boil. Simmer 15 minutes, or until potatoes are tender. Add remaining ingredients. Remove from stove and purée in blender, in batches, until smooth. Cool to room temperature; refrigerate overnight or at least all day. Serve very cold.
Yield: 4 servings

Approximate Per Serving:
Calories: 123
Fat: 0.3 g
Cholesterol: 1.3 mg

Carbohydrates: 21.8 g
Protein: 6.4 g
Sodium: 508 mg

Exchanges: 1 bread; 1 vegetable; 1/4 milk

When chopping onions, put the chopping board on the range top and turn on the exhaust fan in the hood. Helps eliminate odors and tears.

White Gazpacho

(Recipe contains approximately 5% fat)

2 (16 oz.) cans chicken broth
2 c. white dry wine (or broth)
1/2 c. lemon juice
3 cucumbers, chopped
3 tomatoes, peeled, seeded
   & chopped
3/4 c. thinly-sliced green
   onion
1/2 c. minced, fresh parsley
1/4 tsp. Tabasco sauce
White pepper, to taste
1/2 tsp. garlic powder

Put broth, wine, lemon juice and bouillon cubes in a pan and bring to boil. Remove from stove and allow to cool. Chill for at least two hours. Add vegetables, Tabasco sauce, pepper and garlic salt. Purée in blender. Put in large bowl and chill at least six hours. Overnight is even better. Serve in stemmed glasses, cups or paper cups.

Yield: 8 servings

Approximate Per Serving:
Calories: 67
Fat: 0.4 g
Cholesterol: 0.0 mg

Carbohydrates: 6.0 g
Protein: 1.1 g
Sodium: 190 mg

Exchanges: 3 vegetable

To make a liner for a baking pan; shape the foil over the outside of the pan. It will then fit the inside of the pan great.

Tidbits

Cheese Stix

(Recipe contains approximately 23% fat)

1/3 c. flour
1/4 tsp. white pepper
1/4 c. "free" no-fat
   Philadelphia cream cheese
1 T. tub margarine

1 T. boiling water
2 tsp. cheese granules
2 tsp. Worcestershire
   sauce

In a mixing bowl, blend flour, white pepper, cream cheese and margarine, using a pastry blender, until mixture is even in texture. Combine boiling water and cheese granules, stirring until dissolved. Add Worcestershire sauce and drizzle mixture over flour mixture. Blend just until moist. Shape into tight ball. Roll dough out on lightly-floured surface to 1/4-inch thickness. Cut into 3x1/2-inch strips. Place strips onto an ungreased baking sheet. Bake in 450° preheated oven for 6 minutes, or until lightly browned.
Yield: 24 stix

Approximate Per Stick:
Calories: 12
Fat: 0.3 g
Cholesterol: 0.4 mg

Carbohydrates: 1.4 g
Protein: 0.5 g
Sodium: 53 mg

Exchanges: 4 stix = 1/2 bread; 1/4 fat

If you have a cracked egg, you can still boil it if you wrap it in aluminum foil before immersing it into boiling water.

Cheesy Wedges
(Recipe contains approximately 12% fat)

2 oz. low-fat mozzarella
   cheese
10 lg. ripe olives
1/2 c. "fat-free" mayonnaise
6 thinly-sliced green onions
   (use part of green)

1/2 tsp. garlic powder
1/2 tsp. curry powder
8 English muffins split &
   toasted

Combine everything except English muffins. Blend and spread onto 16 toasted English muffin halves. Arrange on baking sheet and put under broiler for about 3 minutes, or until cheese melts. Cut each muffin half into four wedges. Serve hot.
Yield: 64 wedges

Approximate Per Serving:
Calories: 66
Fat: 0.9 g
Cholesterol: 1.0 mg

Carbohydrates: 4.1 g
Protein: 0.9 g
Sodium: 240 mg

Exchanges: 3 wedges = 1 bread

Before measuring syrup, honey or molasses, spray the measuring cup or spoon with cooking spray.

French Bread Appetizer

(Recipe contains approximately 12% fat)

12 (1") slices French bread
1 c. "free" no-fat Italian
  dressing
3 green onions, chopped
1/2 c. chopped green pepper

1 clove garlic, minced
1 T. butter granules
2 T. grated Parmesan cheese
8-second spray of cooking
  spray

Brush each piece of bread with Italian dressing and top with onion, green pepper and garlic. Sprinkle with butter granules and cheese, then spray with cooking spray. Put under broiler for 3 to 5 minutes. Cut each piece of bread into 3 fingers and serve immediately.
Yield: 36 fingers

Approximate Per Finger:
Calories: 37
Fat: 0.5 g
Cholesterol: 0.2 mg

Carbohydrates: 6.5 g
Protein: 1.2 g
Sodium: 89 mg

Exchanges: 2 fingers = 1 bread

*When meat needs marinating, put into a
plastic bag and seal. Requires less marinade.*

Garlic Melba Toast Curls

(Recipe contains approximately 13% fat)

1 loaf unsliced French bread
10-second spray of good-
   grade cooking spray

2 T. garlic powder

Put loaf of bread in freezer for two hours, or until firm, but not frozen. Cut loaf in paper-thin slices using a razor-sharp knife. Put slices on baking sheets. Spray lightly with cooking spray, then sprinkle with garlic powder. Bake in 250° preheated oven, turning occasionally, for 1 hour and 30 minutes, or until bread curls are golden brown. **Yield: 60 curls**

Approximate Per Bread Curl:
Calories: 21
Fat: 0.3 g
Cholesterol: 0.0 mg

Carbohydrates: 3.7 g
Protein: 0.6 g
Sodium: 41 mg

Exchanges: 3 curls = 1 bread

Italian-Italian Bread Slices

(Recipe contains approximately 7% fat)

6 (1") slices French bread,
   toasted
2 T. "free" no-fat Philadelphia
   cream cheese
1 tsp. garlic powder

1/2 c. "free" no-fat shredded
   mozzarella cheese
1 T. fresh parsley, minced
1 tsp. dried basil

Spread cream cheese on toasted French bread and sprinkle with garlic powder. Top with mozzarella cheese and sprinkle with parsley and basil. Broil 6 inches from heat until cheese melts. Serve immediately. **Yield: 6 servings**

Approximate Per Serving:
Calories: 125
Fat: 1.0 g
Cholesterol: 2.3 mg

Carbohydrates: 19.2 g
Protein: 6.7 g
Sodium: 325 mg

Exchanges: 1 1/2 bread; 1/4 milk

Low-Fat Garlic Bread

(Recipe contains approximately 12% fat)

8 slices Vienna bread
3 cloves garlic, peeled
   & halved

Good-grade cooking spray
1 T. butter granules

Rub garlic cloves over bread. Spray with cooking spray and sprinkle with butter granules. Place on baking sheet that has been sprayed with cooking spray. Bake in 350° oven for 10 to 15 minutes, depending on brownness desired.
Yield: 8 servings

Approximate Per Serving:
Calories: 73
Fat: 1.0 g
Cholesterol: 0.0 mg

Carbohydrates: 13.7 g
Protein: 2.0 g
Sodium: 45 mg

Exchanges: 1 bread

Parmesan Slices

(Recipe contains approximately 2% fat)

8 (1/2" thick) slices Vienna
   bread
1 clove garlic, cut crosswise

8-second spray of cooking
   spray
1/4 c. fresh grated Parmesan
   cheese

Put bread slices on baking sheet and bake in 350° for 8 minutes. Remove from oven and rub cut sides of bread with garlic. Spray with cooking spray and sprinkle with Parmesan cheese. Return to oven and bake 8 minutes, or until cheese has melted and bread is crisp. Serve immediately.
Yield: 8 servings

Approximate Per Serving:
Calories: 87
Fat: 2.8 g
Cholesterol: 2.0 mg

Carbohydrates: 26.0 g
Protein: 4.0 g
Sodium: 192 mg

Exchanges: 1 bread; 1/2 fat

Quick Bread Sticks

(Recipe contains approximately 6% fat)

2 whole wheat rolls　　　　　　1 T. butter granules
6-second spray of cooking spray　1 T. minced, fresh parsley
1/4 c. "free" Philadelphia
　　cream cheese

Split rolls in half. Cut each half in quarters. Place breadsticks onto a baking sheet that has been sprayed with cooking spray. Spray breadsticks with cooking spray and brush with mixture of cream cheese, butter granules and minced parsley. Bake in 200° preheated oven for 1 1/2 hours, or until light brown and crisp. Store in airtight container.
Yield: 16 sticks

Approximate Per Stick:
Calories: 15　　　　　　　　Carbohydrates: 0.1 g
Fat: 0.1 g　　　　　　　　　Protein: 0.5 g
Cholesterol: 3.3 mg　　　　　Sodium: 44 mg

Exchanges: 2 sticks = 1/2 bread

For a pretty summer table centerpiece, place washed carrots, celery, green peppers, radishes and cherry tomatoes in a large brandy snifter and sprinkle with crushed ice.

Quick Pizza Wedges

(Recipe contains approximately 3% fat)

1/3 c. tomato sauce	1/4 tsp. basil
1/4 tsp. garlic powder	1/4 tsp. oregano
1 T. finely-chopped onion	3 English muffins, halved
1 T. finely-chopped green pepper	6 slices "free" no-fat American cheese, diced

Blend tomato sauce, garlic powder, onion, green pepper, basil and oregano. Divide among six muffin halves, spreading out evenly over muffin. Top with cheese and bake in 350° preheated oven for 5 to 7 minutes. Remove from oven and cut each muffin half into quarters. Serve immediately.

Yield: 24 wedges

Approximate Per Wedge:

Calories: 30	Carbohydrates: 4.7 g
Fat: 0.1 g	Protein: 4.4 g
Cholesterol: 0.1 mg	Sodium: 167

Exchanges: 3 wedges = 1 bread; 1/4 milk

Slice English muffins in half before freezing. Saves work later on.

Sesame Soda Crackers

(Recipe contains approximately 28% fat)

1 c. enriched all-purpose flour
or whole blend flour
1/4 c. oatmeal
1/4 c. bulgur (cracked wheat)
2 T. sesame seed

3/4 tsp. salt (less, if desired)
1/2 tsp. baking soda
1/2 c. low-fat buttermilk
3 T. diet tub margarine,
melted

Put flour in a mixing bowl and set aside. Put oatmeal and bulgur in a blender and process until fine. Put in bowl with flour. Add sesame seed, salt and baking soda. Stir in buttermilk and melted margarine. Turn dough out onto floured surface and knead until dough is smooth, and even in color and texture. Form dough into ball and wrap in plastic wrap. Chill 30 minutes. Divide dough in half. On floured surface, roll into 10x12-inch rectangle. Place rolled dough onto a baking sheet that has been sprayed with cooking spray. Prick dough with fork; score in 2-inch squares with a knife. Bake in 350° preheated oven for 10 to 15 minutes, or until light brown and crisp. Put on rack to cool, then break into squares. Store loosely covered.

Yield: 60 crackers

Approximate Per Cracker:
Calories: 16
Fat: 0.5 g
Cholesterol: Trace

Carbohydrates: 2.5 g
Protein: 0.5 g
Sodium: 36 mg

Exchange: 4 crackers = 1 bread

*When a screw-top jar won't come open simply wrap a few
rubber bands around the lid to make a firm grip.*

Whole Wheat Pretzels

(Recipe contains approximately 23% fat)

2/3 c. lukewarm water
  (110° to 115°)
2 tsp. sugar
1 pkg. active dry yeast
1 c. whole wheat flour
2 T. tub margarine, melted
1/2 tsp. salt

1 c. enriched all-purpose flour
4-second spray of cooking
  spray
1 egg white, slightly beaten
1 T. water
2 T. sesame seeds

Put water and sugar in a small bowl and sprinkle with yeast. Set aside 10 minutes to proof. In a large mixing bowl, put whole wheat flour, margarine and salt. Add proofed yeast. Blend in enough white flour to make a soft dough. Turn out onto floured surface and knead 10 minutes until smooth and elastic. Place dough in bowl that has been sprayed with cooking spray. Turn once to coat both sides. Cover with plastic wrap and set in warm place one hour, or until dough has doubled in bulk.

Divide dough into 12 pieces. On a floured surface, roll each piece into a 14-inch rope and twist rope into a pretzel. Place 1/2-inch apart on foil-lined baking sheet that has been sprayed with cooking spray. Combine egg white and water. Brush over pretzels. Sprinkle with sesame seeds. Bake in 400° preheated oven 8 to 10 minutes, or until golden. Cool on racks.

Yield: 12 pretzels

Approximate Per Pretzel:
Calories: 96
Fat: 2.4 g
Cholesterol: 0.0 mg

Carbohydrates: 15.9 g
Protein: 3.2 g
Sodium: 46 mg

Exchanges: 1 bread; 1/2 fat

Notes &
Recipes

Pancakes, Waffles & Omelets

Pancakes, Waffles and Omelets

Many of us have a tendency to think of these as high fat products that we cannot have on a diet. They, in themselves, are not high in fat. It's what we put on them or in them.

Most of use like our pancakes swimming with butter and syrup. The syrup won't get us into too much trouble, unless we are diabetic, but the margarine is full of trouble in the fat department.

These are options when it comes to cutting the fat on pancakes and waffles. You might want to try some of the NO-FAT margarine. I have had different reviews on it.

Some find it acceptable; some think it tastes like lard; some don't like its "funny" consistency. I only find the consistency a problem it if is left unrefrigerated for any period of time.

I find it acceptable in small amounts. Don't spread it too thick on your pancakes and waffles, and float them in syrup—regular or sugar-free.

Another way to get the butter taste without the fat is to sprinkle some butter granules into the syrup and heat the syrup, stirring until they are dissolved. There is no written rule that states that pancakes must be swimming in butter or margarine to be good. I find them enjoyable without the butter or margarine.

Jam or jelly (preferably the all-fruit types without sugar added) is another alternative. Jam and jelly on pancakes or waffles can be very good without the butter or margarine.

For a change of taste, try putting NO-FAT cream cheese on your pancakes and then adding syrup. Not too bad.

As for omelets, these can be very low in fat. Avoid all together the cheese or use NO-FAT cheese in your omelets, and be careful of the fat used for cooking them. Use a cooking spray for cooking or a tiny bit of margarine, like a teaspoonful. Or perhaps both.

We all have a little different taste. The key to low-fat cooking is to find the option that cuts the fat, but still pleases our taste buds. Only when this has been accomplished can we be satisfied on a low-fat diet.

It is well-worth the time it takes to explore and discover what your taste buds need to be happy.

Pancakes

Apple Raisin Pancakes
(Recipe contains approximately 5% fat)

1 1/2 c. flour, whole wheat blend, unbleached or enriched all-purpose
6 pkt. Equal or artificial sweetener of choice to = 1/4 c. sugar
2 tsp. baking powder
1/4 tsp. salt (less if desired)
1/2 tsp. ground allspice
1/2 tsp. cinnamon
1 1/4 c. skim milk (room temp.)

Egg substitute to = 2 eggs
1/4 tsp. vanilla
1/4 c. hot water
1 tsp. butter granules
4 lg. Granny Smith apples, peeled, cored & sliced
1/2 c. raisins
3/4 tsp. cinnamon
5 pkt. sweetener, or sweetener of choice to = 3 T. sugar

In a mixing bowl, sift flour, sweetener, baking powder, salt, allspice and cinnamon. In a second bowl, put 1 cup milk, egg substitute and vanilla. Stir wet ingredients into dry ingredients just until moistened. Cover and chill 5 hours.

In a heavy-bottomed skillet, put water and butter granules and bring to boil. Add apples, raisins and 3/4 teaspoon cinnamon and cook until soft, stirring several times. Remove from heat and add sweetener. Set aside, keeping warm.

Stir chilled batter and thin with remaining milk. Using 1/2 cup batter for each pancake, cook on hot griddle or in heavy-bottomed skillet over moderate heat until bubbles cover top. Turn and cook second side. Put pancakes on hot serving plate and top with hot apples.
Yield: 6 pancakes

Approximate Per Pancake:
Calories: 257
Fat: 1.4 g
Cholesterol: 0.8 mg

Carbohydrates: 51.4 mg
Protein: 6.3 g
Sodium: 276 mg

Exchanges: 2 bread, 1 1/2 fruit: 1/4 milk; 1 fat

Applesauce Filled Pancakes

(Recipe contains approximately 5% fat)

Egg substitute to = 2 eggs
1/4 tsp. salt (less if desired)
1 1/4 c. flour, whole wheat
   blend, unbleached or
   enriched all-purpose flour

2 c. skim milk
1/4 tsp. vanilla extract
1/4 tsp. almond extract
2 c. pink unsweetened
   applesauce

In a mixing bowl, put egg substitute and salt. Add flour, 1/2 cup milk and extracts. Beat until smooth. While beating, add remaining milk. Spray a 6-inch skillet with cooking spray and add 2 tablespoons batter to skillet, and tilt skillet so entire skillet surface is coated (as you would for a crepe). Cook until bubbles form; turn for 1 minute. Keep warm while remaining are cooked. Stack pancakes, spreading each pancake with applesauce. Pour remaining applesauce over top of stack. Cut into 4 wedges.
Yield: 4 servings

Approximate Per Serving:
Calories: 268
Fat: 1.6 g
Cholesterol: 2.0 mg

Carbohydrates: 63.9 g
Protein: 10.1 g
Sodium: 228 mg

Exchanges: 2 bread; 1 fruit; 1/2 milk; 1 fat

Place two or three cans of frozen fruit juice wrapped in a paper towel in the center of your picnic basket. This keeps the food cool and the fruit juice is ready to mix and serve.

Banana Pancakes

(Recipe contains approximately 6% fat)

Egg substitute to = 2 eggs
6 pkt. Equal sweetener, or
    sweetener of choice, to =
    1/4 c. sugar
1 1/2 c. buttermilk
1 tsp. butter granules
2 tsp. grated lemon rind
1 tsp. vanilla

2 c. coarsely-chopped bananas
1 1/2 c. flour, whole wheat
    blend, unbleached or
    enriched all-purpose
2 1/2 tsp. baking powder
1/4 tsp. salt
3 lg. egg whites
Pinch of cream of tartar

Blend egg substitute and sweetener in a large mixing bowl. Add buttermilk and beat. Add butter granules, lemon rind and vanilla. Stir in bananas. Add flour, baking powder and salt. Blend. Beat egg whites and cream of tartar until stiff. DO NOT OVERBEAT. Fold into batter. Heat griddle or heavy-bottomed skillet. Spray with cooking spray. Cook over moderate heat, using 1/4 cup batter per pancake. Serve with "light" maple syrup.
Yield: 6 servings (3 pancakes per serving)

Approximate Per Serving:
Calories: 209
Fat: 1.5 g
Cholesterol: 2.3 mg

Carbohydrates: 36.4 g
Protein: 8.4 g
Sodium: 225 mg

Exchanges: 2 bread; 1/2 milk; 1/2 fat

Save time by slicing bananas with a pastry blender.

Blueberry Pancakes Deluxe

(Recipe contains approximately 20% fat)

1 c. whole wheat blend,
   unbleached or enriched
   all-purpose flour
4 tsp. baking powder
1 T. sugar
1 tsp. salt (less if desired)
1/4 tsp. cinnamon
2 c. skim milk

Egg substitute to = 1 egg
2 T. canola oil
1/4 tsp. butter granules
Juice of half a lemon
1/8 tsp. vanilla
1/2 c. canned, drained
   blueberries

Combine flour, baking powder, sugar, salt and cinnamon in a large mixing bowl. Blend well. Stir in milk, egg substitute, oil, butter granules, lemon juice and vanilla. Blend just until moistened. Gently fold in blueberries. Preheat griddle or heavy-bottomed skillet. Spray with cooking spray. Pour 1/4 cup batter on grill for each pancake and cook until bubbles form. Turn and cook second side. Serve immediately.
Yield: 20 pancakes

Approximate Per Pancake:
Calories: 75
Fat: 1.7 g
Cholesterol: 0.4 mg

Carbohydrates: 10.9 g
Protein: 2.4 g
Sodium: 137 mg

Exchanges: 2 pancakes = 1 1/2 bread; 1 fat

*Use a pancake turner to slide sandwiches into sandwich bags.
Keeps sandwiches from coming apart.*

Carrot-Potato Pancakes

(Recipe contains approximately 4% fat)

Egg substitute to = 2 eggs
3 T. enriched all-purpose flour
2 T. skim milk
1 1/2 lb. baking potatoes,
    peeled & shredded fine
2 lg. carrots, peeled & shredded
    fine

1 green onion, minced (use
    part of green)
3 T. minced fresh parsley
1/2 tsp. salt (less if desired)
1/4 tsp. pepper

In a large mixing bowl, put egg substitute, flour and milk. Blend well. Add potatoes, carrots, onions and parsley. Blend. Add salt and pepper and blend. Spray a skillet with cooking spray and heat over moderate heat until hot. Use 1/3 cup batter for each pancake, pouring into skillet and flattening slightly. Cook about 12 minutes per side, or until golden brown and potatoes are done. Serve immediately.
Yield: 6 servings

Approximate Per Serving:
Calories: 125
Fat: 0.6 g
Cholesterol: 0.1 mg

Carbohydrates: 19.3 g
Protein: 6.5 g
Sodium: 178

Exchanges: 1 bread, 1/2 vegetable; 1/2 milk

Write your grocery list on an envelope and you have a handy pocket for the coupons you intend to redeem.

Creamy Blueberry Pancakes with Blueberry Syrup

(Recipe contains approximately 20% fat)

Egg substitute to = 2 eggs
1 c. ricotta cheese
1/3 c. low-fat sour cream
1/4 c. sugar
2/3 c. flour, whole wheat
   blend, unbleached or
   enriched all-purpose

2 tsp. baking powder
1/8 tsp. salt
3/4 c. skim milk
2 c. fresh blueberries
4 egg whites
Pinch of cream of tartar

In a large mixing bowl, blend well, egg substitute, ricotta cheese, sour cream and sugar. Over this mixture sift flour, baking powder and salt. Blend well. Stir in milk, then add blueberries. Stir to blend. Beat egg whites with cream of tartar until stiff. DO NOT OVERBEAT. Heat griddle or heavy-bottomed skillet over medium heat. Spray with cooking spray. Use 3 tablespoons batter for each pancake. Cook until bubbles begin to appear; turn and cook second side. Place on heated platter and serve with blueberry syrup.

BLUEBERRY SYRUP:
2 c. fresh blueberries
1/4 c. sugar (if using sweetener
   add after syrup has cooked)

1/2 c. water
1 tsp. lemon juice
1/8 tsp. vanilla
1/4 tsp. butter granules

Cook 1 cup blueberries, sugar, water, lemon juice and vanilla in a heavy-bottomed saucepan, stirring until sugar has dissolved. Reduce heat and simmer until syrup thickens. Add remaining blueberries and cook about 5 minutes until blueberries are soft. Remove from stove. If using sweetener, add at this time. Add butter granules and stir until dissolved.
Yield: 8 servings

Approximate Per Serving:
Calories: 231
Fat: 5.2 g
Cholesterol: 19 mg

Carbohydrates: 34.6 g
Protein: 8.9 g
Sodium: 162 mg

Exchanges: 1 bread; 1 milk; 1 fruit; 1 fat

Noodle Pancakes

(Recipe contains approximately 14% fat)

8 oz. very thin noodles,
   cooked & drained
Egg substitute to = 2 eggs

1/2 tsp. salt, less if desired
1/4 tsp. pepper
Cooking spray

Put all ingredients, except cooking spray, in a mixing bowl and blend. Spray a griddle with cooking spray and heat over moderate heat until hot. Drop noodle batter in 8 mounds. Cook until browned. Spray top of mounds and turn. Cook second side. Serve immediately.
Yield: 8 servings

Approximate Per Serving:
Calories: 126
Fat: 2.0 g
Cholesterol: 0.0 mg

Carbohydrates: 14.1 g
Protein: 1.3 g
Sodium: 157 mg

Exchanges: 1 bread; 1/2 milk; 1/2 fat

Keep a magnifying glass on a string in your purse. When shopping hang it around your neck so you can read the fine print on labels.

Oatmeal Pancakes

(Recipe contains approximately 8% fat)

3/4 c. quick-cooking oats	1 1/4 c. flour, whole wheat
1 1/2 c. skim milk	blend, unbleached or
Egg substitute to = 2 eggs	enriched all-purpose flour
3/4 c. unsweetened applesauce	1 T. baking powder
1 T. hot water	1 T. sugar
1 tsp. butter granules	1/2 tsp. salt (less if desired)
	1/2 tsp. cinnamon

In a mixing bowl, put oats and milk. Blend, then set aside for 5 minutes. Add egg substitute and applesauce. Blend. Stir butter granules into hot water, stirring until granules dissolve. Add to oats mixture, blending well. In a large bowl, put flour, baking powder, sugar, salt and cinnamon. Blend. Add oats mixture to flour mixture, stirring just until moist. Cook on hot griddle or heavy-bottomed skillet sprayed with cooking spray, using 1/4 cup batter per pancake. Cook until bubbles cover top of pancake; turn and cook second side.

Yield: 12 pancakes (2 pancakes per serving)

Approximate Per Serving:

Calories: 198	**Carbohydrates: 39.1 g**
Fat: 1.7 g	**Protein: 8.1 g**
Cholesterol: 1.0 mg	**Sodium: 267 mg**

Exchanges: 2 bread, 1/2 milk; 1/2 fruit

When shopping during hot weather keep a lightweight foam cooler in the car. Place meat and parishables in cooler until you get home.

Pumpkin Pancakes a'la Apples

(Recipe contains approximately 5% fat)

1 lg. red Delicious apple,
    peeled, cored & sliced thin
1 T. water
1/2 tsp. butter granules
1/2 c. yellow cornmeal
1 c. boiling water
1 c. skim milk
1/2 c. canned pumpkin

Egg substitute to = 2 eggs
1 c. flour, whole wheat blend,
    unbleached or enriched
    all-purpose flour
1 T. sugar
2 1/2 tsp. baking powder
1 tsp. allspice
1/2 tsp. salt (less if desired)

In skillet, over medium heat, put water and butter granules. Stir until butter granules dissolve. Add apples and sauté until softened (3 or 4 minutes). Remove from heat and keep warm. In a large mixing bowl, mix cornmeal and boiling water. Allow to stand 5 minutes. Add milk, pumpkin and egg substitute; blend well. Blend together flour, sugar, baking powder, allspice and salt. Add to pumpkin mixture and stir just until moistened. Cook pancakes on griddle or in heavy bottomed skillet sprayed with cooking oil. When bubbles form on top, turn and cook second side. Keep warm. Put in stacks of flour and top with apples.
Yield: 6 servings

Approximate Per Serving:
Calories: 174
Fat: 0.9 g
Cholesterol: 0.7 mg

Carbohydrates: 34.2 g
Protein: 5.2 g
Sodium: 242 mg

Exchanges: 2 bread; 1/2 fat; 1/2 fruit

*Spare ice cube trays are convenient organizers and
storage containers for small odds and ends.*

Savory Pancakes

(Recipe contains approximately 12% fat)

3/4 c. whole wheat blend or
    enriched all-purpose flour
2 tsp. baking powder
1 tsp. sugar
1/4 tsp. salt

Egg substitute to = 1 egg
1/2 c. plain nonfat yogurt
1/4 c. sparkling water
Cook spray

Combine flour, baking powder, sugar and salt. Add egg substitute, yogurt and sparkling water. Stir with wooden spoon just until flour mixture is moistened. If you have a few lumps don't worry about them, they will cook out. Spray a nonstick skillet or griddle with cooking spray and pour 3 tablespoons of batter in skillet for each pancake. Cook until top is covered with bubbles. Turn and cook second side. Serve immediately.

Yield: 8 pancakes

Approximate Per Pancake:
Calories: 65
Fat: 0.9 g
Cholesterol: 1.0 mg

Carbohydrates: 11.0 g
Protein: 3.0 g
Sodium: 97 mg

Exchanges: 1 bread

Affix a self-adhesive cork square to the inside of one of your kitchen cabinet doors. It's a handy spot for tacking up a recipe or grocery list.

Whole Wheat Pancakes

(Recipe contains approximately 15% fat)

1/2 c. whole wheat flour
1/4 c. enriched all-purpose
   flour
2 tsp. baking powder
1 tsp. honey

Egg substitute to = 1 egg
1/2 c. plain low-fat yogurt
1/4 c. sparkling water
1 tsp. tub margarine, melted

In a large mixing bowl, put flours and baking powder. Mix with wire whisk until even in color. In a small bowl, combine honey, egg substitute, yogurt, sparkling water and margarine. Blend. Make a well in flour mixture and pour in wet mixture. Stir with wooden spoon just until flour mixture is moistened. Don't worry about lumps. Cook pancakes on hot griddle or in nonstick skillet sprayed with cooking spray. Using 3 tablespoons of batter per pancake, cook until top is covered with bubbles. Turn and cook second side.
Yield: 8 pancakes

Approximate Per Pancake:
Calories: 65
Fat: 1.1 g
Cholesterol: 1.0 mg

Carbohydrates: 10.0 g
Protein: 3.0 g
Sodium: 44 mg

Exchanges: 1 bread

*When extra counter space is needed for baking or serving, pull out
a cabinet drawer and place a pastry board or tray across it.*

Waffles

Chocolate Waffles

(Recipe contains approximately 8% fat)

2/3 c. enriched all-purpose
  flour
1/2 tsp. baking powder
1/4 tsp. salt
1 1/2 T. unsweetened cocoa
  powder
Equal sweetener, or sweetener
  of choice, to = 1/3 c. sugar

1/4 c. plain, low-fat yogurt
3 T. hot water
1 tsp. butter granules
Egg substitute to = 1 egg
2 lg. egg whites
Pinch of cream of tartar

Into a large mixing bowl, sift flour, baking powder, salt, cocoa and sweetener or sugar. In a smaller bowl, put yogurt. Blend hot water and butter granules, stirring until granules dissolve. Add to yogurt along with egg substitute. Add wet ingredients to dry ingredients, stirring just until moistened. Beat egg whites and cream of tartar until soft peaks form. Add sweetener or sugar and beat until stiff. DO NOT OVERBEAT. Fold egg whites into batter. Using 1/4 cup batter per waffle, bake until brown. Do not open waffle iron as long as steam is coming from sides.
Yield: 6 servings

Approximate Per Serving:
Calories: 80
Fat: 0.7 g
Cholesterol: 0.6 mg

Carbohydrates: 23.5 g
Protein: 3.9 g
Sodium: 119 mg

Exchanges: 1 bread

If you are short of dining space use your ironing board set at proper height for a table for the children.

Gingerbread Waffles

(Recipe contains approximately 9% fat)

2 T. diet tub margarine
1/4 c. molasses
Egg substitute to = 2 eggs
2 1/4 c. whole wheat blend
  or enriched all-purpose
  flour

2 tsp. ground ginger
1 tsp. cinnamon
1/2 tsp. salt
1/8 tsp. cloves
2 c. boiling water
Cooking spray

In a medium mixing bowl, blend margarine, molasses and egg substitute. Cream very well. In a second bowl, blend flour, ginger, cinnamon, salt and cloves. Add flour mixture to egg substitute mixture alternately with boiling water, beginning and ending with flour; blending well after each addition. Spray an 8-inch square waffle iron with cooking spray. Pour 1 1/2 cups batter onto center of hot waffle iron. Bake at least 8 minutes, or until done. Do not open waffle iron until steam has stopped.
Yield: 12 (4-inch) waffles

Approximate Per Waffle:
Calories: 211
Fat: 2.2 g
Cholesterol: 0.0 mg

Carbohydrates: 35.9 g
Protein: 5.9 g
Sodium: 218 mg

Exchanges: 2 bread; 1 fat; 1/4 milk

*Empty cardboard bathroom tissue rolls make
handy storage sleeves for appliance cords.*

Great Waffles

(Recipe contains approximately 19% fat)

1 3/4 c. flour, whole wheat
   blend or enriched
   all-purpose
2 tsp. baking powder
1/4 tsp. salt
1 T. sugar

Egg substitute to = 2 eggs
2 T. tub margarine
1 c. skim milk
1/2 c. sparkling water (makes
   waffles tender)
3 egg whites

Blend flour, baking powder, salt and sugar in large mixing bowl. Make a well in flour mixture and put egg substitute, margarine, skim milk and sparkling water in well. With swift strokes, combine liquid ingredients with dry ingredients. Blend just until moist. Batter will not be smooth. Beat egg whites just until stiff. Fold into batter just until blended. Heat waffle iron; spray with cooking spray. Cover waffle iron with about 3/4 cup batter, poured into center of waffle iron. Cook 6 to 8 minutes (some irons are slower than others). Do not raise until steam stops.
Yield: 6 waffles (this is 6 batches in waffle iron)

Approximate Per Waffle:
Calories: 218
Fat: 4.6 g
Cholesterol: 1.0 mg

Carbohydrates: 32.0 g
Protein: 13.0 g
Sodium: 236 mg

Exchanges: 1 1/2 bread; 1 milk; 1 fat

Store your flour sifter in a plastic bag.

Seasoned Yogurt Waffles

(Recipe contains approximately 5% fat)

1/4 c. plain low-fat yogurt
Egg substitute to = 2 eggs
2 T. boiling water
1 tsp. butter granules
2 T. sparkling water (makes
    waffles more tender)
1 c. flour, whole wheat blend,
    unbleached or enriched
    all-purpose

1/4 c. snipped green onions
1/4 tsp. baking soda
1/4 tsp. pepper
1/4 tsp. salt (less if desired)
4 egg whites
Pinch of cream of tartar
2 T. sugar

Preheat waffle iron. In a large mixing bowl, put yogurt and egg substitute. Blend boiling water and butter granules until granules dissolve. Add to yogurt mixture along with sparkling water. In a second bowl, put flour, onion, baking soda, pepper and salt. Blend. Stir into wet ingredients and blend well. Beat egg whites and cream of tartar until soft peaks form. Add sugar and beat until stiff. DO NOT OVERBEAT. Fold egg whites into batter, a little at a time. Using 1/4 cup batter per waffle, bake until brown. Do not open waffle iron as long as steam is coming from sides.
Yield: 12 waffles (2 waffles per serving)

Approximate Per Serving:
Calories : 132
Fat: 0.8 g
Cholesterol: 0.6 mg

Carbohydrates: 21.8 g
Protein: 5.8 g
Sodium: 221 mg

Exchanges: 2 bread

Store envelopes of soup, sauce and salad dressing in a napkin holder.

South of the Border Waffles

(Recipe contains approximately 18% fat)

1 1/3 c. skim milk
8 slices no-fat American cheese, diced (be very sure that it is a brand that melts)
2 T. canola oil
Egg substitute to = 1 egg
1 tsp. butter granules
1 c. yellow cornmeal
2/3 c. flour, whole wheat blend, unbleached or enriched all-purpose

1 T. baking powder
1 tsp. chili powder
1/2 tsp. sodium-free salt (opt.)
2 egg whites
Pinch of cream of tartar
Equal artificial sweetener or sweetener of choice to = 2 T. sugar
1/4 c. green chilies, chopped

Preheat waffle iron. In a large mixing bowl, put milk, cheese, oil and egg substitute. Blend. In a second bowl, blend butter granules, cornmeal, flour, baking powder, chili powder and salt. Add dry ingredients to wet ingredients and blend until batter is smooth. Beat egg whites until frothy. Add cream of tartar and sweetener or sugar. Beat until stiff—DO NOT OVERBEAT. Fold into batter, a little at a time. Stir in chilies. Bake in waffle iron until brown. Do not open waffle iron until steam is no longer coming out sides.
Yield: 16 waffles (2 waffles per serving)

Approximate Per Serving:
Calories: 205
Fat: 4.1 g
Cholesterol: 5.6 mg

Carbohydrates: 27.9 g
Protein: 19.6 g
Sodium: 561 mg

Exchanges: 1 3/4 bread; 1/2 milk; 1 fat

Keep a package of pipe cleaners in the kitchen for use in closing bag of food.

Wheat 'N' Date Waffles

(Recipe contains approximately 3% fat)

2 c. skim milk
1/3 c. boiling water
1 T. butter granules
1/3 c. "light" maple syrup
Egg substitute to = 1 egg
1 1/4 c. enriched all-purpose
    flour
3/4 c. whole wheat flour

1/2 c. bran flakes cereal,
    crushed
1 T. baking powder
1/2 tsp. salt, less if desired
1/4 tsp. baking soda
2 egg whites
Pinch of cream of tartar
1 T. sugar
1/2 c. finely-chopped dates

Preheat waffle iron. In a large mixing bowl, put milk. Blend butter granules in boiling water until dissolved, and add to milk along with maple syrup and egg substitute. In a second bowl, put flours, cereal, baking powder, salt and baking soda. Add dry ingredients to wet ingredients and blend. Beat egg whites and cream of tartar until soft peaks form. Add sugar and beat until stiff. DO NOT OVERBEAT. Fold into batter, a little at a time. Stir in dates. Bake in waffle iron until brown. Do not open as long as steam is coming out sides.

Yield: 16 waffles (2 waffles per serving)

Approximate Per Serving:
Calories: 221
Fat: 0.8 g
Cholesterol: 1.0 mg

Carbohydrates: 44.9 g
Protein: 7.3 g
Sodium: 223 mg

Exchanges: 2 bread; 1 milk

Wash knits inside out to prevent snags.

Omelets

Broccoli, Red Pepper and Cheese Omelet

(Recipe contains approximately 23% fat)

1 c. broccoli flowerets, cooked
 until just tender
1/4 c. water
1 tsp. butter granules
1 clove garlic, sliced
1 c. finely-diced onions
1/2 c. diced red bell pepper

Egg substitute to = 6 eggs
1/3 c. evaporated skim milk
1/8 tsp. oregano
1/4 tsp. salt (less if desired)
1/8 tsp. pepper
1/2 c. no-fat shredded
 mozzarella cheese

Cook broccoli and set aside. Put water and butter granules in a skillet and bring to boil. Add garlic. Cook 2 minutes and remove garlic with slotted spoon. Throw garlic away. Add onion and red pepper. Cook until tender (add a little water, if needed). Cook until moisture is absorbed. Remove from stove and cool. Add broccoli and blend. In a mixing bowl, put egg substitute, milk, oregano, salt and pepper. Blend. Add broccoli mixture. Heat a 7-inch skillet and spray with cooking spray. Pour in egg mixture, stir with whisk until mixture begins to set. Cook over low heat for 5 minutes. Sprinkle cheese over top and put under broiler, about 4 inches from heat for 1 to 2 minutes. Slide onto platter and cut in 4 wedges.
Yield: 4 servings

Approximate Per Serving:
Calories: 179
Fat: 4.5 g
Cholesterol: 8.3 mg

Carbohydrates: 11.6 g
Protein: 12.6 g
Sodium: 284 mg

Exchanges: 2 meat; 1 fat; 1 vegetable

When rewrapping prepackaged meat for freezing cut the label from the package and tape it to the newly wrapped package.

Denver Omelet

(Recipe contains approximately 19% fat)

1/4 c. water
1 tsp. butter granules
1/4 c. chopped onion
1/4 c. chopped green pepper
1 med. tomato, seeded & chopped
1/4 tsp. sodium-free seasoned salt (opt.)

1/8 tsp. pepper
1 c. very lean, diced ham
Egg substitute to = 8 eggs
1/3 c. evaporated skim milk
1/4 tsp. salt
1/4 c. no-fat shredded Cheddar cheese

In a skillet, put water and butter granules. Bring to boil and add onions and green pepper. Sauté. Add tomatoes, seasoned salt and pepper. Stir. Add ham and heat through. Remove from stove and set aside, but keep warm. In a mixing bowl, combine egg substitute, milk and salt. Spray a skillet with cooking spray and pour egg substitute mixture into hot skillet. Stir briskly with whisk until mixture begins to set. Cook until done, but a little moist on top. Spread ham mixture over top and sprinkle with cheese. Cover and cook a minute or two until cheese melts. Cut into wedges and serve. **Yield: 6 servings.**

Approximate Per Serving:
Calories: 148
Fat: 3.2 g
Cholesterol: 19.6 mg

Carbohydrates: 6.1 g
Protein: 25.5 g
Sodium: 467 mg

Exchanges: 2 meat; 1 vegetable; 1/4 fat

A soft toothbrush works great as a "mushroom brush".

Mushroom Omelet Puff

(Recipe contains approximately 17% fat)

Egg substitute to = 1 egg
1/4 c. evaporated skim milk
1 tsp. butter granules
1/8 tsp. pepper
1 lg. egg white
1/4 tsp. sodium-free
   seasoned salt

1/4 lb. firm white mushrooms,
   sliced thin
2 T. water
1 tsp. butter granules
Cooking spray
1 tsp. tub margarine

In a bowl, put egg substitute and evaporated skim milk. Add butter granules and beat until a little frothy. Stir in pepper and set aside. Beat egg white and salt until stiff. DO NOT OVERBEAT. In a small skillet, put water and butter granules and bring to boil. Add mushrooms and sauté a few minutes, stirring often. Remove from stove. Put an 8-inch skillet on stove, over moderate heat, and heat until hot. Spray with cooking spray, then add margarine and allow to melt. Fold egg whites into egg substitute and pour into skillet. Stir briskly with a whisk until mixture begins to set. Cook until set on bottom, but still a little moist on top. Spread mushrooms over top. With a spatula, start rolling omelet away from you, completing roll as omelet is turned out onto serving plate. It should be folded in half when it reaches the platter.
Yield: 1 serving

Approximate Per Serving:
Calories: 204
Fat: 3.8 g
Cholesterol: 2.5 mg

Carbohydrates: 13.9 g
Protein: 11.6 g
Sodium: 370 mg

Exchanges: 1 meat; 1 fat; 1 vegetable; 1 milk

To avoid leaving food in freezer too long, attach a list of the items showing the amounts and purchase date and attach to door.
Update as you use the food from freezer.

Oven Omelet

(Recipe contains approximately 18% fat)

Egg substitute to = 8 eggs
1/2 c. evaporated skim milk
1/4 tsp. salt (less if desired)
1/4 tsp. pepper
1 c. diced, very lean ham

1/4 c. finely-chopped green
  pepper
3 T. finely-diced onion
1/2 c. (2 oz.) no-fat shredded mozzarella cheese
2 tsp. cheese granules

Blend egg substitute and milk. Add remaining ingredients and blend well. Pour mixture into a 9x13-inch baking dish that has been sprayed with cooking spray. Bake in a 325° preheated oven 40 to 45 minutes.

Yield: 8 servings

Approximate Per Serving:
Calories: 115
Fat: 2.3 g
Cholesterol: 16 mg

Carbohydrates: 3.0 g
Protein: 10.9 g
Sodium: 272 mg

Exchanges: 2 meat

A dampened sponge placed on the kitchen range makes a good spoon holder and is there handy to wipe up spills.

Potato and Onion Omelet

(Recipe contains approximately 11% fat)

Cooking spray
4 med. red potatoes, peeled
   & diced
1 lg. onion, diced
1/2 tsp. salt (less if desired)

1/4 tsp. garlic powder
1/4 tsp. pepper
Egg substitute to = 8 eggs
1 T. chopped parsley
1/2 tsp. sodium-free salt (opt.)

Spray the bottom of a heavy skillet with cooking spray (3-second spray). Put half of potatoes and onions in skillet and spray top of vegetables with a 3-second spray. Add remaining potatoes and onions and spray with a 3-second spray. Sprinkle with salt, pepper and garlic powder. Put a heavy, tight lid on skillet and cook over medium heat, turning often, until potatoes are tender. The tight lid is very important. Put egg substitute in a mixing bowl and add parsley and salt, if desired. Pour egg mixture over potatoes. Cover and cook 10 minutes, or until set. Invert plate over skillet and turn out on plate. Slide back into skillet to cook second side for 3 minutes. Slide back onto plate and cut into 4 wedges.
Yield: 4 servings

Approximate Per Serving:
Calories: 211
Fat: 2.6 g
Cholesterol: 0.0 mg

Carbohydrates: 20.2 g
Protein: 8.5 g
Sodium: 376 mg

Exchanges: 1 bread; 2 meat; 1/2 fat

Pipe cleaners work well for cleaning hard to reach parts on can openers.

Spinach and Ham Omelet

(Recipe contains approximately 18% fat)

2 T. water	1/4 lb. lean ham, diced
1 tsp. butter granules	Dash of nutmeg
2 T. minced green onion	1/4 tsp. pepper
1/4 tsp. minced garlic	Egg substitute to = 8 eggs
1 c. cooked, squeezed-dry,	1 tsp. tub margarine
chopped spinach	1/2 c. no-fat shredded
1/2 c. low-fat plain yogurt	Cheddar cheese
1/2 c. evaporated skim milk	

Put water and butter granules in a skillet and bring to boil. Add onion and garlic; sauté. Add squeezed-dry spinach and cook 1 minute. Add yogurt and evaporated milk and cook, stirring often, until liquid has been absorbed. Add ham and heat through. In a mixing bowl, put nutmeg, salt, pepper and egg substitute. Blend. Pour over ham mixture. Cover and cook 10 minutes, or until omelet is set. Invert onto plate. Put margarine into skillet; slide omelet back into skillet and cook second side. Sprinkle cheese over top. Cover and cook 1 to 2 minutes, or until cheese melts. Cut into wedges and serve.

Yield: 6 servings

Approximate Per Serving:
Calories: 252 **Carbohydrates: 11.2 g**
Fat: 4.9 g **Protein: 31.6 g**
Cholesterol: 27 mg **Sodium: 649 mg**

Exchanges: 3 meat; 1 vegetable; 3/4 milk

Use a long-handle windshield brush to clean between the kitchen range and adjacent base cabinet.

Tomato and Green Pepper Omelet

(Recipe contains approximately 24% fat)

1/4 c. water
1 tsp. butter granules
1 c. thinly-sliced onions
1 lg. green pepper, diced
2 lg. tomatoes, peeled, seeded & chopped
1 tsp. sweet basil
1 bay leaf
1/4 tsp. salt

1/8 tsp. pepper
2 T. minced parsley
1 green onion, chopped
1 clove garlic, minced
2 T. freshly-grated Parmesan cheese
4 omelets made from "Mushroom Omelet Puff" recipe (see index)

Put water and butter granules in a skillet and bring to a boil. Add onion and sauté for 5 minutes. Add green pepper and sauté for 3 minutes. Add tomatoes, basil, bay leaf, salt and pepper; simmer 15 minutes, or until thick. Add parsley, green onion and garlic. Cook 2 minutes, then remove from stove and keep warm. Make four individual omelets and divide mixture among omelets. Sprinkle each with cheese, before folding in half.

Yield: 4 servings

Approximate Per Serving:
Calories: 261
Fat: 6.9 g
Cholesterol: 4.5 mg

Carbohydrates: 19.8 g
Protein: 14.1 g
Sodium: 461 mg

Exchanges: 3 meat; 1 fat; 2 vegetable

Some recipes require that you finish cooking a dish by placing the skillet in the oven. To prevent the nonmetal part of the handle from burning, wrap it in aluminum foil.

Vegetable Omelet

(Recipe contains approximately 14% fat)

1/4 c. water
1 tsp. butter granules
1/4 c. chopped onion
1/2 c. sliced fresh mushrooms
1/4 c. finely-chopped green
  pepper
1/4 c. finely-chopped sweet
  red pepper

1/2 c. peeled & seeded,
  chopped fresh tomato
1 drop Tabasco sauce
Egg substitute to = 4 eggs
3 T. skim milk
1/4 tsp. pepper
1 tsp. cheese granules

Put water and butter granules in a heavy-bottomed skillet and bring to a boil. Add onion, mushrooms, green and red peppers, tomatoes and Tabasco sauce. Sauté until vegetables are tender and moisture has been absorbed. Remove from skillet with slotted spoon and set aside. Blend egg substitute, milk and pepper. Heat skillet, over medium heat, until hot; spray with cooking spray; pour egg substitute into skillet and stir briskly with whisk until mixture begins to set. Sprinkle top with cheese granules. Cook until set, but still moist on top. Spread vegetable mixture over one-half of omelet. Fold over and slide onto warm plate.
Yield: 2 servings

Approximate Per Serving:
Calories: 173
Fat: 2.7 g
Cholesterol: 1.0 mg

Carbohydrates: 10.5 g
Protein: 8.5 g
Sodium: 128 mg

Exchanges: 2 meat; 1 1/2 vegetable; 1/2 fat

Bread -
Breads, Rolls, Coffeecakes, Muffins & Biscuits

Breads

There is nothing more satisfying than removing a golden loaf of bread from the oven.

However, the best reason for baking your own bread is the control you gain over the ingredients that go into the bread.

For the sodium-restricted it's the best possible way to control the sodium content. Although you can get by without using any salt in bread, there is no disputing that salt does affect the texture of the bread. A dough without salt will not produce the same quality loaf of bread as dough with salt included.

The amount of salt called for in a bread recipe can be reduced without much consequence.

The big consideration when baking bread is the flour used. As we read more and more about putting more fiber in our diets, it only makes sense to use more grains in our bread.

Although using refined white flour is not exactly bad for you, it is not as beneficial as whole grain flours, since white flour has been robbed of its bran and germ in the milling process. This cuts the fiber content compared with whole grain flours.

One of the best discoveries I have made is a whole wheat blend flour manufactured by Gold Medal.

It's a special blend of whole wheat and all-purpose enriched flour that can be substituted cup for cup in a recipe. Although I prefer a mix of whole wheat and unbleached flour, there is no disputing that the whole wheat blend flour is great when it comes to converting recipes. It is also an easy way to include more fiber in the diet.

If you have never made bread before, don't be afraid to give it a try. It is not as difficult as it is cracked up to be.

The secret is to follow the recipe and do exactly as it instructs. Making bread is an art of patience, as it does take a little time to make yeast breads that must be set aside to rise.

However, the presentation of a fresh-baked loaf of bread will not only impress your family, but will give you a feeling of accomplishment that is very satisfying.

When you dry bread for stuffing, place it in a colander.
The holes allow air to circulate and it dries quicker.

Yeast Breads

Basic White Bread

(Recipe contains approximately 7% fat)

2 1/2 c. warm water (110°-115°)	3 T. tub margarine
2 tsp. honey	6 1/2 to 7 1/4 c. enriched
2 pkg. active dry yeast	all-purpose flour
2 tsp. salt	

Put 1/2 cup warm water and honey in small bowl; blend, then sprinkle with yeast. Set aside to proof—10 to 15 minutes. In a large mixing bowl, put 2 cups warm water. Add salt, margarine and yeast sponge. Stir in half of flour. Add as much of remaining flour as can be stirred in with a wooden spoon.

Turn out onto floured surface and knead in as much of remaining flour as possible—knead 10 minutes. Dough should be smooth and elastic.

Spray a large bowl with cooking spray. Form dough into a ball and place in bowl. Turn once to coat both sides. Cover with plastic wrap that has been sprayed with cooking spray. Set in warm place to rise. Allow dough to rise until doubled in bulk, 1 1/2 to 2 hours. Dough is ready when impression of finger springs back when very lightly touched. Punch dough down, cover and allow to rest 10 minutes. Divide dough into 2 pieces. Roll dough into a rectangle, 18x9 inches. Beginning at short side, roll dough up like a jellyroll. Dough must be rolled very tightly.

Cup ends of roll with both hands and press to form a roll that will fit in pan. Put into loaf pan that has been sprayed with cooking spray. Place, seam-side down, after pinching seam tightly together. Repeat with second piece of dough. Allow dough to rise until doubled in bulk, about 1 hour. Bake in 375° preheated oven for 25 to 30 minutes. If top becomes browner than desired, cover with foil to prevent further browning. Bread is done if it sounds hollow when thumped on bottom with finger. Remove from oven, take bread immediately from pans and cool on rack.

Continued on following page.

Continued from preceding page.

Yield: 2 loaves; 16 slices per loaf (1 slice per serving)

Approximate Per Slice:
Calories: 85   Carbohydrates: 17.1 g
Fat: 0.7 g   Protein: 2.4 g
Cholesterol: 0.0 mg   Sodium: 117

Exchanges: 1 1/4 bread

Basil Bread

(Recipe contains approximately 6% fat)

2 T. tub margarine, melted   1/2 tsp. salt
1 1/2 c. low-fat buttermilk   1/4 tsp. pepper
1 1/2 tsp. baking soda   3 c. flour, whole wheat blend,
1/2 tsp. dried basil (do not   unbleached or enriched
    use fresh)   all-purpose

Put margarine and buttermilk into a large bowl. Add baking
soda, basil, salt and pepper. Add flour, one cup at a time. Turn
dough out onto a floured surface and knead 10 minutes. Shape into
a round loaf and put in 7- or 8-inch round pan that has been sprayed
with cooking spray. Sprinkle top generously with flour. Bake in
450° preheated oven for 35 to 40 minutes, or until golden brown.
Cool on rack.
Yield: 1 loaf; 14 slices

Approximate Per Slice:
Calories: 116   Carbohydrates: 21.7 g
Fat: 0.8 g   Protein: 3.6 g
Cholesterol: 1.0 mg   Sodium: 124

Exchanges: 1 1/2 bread; 1/4 fat

Dill Bread
(Recipe contains approximately 16% fat)

1 T. yeast	1/2 c. low-fat plain yogurt
1/4 c. warm water (110°-115°)	2 T. minced onion
1 T. honey	1/4 tsp. baking soda
1 T. canola oil	1 T. dill seed
1 tsp. salt	1 tsp. dill leaf
Egg substitute to = 1 egg	1 c. whole wheat flour
1/2 c. low-fat cottage cheese	1 c. unbleached flour

Put water and honey in a small bowl and sprinkle with yeast. Set aside for 10 minutes to proof. In a large mixing bowl, put proofed yeast and add remaining ingredients in order given. Blend well. Cover with plastic wrap and set in warm, draft-free place to rise until doubled in bulk—about two hours. Stir down; pour into oval ovenproof casserole that has been sprayed with cooking spray. Bake in 350° preheated oven for 30 minutes, or until done.
Yield: 1 loaf; 16 slices

Approximate Per Slice:
Calories: 83
Fat: 1.5 g
Cholesterol: 1.1 mg

Carbohydrates: 13.5 g
Protein: 3.7 g
Sodium: 186 mg

Exchanges: 1 bread; 1/4 fat

To help keep rolls hot and protect the roll basket from grease stains, line the basket with aluminum foil under the napkin.

Honey Wheat Bread

(Recipe contains approximately 15% fat)

2 pkg. active dry yeast	1/4 c. honey
2 1/2 c. warm water (110°-115°)	1/2 c. nonfat dry milk granules
1 T. sugar	2 1/2 c. unbleached or enriched
1 tsp. salt	all-purpose flour
1/4 c. canola oil	5 c. whole wheat flour

Mix sugar and 1/2 cup water in saucer and sprinkle yeast over top. Set aside 10 minutes to proof. In a large mixing bowl, put 2 cups warm water, salt, oil and honey. Blend. Add yeast sponge and allow to stand for 10 minutes. Stir. Add dry milk and stir to blend. Stir in 2 1/2 cups white flour. Beat until smooth. Gradually add whole wheat flour, as much as needed to make a dough that can be handled. Turn dough out onto a floured surface and knead a full 10 minutes. Form into ball and put back into bowl that has been sprayed with cooking spray. Turn once to coat both sides. Cover with plastic wrap that has been sprayed with cooking spray. Set in warm place to rise until doubled in bulk. Knead dough in bowl, five times. Allow to rest 10 minutes, covered. Shape into 2 loaves. Put in loaf pans that have been sprayed with cooking spray, and cover until doubled in size. Bake in 400° preheated oven for 40 to 45 minutes. Remove from pans and cool on rack.
Yield: 2 loaves; 20 slices per loaf

Approximate Per Serving:
Calories: 102	**Carbohydrates: 20.1 g**
Fat: 1.7 g	**Protein: 4.5 g**
Cholesterol: 0.2 mg	**Sodium: 167 mg**

Exchanges: 1 1/2 bread

If grains of rice fall through your steamer while reheating,
try placing a coffee filter on the bottom.

Pita Bread

(Recipe contains approximately 9% fat)

1 pkg. active dry yeast	3 to 3 1/2 c. whole wheat
1 1/3 c. warm water (110°-115°)	blend or enriched
1/2 tsp. sugar	all-purpose flour
1 tsp. salt	Cornmeal
1 T. canola oil	

Put 1/3 cup water in saucer and stir in sugar. Sprinkle with yeast and set aside 10 to 15 minutes until a nice yeast sponge forms. Put yeast sponge into a large mixing bowl. Add 1 cup warm water, salt, canola oil and 1 1/2 cups flour. Beat until smooth. Stir in enough remaining flour to make a dough stiff enough to handle. Turn dough out onto lightly-floured surface and knead a full 10 minutes. Form into ball. Place ball in mixing bowl that has been sprayed with cooking spray. Turn once to coat both sides. Place plastic wrap that has been sprayed with cooking spray over bowl, and set in warm place until doubled in size, about 1 hour.

Punch down. Divide into 6 equal parts. Shape each part into a ball. Allow to rise 30 minutes. Sprinkle ungreased baking sheet with cornmeal. Roll each ball into a circle 1/8-inch thick. It's very important that dough is thin. Place circles in opposite corners of each baking sheet, two circles per sheet. Allow to rise 30 minutes. Bake in 500° preheated oven for about 10 minutes, or until loaves are puffed and light brown. Tear each circle in half crosswise and fill each with filling of choice. These should be served immediately. If not served immediately, place hot unfilled bread in plastic bags and keep moist and pliable until ready to serve.

Yield: 12 servings

Approximate Per Serving:

Calories: 145	**Carbohydrates: 27.3 g**
Fat: 1.5 g	**Protein: 4.0 g**
Cholesterol: 0.0 mg	**Sodium: 179 mg**

Exchanges: 2 bread

A vegetable brush works great to clean muffin tins.

Whole Wheat Pita Bread

(Recipe contains approximately 11% fat)

1 T. active dry yeast	1 1/4 c. whole wheat flour
1/4 c. lukewarm water	1 c. lukewarm water
(110°-115°)	(110°-115°)
1/2 tsp. honey	1 T. canola oil
1 3/4 c. enriched all-purpose	1 tsp. salt
flour	1/4 c. cornmeal

In a small bowl, put 1/4 cup lukewarm water and honey; blend. Sprinkle yeast over top and set aside 10 minutes to proof. In a large mixing bowl, put flours. Stir to blend. Add 1 cup lukewarm water, canola oil, salt and yeast sponge.

Stir with wooden spoon until mixture forms a ball. Turn dough out onto floured surface and knead 10 minutes, adding flour as needed. Divide dough into 6 portions and form each portion into a ball. Roll out each ball until round is 1/4-inch thick. Put rounds on baking sheets sprinkled with cornmeal. Cover with a damp cloth and set in warm draft-free place to rise for 45 minutes. Bake in 500° preheated oven for 12 to 15 minutes, or until puffed and nicely browned. The bread will soften and deflate after being removed from oven. Cut each pita in half and put on racks to cool
Yield: 12 pitas

Approximate Per Serving:

Calories: 131	**Carbohydrates: 25.5 g**
Fat: 1.6 g	**Protein: 4.1 g**
Cholesterol: 0.0 mg	**Sodium: 179 mg**

Exchanges: 2 bread

Store homemade bread crumbs in empty salt box.
Use funnel to fill through spout.

Sourdough Breads

Sourdough breads differ from other breads in the respect that they have a flavor all their own—a bit of a tang to them that other breads do not have.

Sourdough breads were popular way back in the gold rush days. Every prospector carried with him his own crock of sourdough starter to enable him to make his own sourdough breads and sourdough pancakes.

Many people who bake sourdough breads today probably don't realize that the starter they keep in their refrigerator is a step back into time.

True, the refrigerated starters of today are not a true authentic "olden days" starter. However, they give the baker an old-time baking experience, while being more reliable.

Sourdough starters of yesteryear were not kept under refrigeration and no doubt the tang to the bread was anything but the delicate tang of sourdough starters of today.

A good sourdough starter can be kept going for years if properly cared for.

Give sourdough a try. It's an interesting experience in baking, and the bread is very good.

When making stuffing freeze bread first. It cuts much easier.

Sourdough Starter

1 tsp. active dry yeast
1 c. warm water (110°-115°)

1 c. whole wheat blend or
enriched all-purpose flour

In a 1-quart glass bowl, put 1/4 cup warm water. Sprinkle with yeast and set aside to proof for 10 minutes. Add remaining water and stir in flour. Beat with whisk until smooth. Cover with towel or cheesecloth and allow to stand in a warm (80°-85°) draft-free place for about 24 hours, or until starter begins to ferment and bubbles appear on surface of starter. If fermentation has not begun within 24 hours, discard starter and start again.

After starter has begun fermentation, stir well and cover snugly with plastic wrap. Return starter to warm place and allow to stand for 2 to 3 days. When starter becomes foamy, stir and pour into a glass jar that has a tight lid. Store in refrigerator. Starter will be ready to use when a clear liquid has formed on the top.

Always stir before removing starter from jar for baking, and always replace the amount of starter used with water and flour. If you use a cup of starter, replace it with 1/2 cup warm water and 1/2 cup flour. Store at room temperature for about 12 hours, then return to refrigerator.

For a sharper tang to the bread, start the bread the night before and allow it to stand until the next day. However, sourdough breads do not have to stand overnight, and will have a very nice, delicate tang.

When you put your dinner rolls in the oven to bake put a ceramic tile in with them. Put the heated tile in bread basket and put rolls on top. Keeps rolls warm.

Sourdough Bread

(Recipe contains approximately 12% fat)

1 c. sourdough starter, see index
2 c. warm water (110°-115°)
6 1/2 to 6 3/4 c. whole wheat
 blend or enriched all-
 purpose flour
1 tsp. salt
3 T. sugar
1/4 tsp. baking soda
3 T. canola oil
Ice water

Put starter and 2 1/2 cups plus 2 tablespoons warm water in a bowl, and blend with wooden spoon. Cover and let stand 6 hours. Add 3 3/4 cups flour, salt, sugar, baking soda and oil to starter mixture, and stir with wooden spoon until dough is firm enough to form into ball. Add more flour, if needed. Turn dough out onto a floured surface and knead a full 10 minutes. Spray large mixing bowl with cooking spray. Form dough into ball and place in bowl. Turn once to coat both sides. Cover with plastic wrap sprayed with cooking spray. Put in warm place to rise until doubled in bulk. Punch down and allow to rest 10 minutes. Divide into 2 portions and form into two round loaves. Place in opposite corners of a baking sheet sprayed with cooking spray. Flatten tops of loaves slightly, then slash three times with a very sharp knife (about 1/4-inch deep). Cover and let rise until doubled in bulk. Brush with ice water. Bake in 375° preheated oven for 50 minutes. Brush with ice water several times during baking. Remove from pans and cool on wire racks.
Yield: 2 loaves: 26 slices

Approximate Per Serving:
Calories: 147
Fat: 2.0 g
Cholesterol: 0.0 mg
Carbohydrates: 27.5 g
Protein: 3.6 g
Sodium: 90 mg

Exchanges: 2 bread

After baking bread, lay it on its side on a cooling rack.
The wires of the rack leave an impression that works well as a slicing guide.

Sourdough French Bread, San Francisco Style

(Recipe contains approximately 2% fat)

1 1/2 c. lukewarm water (110°-115°)	5 c. flour, whole wheat blend, bleached or enriched all-purpose
1 pkg. active dry yeast	2 tsp. sugar
1 c. sourdough starter	2 tsp. salt
	1 tsp. baking soda

In a large mixing bowl, put water. Sprinkle yeast over water and set aside for 10 minutes to proof. Add starter and blend. Add 3 cups flour, sugar and salt. Stir briskly with wooden spoon, keeping bowl scraped down. Cover with plastic wrap and set in warm draft-free place until double in size, about 1 1/2 to 2 hours. When doubled in bulk, stir in one cup of flour that has been mixed with 1 teaspoon baking soda. Turn dough out onto floured surface and knead 10 minutes, adding as much of remaining flour as needed to make a smooth, elastic dough. Divide dough in half. Form into 2 round loaves and place on baking sheet that has been sprayed with cooking spray. Set in warm, draft-free place 1 to 2 hours, or until doubled in size. Brush loaves with water and make diagonal slashes across loaf with a razor-sharp knife. Place a shallow pan of hot water on bottom rack of oven. Place bread on top shelf and bake in 400° preheated oven for 45 minutes, or until nicely browned.
Yield: 2 loaves; 30 slices

Approximate Per Serving:

Calories: 80	Carbohydrates: 16.9 g
Fat: 0.2 g	Protein: 2.3 g
Cholesterol: 0.0 mg	Sodium: 134 mg

Exchanges: 1 bread

Cut stale bread in shapes with cookie cutter and freeze. When unexpected guests arrive, remove from freezer, spread with low-fat topping and pop under broiler.

Sourdough Pizza Bread

(Recipe contains approximately 12% fat)

1 c. sourdough starter
1/2 c. lukewarm skim milk
2 T. sugar
1 tsp. salt
Egg substitute to = 1 egg
2 T. reduced-calorie tub
   margarine

1/4 tsp. garlic powder
1 tsp. Italian seasoning
3 c. flour, whole wheat blend,
   unbleached or enriched
   all-purpose
Cooking spray
1/2 tsp. butter granules

Put sourdough starter in a large bowl and stir in warm milk. Add sugar, salt, egg substitute, margarine, garlic powder and Italian seasoning. Beat with wooden spoon for 3 minutes, keeping batter scraped from sides of bowl. Stir in flour, 1/2 cup at a time, stirring with a wooden spoon after each addition. At end of flour, dough should pull from sides of bowl. Cover with plastic wrap and set in warm draft-free place for 1 hour. Stir down. Spray 2 bread pans with cooking spray and divide dough between pans. Spread dough out evenly and spray top with cooking spray. Sprinkle with butter granules. Cover with plastic wrap and set in warm, draft-free place for 2 hours. Bake in 375° preheated oven for 30 minutes.
Yield: 1 loaf; 12 slices

Approximate Per Slice:
Calories: 146
Fat: 2.0 g
Cholesterol: 0.0 mg

Carbohydrates: 27.7 g
Protein: 4.9 g
Sodium: 216 mg

Exchanges: 2 bread

To keep cornmeal from getting weevils store it in the freezer.

South of the Border Sourdough Bread

(Recipe contains approximately 13% fat)

1 c. sourdough starter	1/2 tsp. salt
1 1/2 c. yellow cornmeal	1/2 tsp. baking soda
1 1/2 c. skim milk	1 c. whole kernel corn
Egg substitute to = 2 eggs	1/2 c. chopped green onions
2 T. sugar	2 T. cheese granules
4 T. low-fat margarine, melted	1 sm. can green chilies, chopped

In a large mixing bowl, combine sourdough starter, cornmeal, milk, egg substitute and sugar. Blend well. Add melted margarine and blend. Stir in salt, baking soda, corn, onions, cheese granules and green chilies. Blend. Pour into a 9x9-inch pan and bake in 400° preheated oven for 25 to 30 minutes, or until done.
Yield: 9 servings

Approximate Per Serving:
Calories: 218   **Carbohydrates: 35.6 g**
Fat: 3.2 g   **Protein: 5.7 g**
Cholesterol: 0.9 mg   **Sodium: 329 mg**

Exchanges: 2 bread; 1 fat; 1/2 milk

Dip French toast as usual, but cook in waffle iron instead of on top of stove. Great.

Bagels

Plain Good Bagels

(Recipe contains approximately 2% fat)

1 pkg. active dry yeast	1 tsp. salt
2 T. sugar, divided	Cooking spray
1 1/2 c. warm water (110°-115°)	1 T. sugar
4 c. flour, whole wheat blend,	1 gal. water
enriched all-purpose, or	1 egg white, slightly beaten
unbleached	

Put 1 tablespoon sugar and 1 1/2 cups water in large mixing bowl. Blend. Sprinkle with yeast; set aside for 10 minutes to proof. Add flour and salt; blend well. Turn out onto floured surface and knead for 10 minutes. Form dough into ball and put in bowl that has been sprayed with cooking spray. Turn once to coat both sides. Cover and place in warm, draft-free place and allow to rise for 15 minutes. Punch down; turn out onto floured surface and knead 6 or 7 times. Divide dough into 18 pieces and shape each piece into a ball. Push a hole into the center of each ball with floured finger. Pull dough away from center to make a 1 1/2-inch hole. Put bagel back onto floured surface. Cover and let rise 20 minutes. Put 1 tablespoon sugar into water and bring to boil. Pan should have a large surface. Reduce heat to soft boil. Drop 6 bagels into water at a time and boil 2 1/2 minutes. Turn and cook second side 2 1/2 minutes. Drain bagel on paper towel. Place on ungreased baking sheet and bake in 375° preheated oven for 10 minutes. Remove from oven and brush with egg white. Return to oven and bake 20 minutes longer, or until golden brown. Cool on rack.
Yield: 18

Approximate Per Bagel:
Calories: 122

Carbohydrates: 24.7 g
Fat: 0.3 g
Protein: 3.6 g
Cholesterol: 0.0 mg
Sodium: 135 mg

Exchanges: 1 3/4 bread

Sourdough Bagels

(Recipe contains approximately 9% fat)

1 c. sourdough starter	3 c. flour
Egg substitute to = 2 eggs	1 tsp. salt
1 T. canola oil	4 T. sugar
1 tsp. butter granules	1 gal. water
2 T. hot water	

In a large mixing bowl, put sourdough starter, egg substitute and oil. Dissolve butter granules in hot water and add to starter mixture. Blend together 2 1/2 cups flour, salt and 2 tablespoons sugar. Add to starter mixture and blend. If dough does not form and leave sides of bowl, add additional flour. Turn out onto floured surface and knead 10 minutes. Knead in as much remaining flour as necessary. Spray bowl with cooking spray. Form dough into ball and put in bowl, turning once to coat both sides. Cover with plastic wrap and put in warm, draft-free place for 1 to 2 hours, or until doubled in size. Turn out onto floured surface and knead 2 or 3 times. Cover with plastic wrap and let rise 20 minutes. Divide dough into 18 pieces. Shape each piece into a ball. Punch hole in center of each ball with finger. Gently pull to make hole larger. Put back on floured surface, cover with plastic wrap and let rise 20 minutes. Put 2 tablespoons sugar in a gallon of water and bring to boil. Be sure to use large surface pan. Boil, 6 at a time, 3 1/2 minutes. Turn and boil second side 3 1/2 minutes. Remove bagels from boiling water and drain on paper towel. Place on baking sheet that has been sprayed with cooking spray. Bake in 375° preheated oven 25 to 35 minutes, or until golden brown.

Yield: 18 bagels

Approximate Per Bagel:

Calories: 114	**Carbohydrates: 21.6 g**
Fat: 1.2 g	**Protein: 3.0 g**
Cholesterol: 0.0 mg	**Sodium: 142 mg**

Exchanges: 1 1/2 bread

If you put a little artificial sweetener in your pancake batter you won't need syrup for them after they are cooked.

Yeast Rolls

Bread Knots

(Recipe contains approximately 10% fat)

1 1/2 c. warm water (110°-115°)
1 T. sugar
2 pkg. active dry yeast
1 T. canola oil
1 tsp. salt

3 1/2 c. flour, whole wheat
blend, enriched all-purpose
or unbleached
Egg substitute to = 1 egg
1 T. water

In a large mixing bowl, put 1/2 cup water and sugar. Sprinkle with yeast and set aside for 10 minutes to proof. Add oil and beat two minutes with wooden spoon. Stir in salt and 1/2 cup water. Alternately stir in 3 cups flour (one cup at a time) with remaining water. Beat dough until soft and sticky. Sprinkle remaining flour on working surface and turn dough out onto floured surface. Knead 5 minutes, working in flour. Cover dough with plastic wrap and allow to rest 5 minutes. Roll dough out into a 20-inch cylinder. Cut 20 (1-inch) pieces of dough. Let stand 5 minutes. Roll each piece into a cylinder with hand. Tie into knot. Arrange on baking sheet that has been sprayed with cooking spray. Cover with plastic wrap and allow to stand 30 minutes. Beat water into egg substitute and brush rolls with mixture. Bake in 300° oven 30 to 35 minutes, or until brown.
Yield: 20

Approximate Per Knot:
Calories: 93
Fat: 1.0 g
Cholesterol: 0.0 mg

Carbohydrates: 17.5 g
Protein: 2.7 g
Sodium: 216 mg

Exchanges: 1 1/4 bread

*Use a pizza cutter to cut pancakes into bite-size
pieces for the children. Works great.*

Cornmeal Rolls

(Recipe contains approximately 11% fat)

1/4 c. lukewarm water
   (110°-115°)
1 tsp. sugar
2 1/2 tsp. active dry yeast
1 c. skim milk
1/4 c. tub margarine
1 c. yellow cornmeal

Egg substitute to = 2 eggs
3 1/2 c. flour, whole wheat
   blend, unbleached or
   enriched all-purpose
1 tsp. salt
1 egg white
2 tsp. water

Put water and sugar in small bowl. Sprinkle with yeast and set aside for 10 minutes to proof. Heat milk and margarine until margarine is melted. Pour mixture into mixing bowl and add cornmeal. Add egg substitute and 2 cups flour, salt and proofed yeast. Blend. Add enough of remaining flour to form soft dough. Turn dough out onto floured surface and knead 10 minutes, adding flour as needed. Spray mixing bowl with cooking spray; form dough into ball. Put dough in bowl and turn once to coat both sides. Cover with plastic wrap and set in warm, draft-free place until doubled in size (about one hour). Punch down. Roll to 1-inch thick and cut in 2-inch rounds with biscuit cutter. Place on baking sheet that has been sprayed with cooking spray. Cover and let rise for one hour. Bake in 400° preheated oven 15 to 20 minutes, or until brown. Blend egg white and water; brush rolls while they are hot.
Yield: 16

Approximate Per Roll:
Calories: 169
Fat: 2.0 g
Cholesterol: 0.3 mg

Carbohydrates: 28.7 g
Protein: 4.6 g
Sodium: 185 mg

Exchanges: 2 bread; 1/4 milk

*If you store brown sugar, tightly closed,
in the refrigerator it won't get hard.*

Pinwheel Rolls

(Recipe contains approximately 2% fat)

1/2 c. lukewarm water
  (110°-115°)
1 T. sugar
1 pkg. active dry yeast
1/4 c. water
1 tsp. butter granules
1 med. onion, chopped

1 c. skim milk
1/2 tsp. salt (less if desired)
3 1/2 c. flour, whole wheat
  blend, unbleached or bread
  flour
2 tsp. dried dill weed

Put 1/2 cup water and sugar in a large bowl and sprinkle yeast over top. Set aside to proof for 10 minutes. In a small sauté pan, put 1/4 cup water and butter granules. Bring to boil. Add onions and sauté until soft. Remove from stove and set aside. Stir milk and salt into yeast sponge. Add 2 cups flour and beat 3 minutes with an electric beater. Add another cup of flour and stir with wooden spoon. Turn dough out onto floured surface and knead for 10 minutes. Form dough into ball and place in bowl that has been sprayed with cooking spray. Turn once to coat both sides. Put in warm, draft-free place to rise until doubled in size—about 1 1/2 hours. Punch down and knead several times. Roll out on floured surface to 16x11-inch rectangle. Spray surface with cooking spray and sprinkle evenly with onion and dill weed. Roll up jellyroll fashion. Slice in 1-inch slices and place in 10-inch pan that has been sprayed with cooking spray. Allow to rise until double in bulk. Bake in 375° oven for 30 minutes, or until brown.
Yield: 12 rolls

Approximate Per Roll:
Calories: 148
Fat: 0.3 g
Cholesterol: 0.3 mg

Carbohydrates: 30.5 g
Protein: 4.7 g
Sodium: 145 mg

Exchanges: 2 bread

When brown bagging it, use empty pill containers to take ketchup, mustard or mayonnaise in your lunch box.

Quick Dinner Rolls

(Recipe contains approximately 3% fat)

2 1/4 c. warm water
1/4 c. honey
Egg substitute to = 2 eggs
2 pkg. active dry yeast
2 tsp. salt

6 c. whole wheat blend or
enriched all-purpose
flour
1 egg white, slightly beaten

In a large mixing bowl, blend 2 1/4 cups warm water, honey, egg substitute and yeast. Set aside to sponge. Add salt and approximately 6 cups flour—however much it takes to make soft dough. Turn out onto floured surface and knead a full 10 minutes. Allow to rest 10 minutes. Divide dough into 32 pieces and place in a very large round pan or two 9-inch pie pans that have been sprayed with cooking spray. Brush with egg white. Sprinkle with sesame or poppy seeds, if desired. Cover with plastic wrap that has been sprayed with cooking spray. Set in warm place to rise for 25 minutes to 1 hour, or until doubled in bulk. Bake in 350° preheated oven for 25 minutes. Remove from oven and cover rolls with foil. Return to oven and bake, covered, 15 minutes.

Yield: 32 rolls

Approximate Per Serving:
Calories: 106
Fat: 0.3 g
Cholesterol: 0.0 mg

Carbohydrates: 22.4 g
Protein: 2.9 g
Sodium: 139 mg

Exchanges: 1 1/2 bread

When covering a bowl of leftovers with aluminum foil, be sure to write what the contents are on the foil with a felt-tipped pen.

Sour Cream Rolls

(Recipe contains approximately 16% fat)

4 c. flour, whole wheat blend, unbleached or enriched all-purpose	1 c. "light" sour cream
1/4 c. sugar	1/2 c. water
1 tsp. salt (less if desired)	2 T. tub margarine
2 pkg. active dry yeast	1 tsp. butter granules
	Egg substitute to = 2 eggs

In a large mixing bowl, put 3 cups flour, sugar, salt and yeast. Blend well. In a saucepan, put sour cream, water, margarine and butter granules. Heat until very warm to the touch (110°-115°). Add to flour mixture along with egg substitute. Beat at low speed with an electric mixer for 3 minutes. Add remaining flour, 1/2 cup at a time, stirring with wooden spoon until you have a nice, soft dough. Scrape dough from sides; cover with plastic wrap and refrigerate overnight.

In the morning, divide dough in half. Roll out to 1/2-inch thickness and cut in 2-inch rounds with biscuit cutter. Place rolls on baking sheet that has been sprayed with cooking spray, about 1-inch apart. Cover with plastic wrap and allow to rise until doubled in size—about 30 minutes. Bake in 375° preheated oven 12 to 15 minutes, or until brown. Cool on rack.

Yield: 3 dozen

Approximate Per Roll:

Calories: 79	**Carbohydrates: 12.6 g**
Fat: 1.4 g	**Protein: 1.8 g**
Cholesterol: 0.0 mg	**Sodium: 83 mg**

Exchanges: 1 bread

*Add a few drops of green or blue food coloring
to goldfish bowl. Kids love it.*

Sourdough Rolls

Sourdough Cinnamon Rolls

(Recipe contains approximately 5% fat)

1 1/2 c. sourdough starter
3/4 c. skim milk
1 tsp. vanilla
1/4 c. sugar
2 tsp. cinnamon
1 T. tub margarine, melted
1 tsp. salt (less if desired)

2 1/2 c. flour, whole wheat
   blend, unbleached or
   enriched all-purpose
8-second spray of cooking
   spray
1 tsp. butter granules

TOPPING:
1 egg white
1 tsp. water
4 oz. "free" no-fat
   Philadelphia cream cheese

1 tsp. orange juice concentrate
1/2 tsp. grated orange rind
6 pkt. Equal or sweetener of
   choice to = 1/4 c. sugar

Put sourdough starter in a large mixing bowl and add milk, vanilla, sugar, 1 teaspoon cinnamon and melted margarine. Stir in salt. Add enough flour to make a stiff dough. Turn out onto floured surface and knead 10 minutes, adding flour as needed. Dough will be soft. Spray a mixing bowl with cooking spray. Form dough in a ball and put in bowl. Turn once to coat both sides. Set in warm, draft-free place to rise until doubled in bulk. Punch down. Allow to rest 10 minutes. Roll out to a 1/2-inch-thick rectangle and spray with cooking oil. Sprinkle with butter granules and 1 teaspoon cinnamon. Roll up jellyroll fashion. Cut into 18 (1-inch) slices. Place on baking sheet and spray with cooking oil. Allow to rise until doubled in size. Bake in 400° preheated oven 25 to 30 minutes. Blend remaining ingredients and brush on hot rolls when removed from oven.

Yield: 18 rolls

Approximate Per Roll:
Calories: 115
Fat: 0.7 g
Cholesterol: 1.3 mg

Carbohydrates: 21.2 g
Protein: 3.8 g
Sodium: 172 mg

Exchanges: 1 bread; 1/2 milk

Sourdough Cottage-Onion Sandwich Buns

(Recipe contains approximately 5% fat)

1/4 c. lukewarm water
   (110°-115°)
1 pkg. active dry yeast
2 c. sourdough starter
2 c. low-fat cream-style
   cottage cheese
1 tsp. salt

2 T. dry onion soup mix
Egg substitute to = 2 eggs
2 T. sugar
1/2 tsp. baking soda
6 c. flour, whole wheat blend,
   unbleached or enriched
   all-purpose

Put water in a bowl and sprinkle with yeast. Set aside 10 minutes to proof. Put sourdough starter into a large mixing bowl and add yeast sponge. Heat cottage cheese until warm. Add salt, onion soup mix, egg substitute, sugar and baking soda. Stir into sourdough mixture. Gradually add enough flour to make soft dough. Turn out onto floured surface and knead 10 minutes. Form into ball. Put in bowl that has been sprayed with cooking spray. Turn once to coat both sides. Cover with plastic wrap and set in warm, draft-free place for 1 to 2 hours, or until doubled in bulk. Punch down. Allow to rest 10 minutes. Divide dough into 21 pieces, shape into balls and place on baking sheet that has been sprayed with cooking spray. Flatten balls slightly. Cover with plastic wrap and set in warm, draft-free place to rise until doubled in size. Bake in 350° preheated oven for 20 to 25 minutes, or until golden brown.
Yield: 21 buns

Approximate Per Bun:
Calories: 178
Fat: 0.9 g
Cholesterol: 1.8 mg

Carbohydrates: 32.5 g
Protein: 5.4 g
Sodium: 158 mg

Exchanges: 2 bread; 1/2 milk

If you can't stand the "just painted smell" add a few drops of vanilla to the paint before painting.

Sourdough Hard Rolls

(Recipe contains approximately 12% fat)

1 1/2 c. sourdough starter	Egg substitute to = 1 egg
1 T. sugar	2 1/4 c. flour, whole wheat
1/2 tsp. salt	blend, unbleached or
3 T. tub margarine, melted	enriched all-purpose

Put sourdough starter in a large mixing bowl and add sugar, salt and 2 tablespoons melted margarine. Blend, and add egg substitute. Add 1 1/2 cups flour and stir with wooden spoon until dough leaves sides of bowl. Turn out onto floured surface and knead 10 minutes. Add additional flour as needed. Dough should be smooth and elastic. Spray large bowl with cooking spray. Form dough into ball and put in bowl. Turn once to coat both sides. Cover with plastic wrap and set in warm, draft-free place to rise until doubled in size—about 2 hours. Punch down. Form into 18 balls and place on baking sheet sprayed with cooking spray. Brush with melted margarine; cover with plastic wrap and allow to rise until doubled in size. Bake in 400° preheated oven for 12 to 15 minutes.
Yield: 18 rolls

Approximate Per Roll:

Calories: 95	**Carbohydrates: 17.0 g**
Fat: 1.3 g	**Protein: 2.6 g**
Cholesterol: 0.0 mg	**Sodium: 90 mg**

Exchanges: 1 bread; 1/2 fat

When a thick cookbook won't stay open, set a clear glass pie plate over the page. Holds the book open and allows you to read the recipe.

Sweet Breads

Blueberry-Banana Bread

(Recipe contains approximately 11% fat)

1 c. fresh blueberries, or frozen
    blueberries, thawed
1 3/4 c. flour, whole wheat
    blend, unbleached or
    enriched all-purpose
2 tsp. baking powder
1/2 tsp. salt (less if desired)
1/2 tsp. nutmeg

1/4 c. unsweetened applesauce
2 T. tub margarine
1 tsp. butter granules
1/3 c. sugar
Egg substitute to = 2 eggs
1 c. mashed bananas
Cooking spray

Toss blueberries with 2 tablespoons of flour and set aside. Put remaining flour in a mixing bowl and add baking powder, salt and nutmeg. In a large mixing bowl, put applesauce, margarine and butter granules. Blend. Slowly cream in sugar, with an electric mixer at medium speed. Add egg substitute 1/4 cup at a time, beating well after each addition. Add flour mixture alternately with mashed bananas. Gently fold in blueberries. Spray an 8 1/2-inch loaf pan with cooking spray and pour batter into pan. Bake in 350° preheated oven 45 minutes, or until an inserted toothpick comes out clean. Cool in pan on rack for 10 minutes. Remove from pan and cool.

Yield: 1 loaf; 16 slices

Approximate Per Slice:
Calories: 97
Fat: 1.2 g
Cholesterol: 0.0 mg

Carbohydrates: 18.5 g
Protein: 1.9 g
Sodium: 110 mg

Exchanges: 1 bread; 1/2 fruit; 1/4 fat

Bananas are most digestible after a few brown spots appear.

Sourdough Banana-Apricot Bread

(Recipe contains approximately 8% fat)

1/2 c. sourdough starter	1/2 tsp. baking soda
Egg substitute to = 2 eggs	1/2 tsp. salt
1/3 c. unsweetened applesauce	1/3 c. sugar
1/4 c. skim milk	1 c. bran cereal
1 c. mashed, ripe bananas	1/2 c. chopped dried apricots
1 tsp. baking powder	

Put sourdough starter in a large mixing bowl and add egg substitute, applesauce, milk and mashed bananas. Blend. Add remaining ingredients. Blend only until moistened. Spray bread pan with cooking spray. Pour dough into pan. Bake in 350° pre-heated oven 40 to 50 minutes. Cool on rack 10 minutes and remove from pan.

Yield: 1 loaf; 12 slices

Approximate Per Serving:

Calories: 145	**Carbohydrates: 14.5 g**
Fat: 1.8 g	**Protein: 1.8 g**
Cholesterol: 0.1 mg	**Sodium: 93 mg**

Exchanges: 2 bread

Try using hair spray to remove the last bit of sticky glue residue after soaking off a label.

Sourdough Raisin Bread in the Round

(Recipe contains approximately 11% fat)

1 c. sourdough starter
1/4 c. lukewarm milk
  (110°-115°)
1/4 c. brown sugar, firmly
  packed
1/4 c. diet margarine, melted
1 tsp. salt (less if desired)

Egg substitute to = 1 egg
1 1/2 tsp. cinnamon
1 c. seedless raisins
2 c. flour, whole wheat blend,
  unbleached or enriched
  all-purpose

Put starter into large mixing bowl and add milk, sugar, margarine, salt, egg substitute and cinnamon. Toss raisins in a little of flour and add to batter gradually, while stirring with wooden spoon. Stir in flour. Dough should now be stiff. Clean sides of bowl with spatula, cover with plastic wrap and set in warm, draft-free place for 1 hour, or until dough is doubled in size. Stir down batter. Spray a 1-quart casserole with cooking spray and turn dough into casserole. Smooth out top. Bake in 350° preheated oven for 40 to 45 minutes, or until golden brown.
Yield: 1 loaf; 14 slices

Approximate Per Slice:
Calories: 146
Fat: 1.8 g
Cholesterol: 0.1 mg

Carbohydrates: 27.2 g
Protein: 3.1 g
Sodium: 200 mg

Exchanges: 2 bread

Keep a small stapler in your kitchen to staple shut tops of opened bags.

Sourdough Zucchini Bread

(Recipe contains approximately 5% fat)

1/2 c. unsweetened applesauce	1/2 tsp. baking powder
1/4 c. sugar	1/2 tsp. baking soda
Egg substitute to = 1 egg	1/2 tsp. cinnamon
1/2 c. sourdough starter	1/2 tsp. nutmeg
1 c. grated zucchini	1/2 tsp. salt (less if desired)
1/2 c. skim milk	6 pkt. Equal, or sweetener of
2 c. flour, whole wheat blend,	choice to = 1/4 c. sugar
unbleached or enriched	2 T. hot water
all-purpose flour	

In a large mixing bowl, blend applesauce, sugar, egg substitute, sourdough starter, zucchini and milk. Put remaining ingredients, except sweetener and hot water, in a second bowl and blend. Pour into zucchini mixture and blend. Pour batter into a loaf pan that has been sprayed with cooking spray. Bake in 325° preheated oven 60 to 65 minutes, or until done. Cool on rack 5 minutes and remove from pan. Very carefully poke holes in cake with a fork. Blend sweetener and hot water and drizzle very slowly over top of cake. If using sugar, add with 1/4 cup of sugar listed in recipe ingredients.

Yield: 1 loaf; 14 slices

Approximate Per Slice:

Calories: 103	**Carbohydrates: 20.8 g**
Fat: 0.6 g	**Protein: 2.8 g**
Cholesterol: 0.2 mg	**Sodium: 87 mg**

Exchanges: 1 bread; 1 fruit

To keep soap-filled steel wool pads from rusting, wrap in plastic wrap and place in freezer--can be used over and over.

Sweet Breads from a Mix

Many sweet bread box mixes call for quite a bit of oil, making the end product high in fat. As with the muffins, I have discovered that applesauce is a good replacement for the oil. Follow the general instructions that follow when using a box bread mix.

General Instructions for Sweet Bread

Substitute unsweetend applesauce for the oil called for on the box. Use egg substitute or 2 egg whites for each egg called for. Add 1/4 teaspoon baking powder when using egg substitute or egg whites. Use skim milk. With these exceptions, follow package directions.

Apple-Cinnamon Bread   Serves 12
(Approximate 10% fat)

Approximately Per Serving:

Follow General	**Calories**	147	**Carbohydrates**	30.5 g
Instructions	**Fat**	1.6 g	**Protein**	2.3 g
	Cholesterol	0.0 mg	**Sodium**	175 mg

Exchanges: 1 bread; 1 fruit; 1 fat

Banana Bread   Serves 12
(Approximate 12% fat)

Approximately Per Serving:

Follow General	**Calories**	131	**Carbohydrates**	26.4 g
Instructions	**Fat**	1.7 g	**Protein**	2.7 g
	Cholesterol	0.0 mg	**Sodium**	199 mg

Exchanges: 1 bread; 1/2 fruit; 1 fat

Blueberry Bread   Serves 12
(Approximate 7% fat)

Approximately Per Serving:

Follow General	**Calories**	137	**Carbohydrates**	29.5 g
Instructions	**Fat**	1.1 g	**Protein**	2.3 g
	Cholesterol	0.0 mg	**Sodium**	165 mg

Exchanges: 1 bread; 1 fruit; 1/2 fat

Carrot Bread   Serves 12
(Approximate 9% fat)

Approximately Per Serving:

Follow General	**Calories**	122	**Carbohydrates**	22.6 g
Instructions	**Fat**	1.2 g	**Protein**	2.7 g
	Cholesterol	0.0 mg	**Sodium**	159 mg

Exchanges: 1 bread; 1 vegetable; 1/2 fat

Cranberry Bread   Serves 12
(Approximate 10% fat)

Approximately Per Serving:

Follow General	**Calories**	146	**Carbohydrates**	30.3 g
Instructions	**Fat**	1.6 g	**Protein**	2.3 g
	Cholesterol	0.0 mg	**Sodium**	154 mg

Exchanges: 1 bread; 1 fruit; 1/2 fat

Pumpkin Bread   Serves 12
(Approximate 12% fat)

Approximately Per Serving:

Follow General	**Calories**	131	**Carbohydrates**	27.4 g
Instructions	**Fat**	1.7 g	**Protein**	2.7 g
	Cholesterol	0.0 mg	**Sodium**	199 mg

Exchanges: 1 bread; 1/2 vegetable; 1 fat

Coffeecakes

Low-Sugar Yogurt Coffeecake

*(Recipe contains approximately
18% fat sugar-free—15% fat low-fat)*

Egg substitute to = 1 egg
1 (8 oz.) ctn. plain low-fat
  yogurt
1 Estee sugar-free white cake
  mix or Jiffy yellow cake mix

2 c. raisins
3 T. sugar
1/2 tsp. cinnamon

Put egg substitute, yogurt and cake mix in a large mixing bowl and blend well. Stir in raisins. Pour into an 8x8x2-inch baking dish that has been sprayed with cooking spray. In a small mixing bowl, blend sugar and cinnamon; sprinkle over top. Bake in a 350° preheated oven for 30 minutes, or until done.
Yield: 10 servings

Approximate Per Serving (Sugar-Free):
Calories: 147
Fat: 3.0 g
Cholesterol: 1.4 mg

Carbohydrates: 27.6 g
Protein: 1.8 g
Sodium: 22 mg

Exchanges: 2 bread

Approximate Per Serving (Low-Fat):
Calories: 160
Fat: 2.7 g
Cholesterol: 1.4 mg

Carbohydrates: 29.2 g
Protein: 3.1 g
Sodium: 197 mg

Exchanges: 2 bread; 1/4 milk

A drop of vinegar on a tissue is a great way to clean eyeglasses.

Oat 'N' Maple Coffeecake

(Recipe contains approximately 19% fat)

1 c. oat bran
1/2 c. flour, whole wheat blend,
   unbleached or enriched
   all-purpose
2 T. brown sugar, firmly packed
1 T. baking powder
1 tsp. cinnamon
1/2 tsp. cardamom (opt.)
2 T. tub margarine

1/3 c. hot water
1 T. butter granules
Egg substitute to = 1 egg
1 egg white
1/2 c. skim milk
1/4 c. "light" maple syrup
2 tsp. vanilla extract
Cooking spray
1/4 c. granola cereal

In a large mixing bowl, put oat bran, flour, 1 tablespoon brown sugar, 1 tablespoon baking powder, cinnamon and cardamom. Cut in margarine. In a cup, put hot water and stir in butter granules. Toss into oat bran mixture. In a small bowl, blend egg substitute, egg white, milk, maple syrup and vanilla. Add to oat bran mixture, stirring just until moist. Pour into 8-inch round cake pan that has been sprayed with cooking spray; lined with circle of wax paper and sprayed again. Combine granola and 1 tablespoon brown sugar and sprinkle over top. Bake in 375° preheated oven 30 minutes, or until inserted pick comes out clean. Cool on rack; serve warm.

Yield: 1 cake; 10 slices

Approximate Per Slice:
Calories: 112
Fat: 2.4 g
Cholesterol: 0.2 mg

Carbohydrates: 26.0 g
Protein: 2.5 g
Sodium: 153 mg

Exchanges: 1 1/2 bread

To add a nutty flavor to your pie crust, sprinkle pastry board with 3 to 4 tablespoons of quick rolled oats before rolling out the crust.

Sourdough Pineapple Coffeecake

(Recipe contains approximately 3% fat)

Egg substitute to = 1 egg
1/4 c. unsweetened applesauce
1 c. pineapple juice
1/3 c. sugar
1/2 c. sourdough starter

1 2/3 c. flour
2 tsp. baking powder
1/2 tsp. salt
1/4 tsp. baking soda

Blend egg substitute, applesauce, juice, sugar and sourdough starter. Blend well. In a second bowl, combine flour, baking powder, salt and baking soda. Add to starter mixture and blend until smooth. Spray a 9-inch square pan with cooking spray. Pour into pan and bake in 350° preheated oven for 35 minutes, or until done. Remove from oven and cool on rack 5 minutes. Turn out of pan onto serving plate.

TOPPING:
1 (8 oz.) pkg. "free" no-fat
    cream cheese
1 tsp. cinnamon

1/2 c. crushed pineapple,
    drained well
6 pkt. sweetener of choice to =
    1/4 c. sugar

Blend all ingredients and spread over coffeecake.
Yield: 16 servings

Approximate Per Serving:
Calories: 104
Fat: 0.3 g
Cholesterol: 3.0 mg

Carbohydrates: 19.5 g
Protein: 4.0 g
Sodium: 163 mg

Exchanges: 1 bread; 1 fruit

Mix gelatin in a 2-cup glass measure. Pour in the gelatin, add 1 cup boiling water, dissolve gelatin and add 1 cup cold water. Use spout to pour into mold.

Sourdough Raisin-Carrot Bundt

(Recipe contains approximately 3% fat)

1 c. whole wheat blend or enriched all-purpose flour	1/4 c. light brown sugar
1 tsp. baking powder	1/2 c. unsweetened applesauce
1/2 tsp. salt	Egg substitute to = 2 eggs
1/2 tsp. baking soda	1/2 c. sourdough starter
1/2 tsp. cinnamon	1 c. coarsely-grated carrots
2 egg whites	1/2 c. seedless raisins
	1 tsp. lemon extract

In a large mixing bowl, blend flour, baking powder, salt, baking soda and cinnamon. In a second bowl, beat egg whites until soft peaks form. Set aside. In a large mixing bowl, blend sugar, applesauce, egg substitute and sourdough starter. Blend. Stir in carrots, raisins and lemon extract. Add to dry ingredients and stir well. Fold in egg whites. Spray an 8-inch bundt pan with cooking spray and pour batter into pan. Bake in 350° preheated oven for 30 minutes, or until done. Remove from oven and cool 10 minutes. Remove from pan.

Yield: 1 cake; 16 pieces

Approximate Per Piece:

Calories: 65	**Carbohydrates: 27.7 g**
Fat: 0.2 g	**Protein: 2.5 g**
Cholesterol: 0.0 mg	**Sodium: 80 mg**

Exchanges: 1 bread

Roll a marble through the casing of a freshly ironed curtain and the rod will slip through easily.

Muffins

Angel Muffins
(Recipe contains approximately 9% fat)

1 T. tub margarine
1 T. sugar
Egg substitute to = 1 egg
1/2 tsp. butter granules
2 c. flour, whole wheat blend,
    unbleached or enriched
    all-purpose

1 tsp. baking powder
1/2 tsp. salt
1 c. skim milk
2 lg. egg whites

Put margarine, sugar, egg substitute and butter granules in a large mixing bowl. Cream until smooth and light. In a second bowl, sift flour, baking powder and salt. Add to egg substitute mixture alternately with skim milk. Beat egg whites until stiff—DO NOT OVERBEAT. Gently fold egg whites into batter. Spoon batter into 15 (1/3-cup) muffin tins that have been sprayed with cooking spray. Should be half-full. Bake in 350° preheated oven 25 minutes, or until brown.
Yield: 15 muffins

Approximate Per Muffin:
Calories: 81
Fat: 0.8 g
Cholesterol: 0.3 mg

Carbohydrates: 14.4 g
Protein: 2.9 g
Sodium: 111 mg

Exchanges: 1 bread; 1/4 fat

To wash white shoelaces, string them through a buttonhole of a shirt and tie them together before washing. You won't lose the laces and they won't get tangled.

Carrot Bran Muffins

(Recipe contains approximately 3% fat)

1 c. bran flakes cereal, crushed	1/2 tsp. salt
1 c. flour, whole wheat blend, unbleached or enriched all-purpose	1/2 tsp. cinnamon
	1/4 tsp. nutmeg
	1 c. skim milk
1/4 c. firmly-packed brown sugar	Egg substitute to = 1 egg
	3 T. unsweetened applesauce
2 tsp. baking powder	1 c. grated carrots
1/2 tsp. baking soda	1/4 c. raisins

Combine dry ingredients in a large mixing bowl. In a smaller bowl, combine milk, egg substitute and applesauce. Stir into dry ingredients. Add carrots and raisins and blend well. Pour into 10 muffin tins that have been sprayed with cooking spray. Bake in 400° preheated oven 15 minutes, or until an inserted toothpick comes out clean. Cool on rack; serve warm.
Yield: 10 muffins

Approximate Per Muffin:
Calories: 114
Fat: 0.4 g
Cholesterol: 0.4 mg

Carbohydrates: 22.8 g
Protein: 4.1 g
Sodium: 176 mg

Exchanges: 1 1/2 bread

Use shampoo with lanolin when washing leather gloves.
It helps to restore the natural oil in the glove skins.

Fresh Corn Muffins

(Recipe contains approximately 5% fat)

1 c. low-fat buttermilk
Egg substitute to = 1 egg
1 T. butter granules
1/2 c. flour, whole wheat blend,
    unbleached or enriched
    all-purpose
1/2 c. yellow cornmeal

2 T. sugar
1 1/4 tsp. baking powder
1/2 tsp. salt
1 egg white
1/2 c. fresh corn, cut from cob
Cooking spray

In a large mixing bowl, put buttermilk, egg substitute and butter granules. Blend well. In a small bowl, blend dry ingredients. Gradually stir dry ingredients into wet ingredients. Blend just until moistened. Beat egg white just until stiff. DO NOT OVERBEAT. Gently fold into batter. Fold in corn. Spray 12 small muffin tins with cooking spray and divide batter among tins. Bake in 425° preheated oven for 20 minutes, or until lightly browned.

Yield: 12 muffins

Approximate Per Muffin:
Calories: 71
Fat: 0.4 g
Cholesterol: 0.8 mg

Carbohydrates: 13.0 g
Protein: 2.1 g
Sodium: 141 mg

Exchanges: 1 bread

*If you run out of water softener add 1/4 cup of
vinegar to the final rinsewater.*

Mini Hot Muffins

(Recipe contains approximately 23% fat)

3/4 c. yellow cornmeal
1/4 c. whole wheat blend or
    enriched all-purpose flour
2 T. finely-chopped green
    pepper
2 T. finely-chopped green
    onion

1 T. minced jalapeño pepper
1 1/2 tsp. baking powder
1/2 tsp. garlic salt
1/4 tsp. black pepper
1/3 c. skim milk
Egg substitute to = 1 egg
1 T. canola oil

In a medium mixing bowl, put cornmeal, flour, green pepper, green onion, jalapeño pepper, baking powder, garlic salt and pepper. In a small bowl, put milk, egg substitute and oil. Blend. Stir into dry ingredients, stirring just until moist. Spoon into miniature muffin tins that have been sprayed with cooking spray, filling 2/3-full. Bake in 425° preheated oven 10 to 15 minutes, or until lightly browned and done.
Yield: 18 muffins

Approximate Per 2 Muffins:
Calories: 80
Fat: 2.0 g
Cholesterol: 0.2 mg

Carbohydrates: 12.4 g
Protein: 2.0 g
Sodium: 140 mg

Exchanges: 1 bread; 1/4 fat

*Place lace tablecloths, fine lingerie and cutwork in a
mesh bag before laundering them.*

Oatmeal Muffins

(Recipe contains approximately 8% fat)

1 c. old-fashioned oatmeal
1 c. low-fat buttermilk
1/4 c. brown sugar, packed
1/2 c. unsweetened applesauce
Egg substitute to = 1 egg

1 c. flour, whole wheat blend,
   unbleached or enriched
   all-purpose
1 tsp. baking powder
1/2 tsp. baking soda
1/2 tsp. salt

Blend oatmeal and buttermilk in a large mixing bowl. Set aside and allow to stand for 30 minutes. Blend sugar, applesauce and egg substitute and add to oatmeal mixture. Add remaining ingredients. Stir until until moistened. Spray 12 (1-cup) muffin tins with cooking spray and spoon batter into tins, filling 2/3-full. Bake in 400° preheated oven for 20 minutes, or until brown. Cool 5 minutes and serve warm.

Yield: 12 muffins

Approximate Per Muffin:
Calories: 102
Fat: 0.9 g
Cholesterol: 0.8 mg

Carbohydrates: 22.1 g
Protein: 3.3 g
Sodium: 214 mg

Exchanges: 1 1/2 bread

When buying sheets pick a different color or pattern for each size bed.
Makes sorting easier after laundering.

Raised Corn Muffins

(Recipe contains approximately 10% fat)

1 1/2 tsp. active dry yeast
1/4 c. lukewarm water
  (110°-115°)
1/2 tsp. sugar
1 1/2 c. yellow cornmeal
1 c. boiling water

1 1/2 c. skim milk
Egg substitute to = 2 eggs
1 T. tub margarine, melted &
  cooled
1 T. butter granules
1 tsp. salt (less if desired)

Put warm water and sugar into a small bowl. Sprinkle yeast over top and set aside for 10 minutes to proof. In a second bowl, put cornmeal. Pour boiling water over cornmeal and blend. Add milk, egg substitute, margarine and butter granules.

Stir in salt, then add proofed yeast and blend. Cover with plastic wrap and set aside to rise for one hour. Spoon batter into 15 (3-inch) muffin tins that have been sprayed with cooking spray. Bake in 425° preheated oven for 20 minutes, or until brown.

Yield: 15 muffins

Approximate Per Muffin:
Calories: 72
Fat: 0.8 g
Cholesterol: 0.4 mg

Carbohydrates: 12.3 g
Protein: 2.4 g
Sodium: 171 mg

Exchanges: 1 bread

Prevent tangling in the machine by buttoning shirt and
blouse sleeves to front buttons.

Sage Corn Muffins

(Recipe contains approximately 9% fat)

1 1/2 whole wheat blend or
   enriched all-purpose flour
1 1/2 c. yellow cornmeal
1 T. baking powder
1 1/2 tsp. baking soda
1/2 tsp. salt
1 1/2 c. low-fat buttermilk

Egg substitute to = 3 eggs
2 T. tub margarine, melted &
   cooled
1/4 c. hot water
1 T. butter granules
1 T. dried sage

Sift together flour, cornmeal, baking powder, baking soda and salt into a large mixing bowl. In a second bowl, blend buttermilk, egg substitute and margarine. Dissolve butter granules in hot water and add to mixture. Stir in sage. Add wet ingredients to dry ingredients and blend just until moistened. Spoon batter into 12 (1/3-cup) muffin tins that have been sprayed with cooking spray. Tins should be 2/3-full. Bake in 425° preheated oven for 15 to 20 minutes, or until puffed up and golden brown.
Yield: 12 muffins

Approximate Per Muffin:
Calories: 162
Fat: 1.7 g
Cholesterol: 1.2 mg

Carbohydrates: 27.0 g
Protein: 4.8 g
Sodium: 206

Exchanges: 1 bread; 1/2 milk; 1 fat

*If you protect your bath mats with a towel when kids take a
bath it will require laundering less often.*

Sourdough Apple Muffins

(Recipe contains approximately 6% fat)

1 1/2 c. whole wheat blend or
   enriched all-purpose flour
1/4 c. sugar
2 tsp. baking powder
1/2 tsp. salt
1 tsp. cinnamon

Egg substitute to = 1 egg
1/2 c. sourdough starter
2/3 c. skim milk
1/3 c. unsweetened applesauce
1 c. peeled, cored & finely-
   chopped apples

In a mixing bowl, blend flour, sugar, baking powder, salt and cinnamon. With the back of a spoon, make a well in flour mixture. In a second bowl, blend egg substitute, sourdough starter, milk, applesauce and chopped apples. Pour into well in flour mixture. Stir with wooden spoon just until moistened. Spray 12 muffin tins with cooking spray and fill 2/3-full. Bake in 400° preheated oven 20 to 25 minutes, or until done.
Yield: 12 muffins

Approximate Per Muffin:
Calories: 98
Fat: 0.7 g
Cholesterol: 0.3 mg

Carbohydrates: 19.9 g
Protein: 2.5 g
Sodium: 111 mg

Exchanges: 1 bread; 1/2 fruit

*Keep the plant mister handy when ironing clothes--
great for spraying clothes.*

Sourdough Corn Muffins

(Recipe contains approximately 4% fat)

1 c. whole wheat blend or
   enriched all-purpose flour
1 c. yellow cornmeal
2 tsp. baking powder
1/4 tsp. baking soda
1/2 tsp. salt

1 tsp. sugar
1/2 c. sourdough starter
Egg substitute to = 1 egg
1/4 c. unsweetened applesauce
1 c. skim milk

In a mixing bowl, blend flour, cornmeal, baking powder, baking soda, salt and sugar. With the back of a spoon, make a well in center of flour mixture. In a second bowl, blend remaining ingredients. Pour into well in dry ingredients and blend until moistened. Spray 12 muffin tins with cooking spray and fill 2/3-full. Bake in a 400° preheated oven 20 to 25 minutes, or until done.
Yield: 12

Approximate Per Muffin:
Calories: 103
Fat: 0.4 g
Cholesterol: 0.3 mg

Carbohydrates: 20.2 g
Protein: 3.1 g
Sodium: 115 mg

Exchanges: 1 1/2 bread

*A clean catsup dispenser makes an ideal
container for filling steam irons.*

Muffins from a Box

Due to the amount of oil added to box muffins, they are often high in fat content. In experimenting with these box mixes, I have found that by substituting unsweetened applesauce for the oil, the muffins are low in fat and good tasting. You can now buy a little four pack of applesauce that contains 4 (4-ounce) containers of applesauce. These are just great for cooking. It keeps you from opening a large jar when you only need a tablespoon or two. If you do open a large jar, simply freeze some of it in small bags for cooking.

When using box muffin mix, follow the general instructions which follow.

General Instructions for Box Muffins

For the oil called for on the box, substitute unsweetened applesauce. Use egg substitute or 2 egg whites per egg for the eggs called for. When using egg substitute or egg whites, always add 1/4 teaspoon baking soda to the mix. Use skim milk, and with these exceptions, follow package directions.

Light Muffin Mixes

Betty Crocker Light Blueberry Muffins
(Approximate 8% fat)　　　　　Serves 12

Approximately Per Serving:

Follow General	**Calories**	125	**Carbohydrates**	29.3 g
Instructions	**Fat**	1.1 g	**Protein**	2.3 g
	Cholesterol	0.0 mg	**Sodium**	194 mg

Exchanges: 1 1/2 bread; 1/2 fruit

No-Fat Muffin Mixes

Krusteaz, No-Fat, Apple Cinnamon
(no-fat)　　　　　Serves 12

Approximately Per Serving:

Follow General	**Calories**	130	**Carbohydrates**	28.0 g
Instructions	**Fat**	0.0 g	**Protein**	3.0 g
	Cholesterol	0.0 mg	**Sodium**	310 mg

Exchanges: 2 bread

❖

Krusteaz Blueberry Muffins   Serves 12
(no-fat)

Approximately Per Serving:

Follow General	Calories	130	Carbohydrates	30.0 g
Instrucions	Fat	0.0 g	Protein	2.0 g
	Cholesterol	0.0 mg	Sodium	260 mg

Exchanges: 2 bread

Converted Muffin Mixes
Betty Crocker Brand

Apple Cinnamon Muffins   Serves 12
(Approximate 12% fat)

Approximately Per Serving:

Follow General	Calories	116	Carbohydrates	24.2 g
Instructions	Fat	1.6 g	Protein	2.3 g
	Cholesterol	0.0 mg	Sodium	194 mg

Exchanges: 1 bread; 1 fruit

❖

Banana Nut Muffins   Serves 12
(Approximate 17% fat)

Approximately Per Serving:

Follow General	Calories	136	Carbohydrates	24.2 g
Instructions	Fat	2.6 g	Protein	2.3 g
	Cholesterol	0.0 mg	Sodium	194 mg

Exchanges: 1 1/2 bread; 1/2 fruit; 1/2 fat

❖

Cinnamon Streusel Muffin   Serves 12
(Approximate 8% fat)

Approximately Per Serving:

Follow General	Calories	170	Carbohydrates	21.8 g
Instructions	Fat	1.6 g	Protein	2.9 g
	Cholesterol	Tr. mg	Sodium	182 mg

Exchanges: 2 bread; 1 fat HIGH IN SUGAR CONTENT

❖

Twice the Blueberries Muffins
(Approximate 11% fat)   Serves 12
                         Approximately Per Serving:
Follow General **Calories**   126   **Carbohydrates** 25.2 g
  Instructions **Fat**   1.6 g   **Protein**   2.3 g
                Cholesterol   0.0 mg   **Sodium**   184 mg
Exchanges: 1 1/2 bread; 1/2 fruit

❖

Wild Blueberry Muffins   Serves 12
(Approximate 10% fat)
                         Approximately Per Serving:
Follow General **Calories**   146   **Carbohydrates** 29.4 g
  Instructions **Fat**   1.6 g   **Protein**   2.3 g
                Cholesterol   0.0 mg   **Sodium**   214 mg
Exchanges: 1 1/2 bread; 1 fruit

Jiffy Brand Muffin Mixes

Oatmeal Muffins   Serves 8
(Approximate 31% fat)
                         Approximately Per Serving:
Follow General **Calories**   121   **Carbohydrates** 17.6 g
  Instructions **Fat**   4.2 g   **Protein**   2.6 g
                Cholesterol   0.2 mg   **Sodium**   212 mg
Exchanges: 1 bread; 1 fat

❖

Blueberry Muffins   Serves 8
(Approximate 28% fat)
                         Apprxomately Per Serving:
Follow General **Calories**   170   **Carbohydrates** 28.4 g
  Instructions **Fat**   5.2 g   **Protein**   2.8 g
                Cholesterol   Tr. mg   **Sodium**   280 mg
Exchanges: 1 1/2 bread; 1/2 fruit; 1 fat

Robin Hood Brand Mixes

Apple-Cinnamon Muffins   Serves 6
(Approximate 26% fat)

Approximately Per Serving:

Follow General	**Calories**	146	**Carbohydrates**	23.0 g
Instructions	**Fat**	4.2 g	**Protein**	2.1 g
	Cholesterol	Tr. mg	**Sodium**	216 mg

Exchanges: 1 bread; 3/4 fruit; 1 fat

❖

Blueberry Muffins   Serves 6
(Approximate 21% fat)

Approximately Per Serving:

Follow General	**Calories**	136	**Carbohydrates**	24.0 g
Instructions	**Fat**	3.2 g	**Protein**	2.1 g
	Cholesterol	Tr. mg	**Sodium**	226 mg

Exchanges: 1 bread; 1/2 fruit; 1 fat

❖

Caramel Muffins   Serves 6
(Approximate 21% fat)

Approximately Per Serving:

Follow General	**Calories**	138	**Carbohydrates**	24.0 g
Instructions	**Fat**	3.2 g	**Protein**	2.1 g
	Cholesterol	Tr. mg	**Sodium**	226 mg

Exchanges: 1 bread; 1/2 fruit; 1 fat

Biscuits

Baking Powder Biscuits

(Recipe contains approximately 22% fat)

1 c. whole wheat blend or
   enriched all-purpose flour
2 tsp. baking powder
1/4 tsp. yeast

1/4 tsp. salt
1 T. canola oil
6 T. skim milk

Put flour, baking powder, yeast and salt in a small mixing bowl and stir with whisk until well blended. Drizzle oil over top, tossing with fork until oil is evenly distributed. Add milk and stir with wooden spoon until flour is moistened. Turn out onto floured surface and roll into 1/2-inch thickness. Cut with biscuit cutter that has been sprayed with cooking spray. Bake in 450° preheated oven for 12 to 15 minutes, or until lightly browned.
Yield: 10 biscuits

Approximate Per Biscuit:
Calories: 66
Fat: 1.6 g
Cholesterol: Trace

Carbohydrates: 10.0 g
Protein: 2.0 g
Sodium: 64 mg

Exchanges: 1 bread

Starch rag or braided rugs heavily and they'll lay flat.

Cheesy Biscuits

(Recipe contains approximately 13% fat)

1 3/4 c. flour, whole wheat
    blend, unbleached or
    enriched all-purpose
1 T. dried parsley
1 1/2 tsp. baking powder
1 green onion, minced

1/4 tsp. dried oregano
1 T. cheese granules
2 T. tub margarine, melted
3/4 c. low-fat cottage cheese
2 egg whites, slightly beaten

In a large mixing bowl, put flour, parsley, baking powder, green onion and dried oregano. Blend. Put cheese granules into melted margarine and stir until dissolved. Add to flour mixture along with cottage cheese and egg whites. Stir just until moist. Turn out onto floured surface and knead 5 or 6 times. Roll dough to 1-inch thickness and cut into 2-inch rounds. Put on an ungreased baking sheet and bake in 400° preheated oven 10 to 12 minutes, or until golden brown.

Yield: 12 biscuits

Approximate Per Biscuit:
Calories: 97
Fat: 1.4 g
Cholesterol: 1.2 mg

Carbohydrates: 14.6 g
Protein: 4.4 g
Sodium: 124 mg

Exchanges: 1 bread; 1/4 milk; 1/4 fat

*For a better fit of ironing board cover after washing,
put it back on the ironing board while still damp.*

Potato Biscuits

(Recipe contains approximately 4% fat)

1/2 c. skim milk	2 tsp. baking powder
1/2 c. water	Dash of salt
3/4 c. instant potato granules	Egg substitute to = 1 egg
1 c. whole wheat blend or	
enriched all-purpose flour	

Put milk and water in saucepan and bring almost to boil. DO NOT BOIL. Add potato granules and stir with whisk. Set aside a few minutes. Put potatoes in a mixing bowl. Blend together flour, baking powder and salt. Stir into potatoes. Add egg substitute and blend together until thick dough forms. Turn out onto a floured surface and knead 3 or 4 minutes. Roll out dough to 3/4-inch thickness. Cut in rounds. Place on baking sheet that has been sprayed with cooking spray. Bake in 450° preheated oven 15 to 20 minutes. Cool on rack. Serve warm.
Yield: 12 biscuits

Approximate Per Biscuit:

Calories: 67	**Carbohydrates: 13.0 g**
Fat: 0.3 g	**Protein: 2.2 g**
Cholesterol: 0.2 mg	**Sodium: 65 mg**

Exchanges: 1 bread

When ironing flat pieces, turn your ironing board around so the iron rests on the narrow end of the board. Gives you more ironing surface.

Sourdough Biscuits

(Recipe contains approximately 24% fat)

1/2 c. sourdough starter	1 T. sugar
1 c. skim milk	1 T. baking powder
2 1/2 c. flour, whole wheat	1/2 tsp. baking soda
blend, unbleached or	1 T. tub margarine, melted
enriched all-purpose	1 tsp. butter granules
1/2 tsp. salt	1 T. canola oil

In a large mixing bowl, put sourdough starter, milk and 1 cup flour. Blend. Cover with plastic wrap and place in warm place and allow to stand overnight. In the morning, add 1 cup flour and beat with wooden spoon. Blend together salt, sugar, baking powder, baking soda and 1/2 cup flour. Pour into starter mixture and blend to form a dough. Turn out onto floured surface and knead several times. Form dough in ball and roll out to 1/2-inch thickness. Blend together melted margarine and butter granules, along with oil. Brush over top of biscuits; cover with plastic wrap and set in warm, draft-free place to rise for 30 to 40 minutes. Bake in 375° preheated oven for 30 to 35 minutes. Serve hot.

Yield: 12 biscuits

Approximate Per Biscuit:

Calories: 78	**Carbohydrates: 17.2 g**
Fat: 2.1 g	**Protein: 1.7 g**
Cholesterol: 0.0 mg	**Sodium: 111 mg**

Exchanges: 1 bread

If you spill something on your clothes while eating out, ask the waiter for a glass of club soda; use a clean napkin to remove spot.

Sourdough Bran Biscuits

(Recipe contains approximately 21% fat)

1 c. sourdough starter
1 tsp. active dry yeast
1/2 c. lukewarm water
    (110°-115°)
2 T. brown sugar, firmly
    packed
Egg substitute to = 1 egg

3 T. canola oil
1/2 c. whole bran cereal
1 tsp. salt
2 1/4 c. flour, whole wheat
    blend or enriched
    all-purpose

In a large mixing bowl, put sourdough starter and set aside for one hour at room temperature. Put lukewarm water in a saucer and sprinkle with yeast. Set aside 10 minutes to proof. Add yeast sponge to starter, along with brown sugar, egg substitute, oil and bran. Mix well. Sift together salt and flour. Add enough flour to starter mixture to make a nonsticky, soft dough. Spray a bowl with cooking spray. Form dough into a ball and place in bowl. Turn once to coat both sides. Cover with plastic wrap and set in warm, draft-free place until dough is doubled in bulk—about 1 1/2 hours. Spray hands with cooking spray and punch dough down. Allow to rest 10 minutes. Spray hands again and form dough into 24 half-inch balls. Put balls into two 9-inch cake pans that have been sprayed with cooking spray. Cover with plastic wrap and set in warm, draft-free place for 50 minutes to rise. Bake in a 350° preheated oven for 20 to 25 minutes.
Yield: 24 rolls

Approximate Per Roll:
Calories: 85
Fat: 2.0 g
Cholesterol: 0.0 mg

Carbohydrates: 18.1 g
Protein: 2.0 g
Sodium: 111 mg

Exchanges: 1 bread; 1/4 fat

*There is nothing better for removing gum than Energine Spot Remover.
Ask for it at your local drug store. Gum almost melts away.*

Sourdough Cinnamon-Raisin Biscuits

(Recipe contains approximately 18% fat)

1 1/2 c. whole wheat blend or
   enriched all-purpose flour
1 T. baking powder
1/2 tsp. salt
1/4 tsp. baking soda

1/4 c. diet tub margarine
1/2 c. raisins
Egg substitute to = 1 egg
1 c. sourdough starter

In a medium mixing bowl, sift together flour, baking powder, salt and baking soda. Cut in margarine until the texture of cornmeal. Stir in raisins. In a second bowl, blend egg substitute and starter. Using a fork, toss wet mixture into dry mixture. Turn out onto a lightly-floured surface and knead 10 to 12 times. Roll dough to 1/2-inch thickness. Cut with floured biscuit cutter. Place on ungreased baking sheet. Cover and let rise 30 minutes. Bake in a 425° preheated oven 12 to 15 minutes, or until golden brown.
Yield: 12 biscuits

Approximate Per Biscuit:
Calories: 107
Fat: 2.1 g
Cholesterol: 0.0 mg

Carbohydrates: 18.3 g
Protein: 2.4 g
Sodium: 155 mg

Exchanges: 1 1/2 bread

Orange Cheese Spread

(Contains only a trace of fat)

1 (8 oz.) pkg. "free" no-fat
   Philadelphia cream cheese

1/2 c. "all fruit" orange
   marmalade

Blend ingredients together until soft and smooth.
Yield: 24 tablespoons

Approximate Per Tablespoon:
Calories: 27
Fat: Trace
Cholesterol: 1.7 mg

Carbohydrates: 6.2 g
Protein: 1.3 g
Sodium: 58 mg

Exchanges for 2 Tablespoons: 1 fruit

Salads-
Vegetable, Fruit, Gelatin, Pasta & Rice

Salads

Salads are a very important part of the meal. Not only do they provide a lot of nutrition by way of vitamins and minerals, but they are easy to use to round out a meal—a vegetable salad if the day is short of vegetables—a fruit salad if fruit is needed—a pasta or rice salad if the day needs more starch.

The pitfall to salads is what lands on them or in them. As long as the ingredients are selected with fat in mind—staying from away from such things as high-fat cheeses, bacon, ham, etc., a salad can be an important part of the meal.

Many salads are also low in calories and can round out the meal without adding a lot in calories and fat.

The salad dressing must be chosen with care. Manufacturers are coming up with some real great no-fat salad dressings. Add don't overlook the flavored vinegar you can make yourself. There's some waiting time involved with making flavored vinegars, but it lasts a long time and is well-worth the wait.

When I use the flavored vinegar as a salad dressing I like to spray the salad itself with a little cooking spray (I like the olive oil flavored cooking spray best for salads.

There are a variety of salads listed in this chapter. Use them as needed to round out a meal. And don't overlook using a chef's, pasta or rice salad as the entrée for a light meal.

Use a grapefruit spoon with a serrated tip to
scoop out tomatoes for stuffing.

Gelatin Salads

Applesauce Salad
(Recipe contains approximately 3% fat)

2 1/2 c. boiling water
2 (3 oz.) pkg. lemon gelatin
1 (16 oz.) can unsweetened
   applesauce
1 tsp. cinnamon

1 (8 oz.) pkg. "free" no-fat
   Philadelphia cream cheese
2 T. skim milk
1/2 tsp. lemon extract

Dissolve gelatin in boiling water. Add applesauce and cinnamon. Pour into 8x8-inch baking dish and chill until set. Blend cream cheese, milk and lemon extract. Spread over gelatin.
Yield: 9 servings

Approximate Per Serving:
Calories: 55
Fat: 0.2 g
Cholesterol: 4.5 mg

Carbohydrates: 13.6 g
Protein: 3.8 g
Sodium: 162 mg

Exchanges: 1/2 fruit; 1/2 milk

*The pointed end of a beer-can opener is an
excellent tool for deveining shrimp.*

Apricot Salad Deluxe

(Recipe contains approximately 2% fat)

1 (6 oz.) pkg. sugar-free
    orange gelatin
2 c. boiling water
2 c. mini marshmallows
2 (16 oz.) cans "light" apricots,
    drained & diced (reserve
    juice)
1 (16 oz.) can "light" crushed
    pineapple, drained (reserve
    juice)

2 T. flour
Artificial sweetener to =
    1/2 c. sugar
Egg substitute to = 1 egg
1 (8 oz.) ctn. "light" Cool
    Whip
1/2 c. "free" no-fat shredded
    Cheddar cheese

Dissolve gelatin in 2 cups boiling water. Add marshmallows and stir until dissolved and mixture is smooth. Set 1/2 cup juice aside. Add water to remaining juice to make 1 1/2 cups. Add to gelatin. Add diced apricots and crushed pineapple. Blend well and pour into 9x13-inch dish (a 10x15-inch dish is even better). Chill until set. In a saucepan, blend flour, and sugar, if using. Do not add sweetener at this point. Slowly blend in 1/2 cup juice. Blend in egg substitute. Cook over medium heat, stirring constantly, until thick. Stir in artificial sweetener, if using. Cool. Fold in Cool Whip and spread mixture over gelatin. Sprinkle with cheese. Refrigerate until set.

Yield: 16 servings

Approximate Per Serving:
Calories: 82 g
Fat: 0.2 g
Cholesterol: 0.6 mg

Carbohydrates: 8.5 g
Protein: 3.9 g
Sodium: 45 mg

Exchanges: 1 fruit; 1/2 milk

Use the tip of a potato peeler to pit cherries.

Carrot Pineapple Gelatin

(Recipe contains approximately 1% fat)

1 (3 oz.) pkg. sugar-free orange
    gelatin
1 c. boiling water
1 c. cold water

1 sm. can crushed pineapple,
    canned in own juice, drained
1 c. shredded carrots

Dissolve gelatin in boiling water. Add cold water. Chill until gelatin is the consistency of egg white. Stir in pineapple and carrots. Chill until set.
Yield: 4 servings

Approximate Per Serving:
Calories: 63
Fat: 0.1 g
Cholesterol: 0.0 mg

Carbohydrates: 10.3 g
Protein: 3.5 g
Sodium: 18 mg

Exchanges: 1 fruit; 1 vegetable

Easy Gelatin Salad

(Recipe contains approximately 2% fat)

1 box sugar-free red gelatin
1 c. boiling water
1 c. cold water

1 (16 oz.) can of canned in own
    juice fruit cocktail, drained

Dissolve gelatin in boiling water. Add cold water and set aside. Divide drained fruit cocktail among 4 custard cups or 4 stemmed sherbets and add 1/2 cup gelatin. Chill until set.
Yield: 4 servings

Approximate Per Serving:
Calories: 37
Fat: 0.1 g
Cholesterol: 0.0 mg

Carbohydrates: 7.3 g
Protein: 2.3 g
Sodium: 11 g

Exchanges: 1 fruit

Lemon-Cheese and Horseradish Salad

(Recipe contains approximately 4% fat)

2 (3 oz.) pkg. sugar-free
  lemon gelatin
2 c. boiling water
1 (8 oz.) pkg. "free" no-fat
  Philadelphia cream cheese
3 T. "light" mayonnaise

2 c. chopped celery
1 sm. can crushed pineapple,
  drained
1 jar pimento, drained &
  chopped
1 tsp. horseradish

Dissolve gelatin in boiling water and add cream cheese, stirring until melted and mixture is well blended. Stir in mayonnaise and blend until smooth. Set aside to cool to room temperature. Add remaining ingredients and pour into 9x13-inch baking dish. Chill until set. Cut in squares and serve on lettuce leaf.
Yield: 16 servings

Approximate Per Serving:
Calories: 47
Fat: 0.2 g
Cholesterol: 2.5 mg

Carbohydrates: 2.8 g
Protein: 3.2 g
Sodium: 130 mg

Exchanges: 1/2 fruit; 1 vegetable

Use a soup ladle when filling molds with gelatin.

Lemon Cottage Salad

(Recipe contains approximately 21% fat)

1 (3 oz.) pkg. sugar-free lemon
   flavored gelatin
1/2 c. boiling water
1 sm. ctn. small-curd, low-fat
   cottage cheese, drained well

4 ribs celery, chopped fine
1 sm. can "light" crushed
   pineapple, drained
1 c. "light" Cool Whip

Dissolve gelatin in boiling water. Cool. Refrigerate until the consistency of egg whites. Stir in cottage cheese, celery and pineapple. Fold in Cool Whip. Put in serving dish or mold. Refrigerate until set.

Yield: 8 servings

Approximate Per Serving:
Calories: 77
Fat: 1.8 g
Cholesterol: 3.6 mg

Carbohydrates: 7.1 g
Protein: 12.8 g
Sodium: 185 mg

Exchanges: 1/4 milk; 1/2 vegetable; 1 fruit

Lime Gelatin with Pear Halves

(Recipe contains approximately 7% fat)

1 (3 oz.) pkg. sugar-free
   lime gelatin
1 c. boiling water

1 c. cold water
4 canned pear halves, canned
   in own juice

Dissolve gelatin in boiling water. Add cold water and set aside. Put pear half in 4 custard cups or stemmed sherbets and add 1/2 cup of gelatin. Chill until set.

Yield: 4 servings

Approximate Per Serving:
Calories: 66
Fat: 0.5 g
Cholesterol: 0.0 mg

Carbohydrates: 12.5 g
Protein: 2.5 g
Sodium: 8 mg

Exchanges: 1 1/2 fruit

Mmmmm Good Salad

(Recipe contains approximately 10% fat)

1 pkg. sugar-free lemon gelatin
14 lg. marshmallows
1/2 of 8 oz. ctn. of "free" no-fat
   Philadelphia cream cheese
2 c. boiling water
1 (8 oz.) ctn. "light" Cool
   Whip
1 c. drained, crushed
   pineapple
1 c. grated carrots

Put gelatin, marshmallows and cream cheese in a bowl. Add boiling water and stir until marshmallows and cheese melts, and gelatin dissolves. Chill until mixture is the consistency of egg white. Lightly whip gelatin mixture with an electric mixer. Stir in Cool Whip, blending until smooth. Fold in remaining ingredients and chill until set.
Yield: 8 servings

Approximate Per Serving:
Calories: 101
Fat: 1.1 g
Cholesterol: 2.5 mg
Carbohydrates: 19.9 g
Protein: 3.8 g
Sodium: 100 mg

Exchanges: 1 milk; 1 vegetable

Wear an oven mitt to hold on to a pineapple while cutting it.

Mandarin Orange Gelatin

(Recipe contains only a trace of fat)

1 (3 oz.) pkg. sugar-free orange
   gelatin
1 c. boiling water

1 c. cold water
1 (11 oz.) can mandarin
   oranges, drained

Dissolve gelatin in boiling water. Add cold water and set aside.
Divide mandarin oranges among 4 small serving dishes. Add 1/2
cup gelatin. Chill until set.
Yield: 4 servings

Approximate Per Serving:
Calories: 42
Fat: Trace
Cholesterol: 0.0 mg

Carbohydrates: 10.3 g
Protein: 2.3 g
Sodium: 12 mg

Exchanges: 1 fruit

Melon Gelatin

(Recipe contains approximately 3% fat)

2 c. cantaloupe
1 pkg. sugar-free orange gelatin

1 c. boiling water
1 c. cold water

Put 1/2 cup melon balls in 4 small berry dishes. Dissolve gelatin
in hot water. Add cold water. Pour 1/2 cup gelatin over melon balls.
Chill until set.
Yield: 4 servings

Approximate Per Serving:
Calories: 32
Fat: 0.1 g
Cholesterol: 0.0 mg

Carbohydrates: 6.0 g
Protein: 2.6 g
Sodium: 8 mg

Exchanges: 1 fruit

Seafoam Salad

(Recipe contains approximately 12% fat)

1 (16 oz. can pears, canned in
    own juice (reserve juice)
1 (8 oz.) ctn. "free" no-fat
    Philadelphia cream
    cheese

2 T. skim milk
1 (3 oz.) pkg. sugar-free lime
    gelatin
1 c. cold water
1 c. "light" Cool Whip

Drain pears and set juice aside. Mash pears and set aside. In a mixing bowl, blend cream cheese and milk. Whip until smooth. Add enough water to pear juice to make 1 cup. Heat juice and add gelatin; stir until dissolved. Pour into cream cheese mixture. Add cold water and blend until smooth. Add mashed pears and blend until smooth. Add 1 cup Cool Whip, stirring until smooth. Pour into serving dish or 6 individual dishes.
Yield: 6 servings

Approximate Per Serving:
Calories: 109
Fat: 1.4 g
Cholesterol: 6.8 mg

Carbohydrates: 14.9 g
Protein: 6.0 g
Sodium: 235 mg

Exchanges: 1 milk; 1/2 fruit

Use a potato peeler to cut orange or lemon rind peels.

Strawberry-Cheese Salad
(Recipe contains approximately 21% fat)

2 (3 oz.) pkg. strawberry
flavored sugar-free gelatin
2 c. boiling water
2 (10 oz.) pkg. frozen,
unsweetened strawberries
1 (13 1/2 oz.) can crushed
pineapple, drained

2 lg. bananas, sliced
1 (8 oz.) pkg. "free" no-fat
Philadelphia cream cheese
2 T. skim milk
1 c. "light" Cool Whip

Dissolve gelatin in 2 cups boiling water. Stir in strawberries and stir until strawberries have thawed. Stir in pineapple and bananas. Pour 1/2 of mixture in a 9x13-inch baking dish. Refrigerate until set. With an electric mixer, blend cheese, milk and Cool Whip, beating until smooth. Spread evenly over set gelatin. Add remaining gelatin, cover and refrigerate until set.
Yield: 16 servings

Approximate Per Serving:
Calories: 52
Fat: 1.2 g
Cholesterol: 2.5 mg

Carbohydrates: 8.1 g
Protein: 2.4 g
Sodium: 90 mg

Exchanges: 1 fruit; 1/4 fat

Remove the cores from pears with a melon baller scoop.
If pear is to be served whole, core from bottom of pear.

Strawberry Gelatin with Strawberries

(Recipe contains approximately 11% fat)

2 c. sliced, fresh strawberries
1 (3 oz.) pkg. sugar-free
   strawberry gelatin

1 c. boiling water
1 c. cold water

In four small berry dishes, put 1/2 cup sliced strawberries. Dissolve gelatin in boiling water. Add cold water. Pour 1/2 cup gelatin over each dish of strawberries. Chill until set.
Yield: 4 servings

Approximate Per Serving:
Calories: 33
Fat: 0.4 g
Cholesterol: 0.0 mg

Carbohydrates: 6.3 g
Protein: 2.5 g
Sodium: 9 mg

Exchanges: 1 fruit

Fruit Salads

Easy Apple Salad

(Recipe contains approximately 22% fat)

3 med. apples, cored & diced
1 banana, peeled & sliced
1 c. seedless grapes, halved

1 (16 oz.) can crushed
   pineapple, drained
6 oz. "light" Cool Whip
2 T. "free" no-fat mayonnaise

Put all of fruit in a mixing bowl. Combine Cool Whip and mayonnaise. Pour into fruit and gently toss.
Yield: 8 servings

Approximate Per Serving:
Calories: 82
Fat: 2.0 g
Cholesterol: 0.0 mg

Carbohydrates: 18.9 g
Protein: 0.2 g
Sodium: 49 mg

Exchanges: 2 fruit

Simple Fruit Salad

(Recipe contains approximately 7% fat)

1 lg. red Delicious apple,
    cored & diced
1 med. banana, peeled & sliced
1/4 c. lemon juice
2 c. fresh strawberries, sliced

1/4 c. unsweetened orange juice
1 1/2 tsp. cornstarch
1 T. honey
1/4 tsp. butter granules

Put apples and bananas in a bowl and sprinkle with 2 tablespoons lemon juice, toss to coat fruit (the lemon juice keeps the fruit from turning dark). Add strawberries and toss.

In a small saucepan, put the remaining 2 tablespoons lemon juice and cornstarch. Stir until smooth. Add honey and bring mixture to a boil. Add butter granules and stir until thick and bubbly. Remove from heat and allow to cool, covered. Pour over fruit, tossing gently to blend. Chill until ready to serve.

Yield: 8 servings

Approximate Per Serving:
Calories: 53
Fat: 0.4 g
Cholesterol: 0.0 mg

Carbohydrates: 13.3 g
Protein: 0.5 g
Sodium: 25 mg

Exchanges: 1 1/4 fruit

To prevent salads from getting soggy, place an inverted saucer in the bottom of the salad bowl.

Six-Cup Salad

(Recipe contains approximately 4% fat)

1 c. pineapple chunks, drained
1 c. mandarin oranges, drained
1 c. sliced peaches, drained &
    halved
1 c. small marshmallows

1 c. "free" Philadelphia
    cream cheese
1 c. low-fat plain yogurt
12 pkt. artificial sweetener, or
    sweetener of choice to =
    1/2 c. sugar

Put drained fruit in large mixing bowl, along with marshmallows. Blend cream cheese, yogurt and sweetener until smooth. Pour over fruit and gently toss to blend.
Yield: 10 servings

Approximate Per Serving:
Calories: 105
Fat: 0.5 g
Cholesterol: 5.4 mg

Carbohydrates: 14.1 g
Protein: 4.8 g
Sodium: 159 mg

Exchanges: 2 fruit; 1/4 milk

*When onions and green pepper are cheap and plentiful buy,
slice and store in 1/2 packages in the freezer.*

Vegetable Salads

Black Bean Salad
(Recipe contains approximately 13% fat)

1 (16 oz.) can black beans,
    drained & rinsed
1 lg. green pepper, diced
1 lg. tomato, seeded & diced
2 green onions, sliced thin
    (include some green)

1/2 tsp. chicken bouillon
    granules
1/4 c. hot water
Cooking spray
1/4 tsp. salt
1/4 tsp. black pepper

In a mixing bowl, put beans, green pepper, tomato and onion. Toss to blend. Combine bouillon and hot water; stir until dissolved. Set aside to cool slightly. As you toss salad, spray with cooking spray for 6 seconds. Drizzle bouillon over salad. Add salt and pepper; toss to blend. Refrigerate until ready to serve.
Yield: 4 servings

Approximate Per Serving:
Calories: 98
Fat: 1.4 g
Cholesterol: 0.0 mg

Carbohydrates: 28.1 g
Protein: 9.1 g
Sodium: 141 mg

Exchanges: 1 bread; 1 vegetable

---

*Hang belts--or your daughter's hair ribbons--on a rotating necktie
rack to keep them in order and easily accessible.*

Marinated Salad

(Recipe contains approximately 26% fat)

1 (17 1/2 oz.) can garbanzo
  beans, drained
1 (16 oz.) can pitted black
  olives, drained
1 (8 1/2 oz.) can artichoke
  hearts, water-packed,
  drained
1 (8 oz.) can green beans,
  drained

1 (4 oz.) jar pimentos, drained
1 cucumber, peeled & chopped
1 (16 oz.) btl. "free" Italian
  dressing
1 tsp. dried dill weed
1 tsp. dried oregano
1/4 tsp. pepper

In a mixing bowl, put first 6 ingredients. Blend remaining ingredients and pour over vegetables. Cover and chill for several hours. Transfer salad from mixing bowl to serving dish with slotted spoon.
Yield: 6 servings

Approximate Per Serving:
Calories: 169
Fat: 4.8 g
Cholesterol: 0.0 mg

Carbohydrates: 22.7 g
Protein: 5.9 g
Sodium: 118 mg

Exchanges: 1 1/2 bread; 1/2 vegetable; 1 fat

Parsley will keep a long time in the refrigerator, if after washing you place it in a jar with tight lid while still slightly damp. Parsley can also be frozen for use later.

New Potato Salad

(Recipe contains approximately 19% fat)

2 lb. sm. new red potatoes,
  scrubbed
2 T. hot water
1/2 tsp. chicken bouillon
  granules
1 T. olive oil
2 T. balsamic vinegar

1 tsp. Dijon mustard
1/2 tsp. garlic powder
1/2 tsp. salt (less if desired)
1/8 tsp. black pepper
1/2 c. chopped green onions,
  include some green
1 clove garlic, minced

In a saucepan, put new potatoes and cover with water. Bring to boil, reduce heat and simmer until potatoes are tender (about 15 to 20 minutes). In a cup, blend hot water and bouillon granules and stir until dissolved. Set aside to cool. When cool, add olive oil, vinegar, mustard, garlic powder, salt and pepper; blend. In a mixing bowl, put green onion and garlic. Allow potatoes to cool, then cut in quarters and add to garlic mixture. Drizzle dressing over potato mixture and toss gently to blend. Refrigerate 2 hours before serving.

Yield: 8 servings

Approximate Per Serving:
Calories: 90
Fat: 1.9 g
Cholesterol: 0.0 mg

Carbohydrates: 16.0 g
Protein: 1.0 g
Sodium: 148 mg

Exchanges: 1 1/4 bread

Citrus fruit yields nearly twice the amount of juice if dropped into hot water for a few minutes before squeezing.

Pea and Potato Salad

(Recipe contains approximately 18% fat)

24 sm. new red potatoes, scrubbed
1 T. canola oil
2 T. cool water
3 T. balsamic vinegar
1/2 tsp. Mrs. Dash's Italian salad dressing mix

2 c. fresh peas, cooked; or frozen peas, thawed & drained
1/2 c.. "free" no-fat mayonnaise
1/4 tsp. salt (less if desired)
1/4 tsp. pepper
1/2 tsp. garlic powder

In a saucepan, put potatoes and cover with water. Cover with lid, put on stove, bring to boil; reduce heat and simmer until potatoes are tender (12 to 15 minutes). Drain and cover with cold water. While potatoes are still warm, quarter each potato and put in mixing bowl. Mix oil, water, vinegar and Italian salad mix. Allow to stand 5 minutes, then drizzle over potatoes. Toss to coat. Refrigerate at least 2 hours. Add peas and toss. Blend mayonnaise, salt, pepper and garlic powder. Gently toss into potato mixture. Put into serving dish. Allow salad to reach room temperature before serving.

Yield: 8 servings

Approximate Per Serving:
Calories: 98
Fat: 2.0 g
Cholesterol: 0.0 mg

Carbohydrates: 17.3 g
Protein: 3.1 g
Sodium: 332 mg

Exchanges: 1 1/2 bread

To peel a tomato easily spear it with a kitchen fork and plunge it into boiling water for 30 seconds. The skin will slide right off.

Simple Potato Salad

(Recipe contains only a trace of fat)

8 sm. new red potatoes, scrubbed & boiled until tender
1/2 c. "free" no-fat mayonnaise
1/2 tsp. sour cream granules
1/8 tsp. ground dill or dill seeds
1/4 tsp. parsley flakes
2 T. chopped green pepper
1 green onion, minced (include green)
1/4 tsp. garlic powder
1/8 tsp. pepper

Cool potatoes slightly. Cut into quarters and place on a serving plate. Blend remaining ingredients and spoon over potatoes. Serve hot.
Yield: 4 servings

Approximate Per Serving:
Calories: 66
Fat: Trace
Cholesterol: 0.1 mg
Carbohydrates: 14.5 g
Protein: 1.0 g
Sodium: 405 mg

Exchanges: 1 bread

Tomato Salad

(Recipe contains approximately 8% fat)

1 c. chopped lettuce
4 med. tomatoes, quartered
1/4 c. low-fat plain yogurt
1/4 c. "free" no-fat mayonnaise
1 tsp. sour cream granules
1 1/2 tsp. vinegar
1/4 tsp. garlic powder
1/2 tsp. basil
1 T. chopped parsley

Put chopped lettuce on serving plate and spread evenly. Arrange tomato wedges on top of lettuce bed. Combine remaining ingredients and drizzle over lettuce and tomato wedges. Sprinkle with parsley.
Yield: 8 servings

Approximate Per Serving:
Calories: 32
Fat: 0.3 g
Cholesterol: 0.6 mg
Carbohydrates: 6.9 g
Protein: 1.5 g
Sodium: 119 mg

Exchanges: 1 vegetable

Tossed Salads

Chef's Salad Deluxe
(Recipe contains approximately 13% fat)

2 c. shredded lettuce
   (or greens of choice)
2 radishes, sliced
1/2 rib celery, diced
1/4 c. chopped green pepper
2 green onions, sliced
1/2 carrot, shredded

1 sm. solid tomato, quartered
2 oz. cooked chicken breast,
   cubed
2 T. no-fat Cheddar cheese
1 tsp. soy bacon bits
2 T. "free" salad dressing of
   choice (see below)

Toss together lettuce, radishes, celery, green pepper and onion and put in salad bowl. Sprinkle with grated carrots. Place tomato quarters in bowl and arrange chicken cubes around them. Sprinkle with shredded cheese and bacon bits. Drizzle with salad dressing of choice.
Yield: 1 serving

Approximate Per Serving:
Calories: 294
Fat: 4.1 g
Cholesterol: 47 mg

Carbohydrates: 32.6 g
Protein: 29.0 g
Sodium: 694 mg

Exchanges: 3 meat; 3 vegetable; 1 fat

SALAD DRESSING CHOICES:
Any fat-free dressing
Any dressing prepared with no-fat mayonnaise and other no-fat ingredients.
Any vinegar dressing using olive oil spray for greens.

Tomatoes cut vertically bleed less.

Deluxe Tossed Salad

(Recipe contains approximately 4% fat)

6 c. shredded lettuce
10 sm. radishes, sliced
1/4 green pepper, large dice
2 med. tomatoes, seeded &
    diced

12 T. low-fat dressing
    (see below)
2 T. soy bacon bits

Put prepared vegetables in large mixing bowl and toss. Divide among 6 salad bowls. Drizzle each salad with 2 tablespoons dressing. Sprinkle with 1 teaspoon bacon bits.
Yield: 6 salads

Approximate Per Salad:
Calories: 44
Fat: 0.2 g
Cholesterol: 0.0 mg

Carbohydrates: 6.8 g
Protein: 1.8 g
Sodium: 64 mg

Exchanges: 2 vegetable

SALAD DRESSING CHOICES:
Any of the following "free" no-fat dressings:
Blue Cheese
Ranch
Catalina
Peppercorn Ranch

Honey Dijon
1000 Island
French

Store cottage cheese upside down.
The cottage cheese will keep twice as long.

Tossed Salad

(Recipe contains approximately 19% fat)

6 c. shredded lettuce
10 radishes, sliced
1/4 green pepper, large dice
1 stalk celery, diced

2 tomatoes, seeded & chopped
1/3 c. dressing (see below)
6-second spray of olive oil
   cooking spray

CHOICE OF DRESSING (see index):
Italian "free" no-fat
Herbal Vinegar
Dill Vinegar

Garlic Vinegar
Grapefruit-Orange vinegar

Prepare vegetables and spray with olive oil spray. Divide among 6 salad bowls and drizzle with choice of dressing.
Yield: 6 servings

Approximate Per Serving:
Calories: 28
Fat: 0.2 g
Cholesterol: 0.0 mg

Carbohydrates: 5.8 g
Protein: 2.8 g
Sodium: 64 mg

Exchanges: 1 vegetable

*Wrap onions individually in foil to prevent them
from becoming soft or sprouting.*

Vinegar Salad Dressings

Dill Vinegar
(Recipe contains only a trace of fat)

Enough fresh dill to loosely fill **4 c. cider vinegar**
  a 1 1/2-quart jar 2/3-full plus **3 T. crushed dill seed**
  some additional dill **2 cloves garlic, split**

Rinse dill. Pack into a 1 1/2-quart glass jar loosely. Jar should have a non-metallic lid. Add vinegar and allow to stand two days, covered. Stir. Push down dill so all of it is covered with vinegar. Cover and allow to stand in cool place for 12 days. Strain vinegar through fine sieve or cheesecloth. Rinse remaining dill and pack loosely in jar, along with dill seed and garlic. Add vinegar and allow to stand for 2 days. Push dill down so all of it is covered with vinegar. Cover and allow to stand 12 days. Stain. Pour into sterilized jar with lid and store in cool place.
Yield: 4 cups or 64 tablespoons

Approximate Per Tablespoon:
Calories: 3   **Carbohydrates: 1.0 g**
Fat: Trace   **Protein: Trace**
Cholesterol: 0.0 mg   **Sodium: Trace**

Exchanges: Free

Cover peeled potatoes with cold water to which a few drops of vinegar have been added. Keep in refrigerator. Will last 3 or 4 days.

Garlic Vinegar

(Recipe contains only a trace of fat)

8 cloves garlic, crushed   1 T. crushed peppercorns
4 c. cider vinegar   1 tsp. turmeric

In a 1 1/2-quart glass jar with non-metallic lid, put garlic and vinegar. Put in a cool place for 2 weeks. Strain and discard garlic. Put back into jar and add peppercorns and turmeric. Allow to stand for 5 days. Strain and put in sterilized jar, seal and put in cool place.
Yield: 4 cups

Approximate Per Tablespoon:
Calories: 3   **Carbohydrates: 1.0 g**
Fat: Trace   **Protein: Trace**
Cholesterol: 0.0 mg   **Sodium: Trace**

Exchanges: Free

Grapefruit-Orange Vinegar

(Recipe contains only a trace of fat)

1/2 sm. grapefruit, thinly sliced   1 qt. white wine vinegar
1/2 orange, thinly sliced

Put fruit in 1 1/2-quart jar with a non-metallic lid. Bring vinegar to a boil. Remove from stove and pour over fruit. Put on lid and set in a cool place for 10 days. Strain and put in a sterilized jar, seal and store in cool place.
Yield: 4 cups

Approximate Per Tablespoon:
Calories: 3   **Carbohydrates: 1.1 g**
Fat: Trace   **Protein: Trace**
Cholesterol: 0.0 mg   **Sodium: Trace**

Exchanges: Free

Herbal Vinegar

(Recipe contains only a trace of fat)

3 T. crushed allspice
2 T. crushed coriander seeds
1 T. crushed mustard seeds
3 T. peeled & chopped
   gingerroot

1 bay leaf
1 c. hot water
4 c. cider vinegar

In a heat-proof 1 1/2-quart glass jar with a non-metallic lid, allow the herbs to soak in 1 cup hot water for 5 minutes. In a saucepan, bring vinegar to a simmer. Remove from stove and add to jar. Put tight lid on jar. Shake, then put in cool place to marinate for 2 weeks. Strain and put in sterilized glass jar. Seal with lid and put in cool place.
Yield: 5 cups

Approximate Per Tablespoon:
Calories: 4
Fat: Trace
Cholesterol: 0.0 mg

Carbohydrates: 0.7 g
Protein: 0.0 mg
Sodium: Trace

Exchanges: Free

Raspberry Vinegar

(Recipe contains approximately 0% fat)

4 c. cider vinegar

1 c. fresh raspberries

In a 1 1/2-quart glass jar with non-metallic lid, put vinegar and raspberries. Put in cool place for 2 weeks. Strain and put in jar. Seal and put in cool place.
Yield: 4 cups or 64 tablespoons

Approximate Per Tablespoon:
Calories: 3
Fat: Trace
Cholesterol: 0.0 mg

Carbohydrates: 1.2 g
Protein: 0.0 g
Sodium: Trace

Exchanges: Free

Spicy Vinegar

(Recipe contains only a trace of fat)

3 T. crushed allspice
2 T. crushed coriander seeds
1 T. crushed mustard seeds
3 T. peeled & chopped
   gingerroot

1 bay leaf
1 c. hot water
4 c. cider vinegar

Put herbs and hot water in a heat-proof 1 1/2-quart glass jar with a non-metallic lid. Allow to soak for 5 minutes. In a saucepan, bring vinegar to a simmer. Add to jar. Put lid on jar. Shake. Put in cool place to marinate for 2 weeks. Strain vinegar and put in sterilized glass jar with lid. Store in cool place.

Yield: 5 cups or 80 tablespoons

Approximate Per Tablespoon:
Calories: 3
Fat: Trace
Cholesterol: 0.0 mg

Carbohydrates: 1.0 g
Protein: Trace
Sodium: Trace

Exchanges: Free

Marshmallows will not dry out if stored in freezer.

Pasta Salads

Easy Cheesy Pasta Salad

(Recipe contains approximately 9% fat)

1 box Kraft macaroni & cheese
1/4 c. skim milk
1/4 c. "free" no-fat mayonnaise
2 tsp. butter granules

1/4 c. diced celery
1/4 c. diced onion
2 T. sweet pickle relish
3/4 c. diced green pepper

Cook macaroni per package directions, adding the mayonnaise and butter granules instead of the margarine. Cool to room temperature and add remaining ingredients. Chill several hours before serving.
Yield: 8 servings

Approximate Per Serving:
Calories: 115
Fat: 1.1 g
Cholesterol: 4 mg

Carbohydrates: 22.4 g
Protein: 4.5 g
Sodium: 375 mg

Exchanges: 1 1/2 bread; 1/2 vegetable

Cranberries will grind very nicely when frozen.
Wash berries, pat dry and freeze.

Mac and Cheese Pasta Salad

(Recipe contains approximately 6% fat)

2 c. sm. macaroni, cooked
1 T. tub margarine
2 T. cheese granules
1/4 c. skim milk
1 T. sweet pickle relish
1/4 c. finely-chopped celery
1/4 c. finely-chopped onion

1/4 c. finely-chopped green
   pepper
2 tomatoes, seeded & chopped
1/3 c. "free" no-fat
   mayonnaise
1 tsp. balsamic vinegar

Cook macaroni and drain. To hot macaroni, add margarine, cheese granules and milk. Stir, blending well. Add remaining ingredients, except mayonnaise and vinegar, and blend. Combine mayonnaise and vinegar and pour over salad. Toss to blend. Chill.
Yield: 8 servings

Approximate Per Serving:
Calories: 166
Fat: 1.1 g
Cholesterol: 0.9 mg

Carbohydrates: 10.6 g
Protein: 1.8 g
Sodium: 254 mg

Exchanges: 2 bread; 1 vegetable

*Thaw fish in milk. The milk draws out the frozen taste
and provides a fresh-caught flavor.*

Pasta and Salmon Salad

(Recipe contains approximately 11% fat)

2 c. sm. shell macaroni, cooked
Cooking spray
1 (6 1/2 oz.) can pink salmon,
 drained, skin discarded;
 bones mashed & stirred in
 with flaked salmon
1/4 c. sweet pickle relish

1/4 c. diced celery
1/4 c. diced sweet onion
1/3 c. "free" no-fat
 mayonnaise
1 tsp. balsamic vinegar
1 tsp. prepared yellow
 mustard

Cook macaroni, drain and run under hot water and then under cold water until cool. Drain and spray with cooking spray. Stir in salmon, relish, celery and onion. Blend remaining ingredients. Pour over salad and toss gently to blend. Chill.
Yield: 8 servings

Approximate Per Serving:
Calories: 182
Fat: 2.2 g
Cholesterol: 7.6 mg

Carbohydrates: 29.4 g
Protein: 9.1 g
Sodium: 293 mg

Exchanges: 1 meat; 1 1/2 bread; 1 vegetable

The fish smell can be removed from your hands by washing with vinegar and water or salt and water.

Pasta Primavera Salad

(Recipe contains approximately 12% fat)

1 lb. linguini, cooked
1/2 bunch broccoli, steamed
   al denté, chopped
1 lg. tomato, seeded & chopped
1/4 of lg. red onion, chopped
1 red sweet pepper, chopped
1 green pepper, chopped
1 c. snow peas
1/4 c. boiling water

1 tsp. chicken bouillon
   granules
1 c. buttermilk
2 T. Dijon mustard
1/4 c. red wine vinegar
2 cloves garlic
1 tsp. dried basil
1/2 tsp. seasoned salt
2 T. grated Parmesan cheese

Put linguini, broccoli, tomatoes, onions, green and red peppers and snow peas in a large mixing bowl and toss to blend. In a cup, dissolve bouillon granules in boiling water and set aside to slightly cool. In a small mixing bowl, put buttermilk, mustard, vinegar, garlic, basil and salt. Add cooled bouillon. Put in blender and purée until smooth. Pour over linguini mixture, tossing to blend. Pour into serving dish. Top with grated cheese. Put in refrigerator until ready to serve.
Yield: 12 servings

Approximate Per Serving:
Calories: 184
Fat: 2.5 g
Cholesterol: 1.0 mg

Carbohydrates: 33.1 g
Protein: 7.7 g
Sodium: 165 mg

Exchanges: 2 bread; 1 vegetable; 1/2 fat

Put spaghetti in a deep-fryer basket before boiling.
No sticking to the bottom and easy to drain.

Taco Pasta Salad

(Recipe contains approximately 12% fat)

1 (8 oz.) pkg. macaroni, cooked until almost tender
1/4 c. water
1 tsp. butter granules
1 pkg. taco mix
1 c. water
1/2 c. chopped onion
1/2 c. chopped green pepper
1/2 c. chopped celery
2 med. tomatoes, seeded & diced
10 ripe olives, sliced
1/2 c. "free" no-fat ranch dressing

Put 1/4 cup water and butter granules in a large skillet and bring to boil. Add cooked macaroni and toss well to coat. Add taco mix and 1 cup of water and simmer until liquid is absorbed. Pour into large mixing bowl—allow to cool to room temperature. Add vegetables and olives, tossing to blend. Gently stir in dressing. Chill several hours.
Yield: 8 servings

Approximate Per Serving:
Calories: 128
Fat: 1.7 g
Cholesterol: 0.0 mg
Carbohydrates: 23.8 g
Protein: 4.0 g
Sodium: 498 mg

Exchanges: 1 bread; 1 vegetable; 1/2 fat

To keep spaghetti straight while cooking, cook in large oval roaster pan on top of stove.

Rice Salads

Bean, Corn and Rice Salad
(Recipe contains approximately 26% fat)

3 1/2 c. cooked brown rice
1 (16 oz.) can pink kidney beans,
   drained & rinsed
1 (16 oz.) can whole kernel corn,
   drained
1/3 c. finely-sliced green onion
1/4 c. canola oil

2 T. fresh lime juice
1 T. cider vinegar
1 T. brown sugar (can use
   artificial sweetener)
1 tsp. chili powder
1/4 tsp. salt (less if desired)
1/2 tsp. ground cumin

In a large bowl, put rice, beans, corn and onion. Blend. In a smaller bowl, blend oil, lime juice, vinegar, brown sugar, chili powder, salt and cumin. Mix well, then drizzle dressing over salad. Toss to blend. Allow to stand at room temperature 4 hours before serving. Will keep in refrigerator for about 3 days.
Yield: 10 servings

Approximate Per Serving:
Calories: 216
Fat: 6.3 g
Cholesterol: 0.0 mg

Carbohydrates: 36.6 g
Protein: 5.7 g
Sodium: 204 mg

Exchanges: 2 bread; 1 vegetable; 1 fat

When you need a lot of celery sliced, leave in bunch and use an electric knife to cut through the whole bunch at once.

Oriental Potato Salad

(Recipe contains approximately 3% fat)

2 c. cooked brown rice
2 c. cooked & diced potatoes
1/4 c. finely-chopped celery
1/4 c. finely-chopped onion
1/4 c. finely-chopped green
   pepper
1 can water chestnuts, diced

1/3 c. "free" no-fat
   mayonnaise
1 tsp. balsamic vinegar
1 T. "light" soy sauce
1/2 tsp. garlic powder
1/2 tsp. sodium-free seasoned
   salt

Put rice, potatoes, celery, onion, green pepper and water chestnuts in a large mixing bowl and blend. Combine remaining ingredients, blending well, and pour over salad. Toss gently to blend. Chill before serving.
Yield: 8 servings

Approximate Per Serving:
Calories: 107
Fat: 0.4 g
Cholesterol: 0.0 mg

Carbohydrates: 23.7 g
Protein: 2.5 g
Sodium: 215 mg

Exchanges: 1 1/2 bread

*Use a wire cheese slicer to make paper-thin slices of
cold cooked potatoes for potato salad.*

Rice and Broccoli Salad

(Recipe contains approximately 5% fat)

3 c. cooked brown rice
1 pkg. frozen, chopped broccoli,
   cooked
2 green onions, sliced thin
1 T. sweet pickle relish
1/4 c. finely-diced celery

1/3 c. "free" no-fat
   mayonnaise
1 tsp. balsamic vinegar
1/2 tsp. garlic powder
1/2 tsp. sodium-free seasoned
   salt

Put rice, cooked chopped broccoli, onion, sweet relish and celery in mixing bowl and blend. Combine mayonnaise, vinegar, garlic powder and seasoned salt. Pour over rice mixture and blend. Chill. **Yield: 8 servings**

Approximate Per Serving:
Calories: 108
Fat: 0.6 g
Cholesterol: 0.0 mg

Carbohydrates: 23.4 g
Protein: 3.1 g
Sodium: 151 mg

Exchanges: 1 bread; 1 1/2 vegetable

If you have a lot of potatoes to dice, put them through the French fry cutter first, then simply cut across them.

Salad in the Rice

(Recipe contains approximately 2% fat)

1 c. brown rice, cooked per pkg. directions	1/2 c. "free" no-fat Italian salad dressing
1 c. frozen peas, cooked	1 T. prepared mustard
1 c. sliced carrots, cooked	Dash of Worcestershire sauce
1/2 c. diced celery	1 drop Tabasco sauce
1/4 c. dill pickle relish	1/2 tsp. garlic powder
1/2 c. green pepper, diced	1/2 tsp. sodium-free seasoned salt
2 green onions, sliced thin	

In large mixing bowl, blend peas, carrots, celery, pickle relish, green pepper and onion. Add to cooked rice. Toss to blend. In a small bowl, blend Italian dressing, mustard, Worcestershire sauce, Tabasco sauce, garlic powder and salt. Blend, then pour over rice mixture and toss to blend. Chill.

Yield: 8 servings

Approximate Per Serving:
Calories: 138   **Carbohydrates: 28.1 g**
Fat: 0.3 g   **Protein: 5.2 g**
Cholesterol: 0.0 mg   **Sodium: 164 mg**

Exchanges: 1 1/2 bread; 1 vegetable

If celery goes limp don't discard it. Clean it and put it in ice water and store in refrigerator for an hour or so. It will crisp right up.

Waldorf Rice Salad

(Recipe contains approximately 3% fat)

1 T. water
1 tsp. butter granules
3/4 c. uncooked brown rice
1 1/2 c. unsweetened apple
   juice
1/2 c. chopped celery

1 med. yellow Delicious
   apple, diced
1 med. red Delicious apple,
   diced
1 med. banana, sliced
1 T. lemon juice
6 maraschino cherries, halved

Put 1 tablespoon water and butter granules in a heavy-bottomed skillet and bring to boil. Add rice and stir until water is absorbed. Add apple juice and bring to boil. Cover and cook over low heat 30 to 35 minutes, or until rice is done. Add more liquid, if needed. Remove from stove and put in bowl. Allow to cool, then add celery. Put lemon juice in second bowl and add apples and banana. Toss in lemon juice to coat. Add to rice mixture, along with cherries.
Yield: 8 servings

Approximate Per Serving:
Calories: 127
Fat: 0.4 g
Cholesterol: 0.0 mg

Carbohydrates: 34.3 g
Protein: 1.4 g
Sodium: 5 mg

Exchanges: 1 1/2 fruit; 1 bread

Notes & Recipes

Sandwiches

Sandwiches

At one time or another, we all find ourselves with a sandwich in our hands.

There are some pitfalls when it comes to sandwiches. First, the margarine that goes onto the bread. If you must use margarine on the bread, use the NO-FAT brand of margarine that is available.

However, keep in mind that when you order a sandwich in a fast-food restaurant, or most other restaurants, for that matter, they do not butter the bread. So why must the bread be buttered at home? Not putting margarine on sandwiches (or using the NO-FAT brand, if you do) is a great way to cut fat and is also a somewhat painless sacrifice.

Mayonnaise is another area that must be watched. Use a NO-FAT mayonnaise when using mayonnaise for sandwiches, or anything else for that matter. Actually, the NO-FAT mayonnaise now tastes very good.

LUNCHEON MEATS are another big pitfall. Stick to the thin-sliced turkey, thin-sliced chicken and if it must be beef or ham, use only the thin-sliced. Read the label when buying meat for sandwiches. Many are very high in fat content and loaded with sodium. And don't be fooled by the label "light"—on a package. Find out just how light it really is. Remember, some of the fat has been removed to allow the labeling of "light" it does not mean that enough fat has been removed to make it acceptable on a fat-restricted diet.

To help you in this area, I have included a list of luncheon type thin-sliced meats containing acceptable amounts of fat.

Mustard and ketchup are okay. Shredded lettuce or cabbage on a sandwich helps to make it moist and palatable without the fat. And don't overlook the low-calorie slice of tomato, a good way to add extra taste without the fat. Pickles are okay, but are very high in sodium content.

As for the bread used, if you stick to the reduced-calorie breads they contain only half the calories and fat. However, this does not mean that you cannot have regular bread. A slice of regular bread contains only 1 gram of fat, usually, and can be used, if desired.

Continued on following page.

Continued from preceding page.

The big thing when it comes to bread is to use whole grain breads. They are so very much better for you because of the fiber they contain.

Don't be afraid of sandwiches, but be sure you know what has gone into them if you did not prepare them yourselves. Most "fast food" sandwiches are not only high in fat content, but loaded with sodium. Avoid burgers and fried chicken patties, etc. If you must eat in fast-food establishments stick to the turkey sub or that type of sandwich. You might even want to ask that they leave the dressing off and give you some low-fat mayonnaise on the side.

"Bacon" and Tomato Sandwich

(Recipe contains approximately 11% fat)

2 tomatoes, seeded & chopped
4 tsp. low-fat bacon bits (made with soy)
1 c. shredded lettuce
1/4 tsp. salt (opt.)
1/8 tsp. pepper
3 T. "free" mayonnaise
8 slices "light" whole wheat bread

Put all ingredients, except bread, in a bowl and blend. Toast bread. Divide tomato mixture among four slices of bread and top with second slice of bread. Cut in fourths cornerwise.
Yield: 4 sandwiches

Approximate Per Sandwich:
Calories: 127
Fat: 1.5 g
Cholesterol: 0.0 mg
Carbohydrates: 20.5 g
Protein: 4.0 g
Sodium: 435 mg

Exchanges: 1 bread; 1 vegetable; 1/2 fat

Broiled Crabmeat Open Sandwich

(Recipe contains approximately 17% fat)

1 (6 1/2 oz.) can crabmeat,
   drained & sorted
2 T. chopped green pepper
1 T. chopped green onion
6 chopped ripe olives
1/4 tsp. salt (opt.)
3 T. "free" no-fat mayonnaise

1 tsp. lemon juice
1/2 tsp. horseradish
4 slices 1" thick French
   bread, toasted
2 slices "free" no-fat American
   cheese, halved

In a mixing bowl, blend flaked crab, green pepper, onion, olives, salt, mayonnaise, lemon juice and horseradish. Divide among French bread slices. Top with 1/2 slice of American cheese. Put under broiler 2 to 4 minutes, or until cheese melts and sandwich is heated through.
Yield: 4 servings

Approximate Per Serving:
Calories: 194
Fat: 3.6 g
Cholesterol: 53.1 mg

Carbohydrates: 25.1 g
Protein: 19.3 g
Sodium: 1196 mg

(To eliminate some of the sodium, omit the cheese and use a sprinkle of Parmesan.)

Exchanges: 2 meat; 1 bread; 1/2 vegetable

For the brown bagger--use chopped celery on sandwiches instead of lettuce. It won't get limp and tastes great.

Chicken Strip Sandwich

(Recipe contains approximately 18% fat)

2 T. water
1 tsp. butter granules
12 oz. boneless, skinless
  chicken breast, cut in strips
4 "light" whole wheat buns

Cooking spray
4 oz. "free" Philadelphia
  cream cheese
1 c. shredded lettuce
4 slices tomato

Put water and butter granules in a skillet and bring to boil. Add chicken strips and sauté until chicken is done and tender. Remove from heat and keep warm. Spray each bun half lightly with cooking spray and toast in toaster oven. Spread 4 bun halves with cream cheese. Top with lettuce, tomato and chicken strips. Top with second half of bun. Serve.
Yield: 4 sandwiches

Approximate Per Sandwich:
Calories: 271
Fat: 5.3 g
Cholesterol: 71 mg

Carbohydrates: 17.0 g
Protein: 34.4 g
Sodium: 471 mg

Exchanges: 3 meat; 1 bread; 1 1/2 vegetable

Cream Cheese and Olive Sandwich

(Recipe contains approximately 23% fat)

4 English muffins, split &
  toasted
1 (8 oz.) ctn. "free" Philadelphia cream cheese

10 lg. ripe olives, chopped
10 med. pimento-stuffed green
  olives, chopped

Blend cream cheese and olives. Spread over muffin halves.
Yield: 8 servings

Approximate Per Serving:
Calories: 118
Fat: 3.0 g
Cholesterol: 5.0 mg

Carbohydrates: 16.5 g
Protein: 6.5 g
Sodium: 547 mg

Exchanges: 1 bread; 1 fat

Cream Cheese and Vegetable Sandwich

(Recipe contains approximately 5% fat)

1 (8 oz.) ctn. "free" Phila-
    delphia cream cheese
1 tomato, seeded & chopped
2 T. chopped green pepper

1 green onion, sliced
1/4 c. cauliflower, chopped
4 English muffins, toasted

Put all ingredients in mixing bowl, except English muffins, and blend well. Divide cream cheese mixture among 8 English muffin halves. Serve.
Yield: 8 servings

Approximate Per Serving:
Calories: 104
Fat: 0.6 g
Cholesterol: 5.0 mg

Carbohydrates: 16.3 g
Protein: 7.0 g
Sodium: 361 mg

Exchanges: 1 bread; 1/2 milk

A quick way to clean dirty, smuged eyeglasses is with white vinegar. A small squeeze bottle in purse, home or office allows quick cleaning. Rub on and wipe off with tissue.

Creamy Salmon Salad Sandwich

(Recipe contains approximately 24% fat)

1 (15 1/2 oz.) can red salmon,
   drained, skin discarded;
   bones mashed & stirred
   into flaked salmon
1/4 c. thinly-sliced celery
1/4 c. chopped onion

1/2 tsp. dill weed
4 T. "free" no-fat Phila-
   delphia cream cheese
1 T. skim milk, heated
1 tsp. butter granules
6 reduced-calorie buns

Put flaked salmon, celery, onion and dill weed into a small mixing bowl and blend. Put cream cheese in small bowl. Blend heated milk and butter granules until granules dissolve. Add to cream cheese mixture. Stir into salmon mixture until even in texture. Chill at least 1 hour. Spread on buns and serve.
Yield: 6 servings

Approximate Per Serving:
Calories: 220
Fat: 5.9 g
Cholesterol: 28.0 g

Carbohydrates: 13.9 g
Protein: 18.2 g
Sodium: 584 mg

Exchanges: 2 1/2 meat; 1 bread; 1/4 milk

Deluxe Cheeseburger

(Recipe contains approximately 14% fat)

Same as Deluxe Hamburger
   (see index)

4 slices "free" no-fat American
   cheese

Yield: 4 servings

Approximate Per Serving:
Calories: 332
Fat: 5.3 g
Cholesterol: 74 mg

Carbohydrates: 27.9 g
Protein: 55.8 g
Sodium: 950 mg

Exchanges: 3 1/2 meat; 1 bread; 1/2 milk; 1 vegetable

Deluxe Hamburgers

(Recipe contains approximately 17% fat)

1/2 lb. ground turkey breast
1/4 lb. ground round
1/2 c. fine cracker crumbs
1 T. Worcestershire sauce
2 T. skim milk
2 T. finely-chopped onion
1/4 tsp. sodium-free
  seasoned salt
1/2 tsp. garlic powder
1/8 tsp. pepper

2 egg whites
Cooking spray
4 "light" whole wheat
  hamburger buns
Mustard or ketchup
16 dill pickle slices
4 thin slices tomato
4 thin slices onion
1 c. shredded lettuce

Put ground meat in bowl and add cracker crumbs, Worcestershire sauce, milk, chopped onion, seasoned salt, garlic powder, pepper and egg whites. Form mixture into 4 patties. Spray hot skillet with cooking spray and cook burgers until done and brown (or cook on barbecue grill). Put mustard or ketchup on buns and add pickle, tomato, onion and lettuce. Top with burgers.
Yield: 4 hamburgers

Approximate Per Burger:
Calories: 287
Fat: 5.3 g
Cholesterol: 68.6 g
Carbohydrates: 23.9 g
Protein: 40.8 g
Sodium: 519 mg

Exchanges: 3 meat; 1 1/2 bread; 1/2 vegetable

A convenient way to store belts is to hang them on cup hooks screwed to the underside of a wooden clothes hanger.

Deluxe Scrambled Egg Sandwich

(Recipe contains approximately 17% fat)

4 T. "free" no-fat Philadelphia
  cream cheese
4 tsp. low-fat bacon bits
2 T. water
1 tsp. butter granules
1 c. sliced, fresh mushrooms

1/4 c. diced green pepper
1 tsp. tub margarine
Egg substitute to = 4 eggs
1/4 tsp. sodium-free salt (opt.)
1/4 tsp. pepper
4 reduced-calorie buns

Blend cream cheese and bacon bits and set aside. In a small saucepan, put water and butter granules and bring to boil. Add mushrooms and green pepper; sauté until tender. In a small skillet, put 1 teaspoon margarine. Blend egg substitute, salt and pepper; pour into skillet. Stir as mixture cooks, until eggs are set. Spread buns with cheese mixture and top with scrambled egg mixture and then mushrooms and green pepper.

Yield: 4 servings

Approximate Per Serving:
Calories: 183
Fat: 3.4 g
Cholesterol: 2.5 mg

Carbohydrates: 17.1 g
Protein: 8.9 g
Sodium: 608 mg

Exchanges: 1 meat; 1 bread; 1/2 milk; 1/2 fat

*To keep scissors closed while storing simply
slip points into a piece of cork.*

Deluxe Turkey Sandwich

(Recipe contains approximately 12% fat)

4 T. "free" no-fat Philadelphia
    cream cheese
1 T. skim milk, hot
1 tsp. Dijon mustard
2 tsp. butter granules

1/4 tsp. dried dill weed
4 reduced-calorie buns
4 (1 oz.) slices turkey breast
4 slices fresh tomato
1/2 c. shredded lettuce

In a small bowl, put cream cheese, milk, mustard, butter granules and dill weed. Blend. Spread on buns and top with turkey breast, tomato and lettuce.
Yield: 4 servings

Approximate Per Serving:
Calories: 155
Fat: 2.0 g
Cholesterol: 25.1 mg

Carbohydrates: 16.0 g
Protein: 13.1 g
Sodium: 333 mg

Exchanges: 1 1/2 meat: 1 bread

A plastic toothbrush holder makes a good crochet hook holder.

Egg Salad Sandwich

(Recipe contains approximately 12% fat)

Egg substitute to = 4 eggs
1 boiled egg, yolk discarded,
   white chopped
1/4 c. chopped celery
2 T. chopped green pepper
1 green onion, chopped
2 T. "free" Philadelphia
   cream cheese

2 T. "free" mayonnaise
1/4 tsp. sodium-free
   seasoned salt
1/8 tsp. pepper
8 slices whole wheat "light"
   bread

Scramble egg substitute (microwave is best and easiest). Cool, then chop up fine. Add chopped egg whites and blend. Add celery, green pepper and onion. Blend. In a small bowl, blend cream cheese, mayonnaise, salt and pepper. Pour over egg mixture and blend. Divide mixture among four slices of bread. Top with second slice of bread. If desired, chopped lettuce can be put on sandwich. **Yield: 4 sandwiches**

Approximate Per Sandwich:
Calories: 160
Fat: 2.2 g
Cholesterol: 1.3 mg

Carbohydrates: 16.2 g
Protein: 19.9 g
Sodium: 349 mg

Exchanges: 1 meat; 1 bread; 1/2 milk

Before sewing on a row of buttons, tape each one where it belongs with transparent tape. After the first stitches through buttons are made remove the tape.

Fajita Sandwich

(Recipe contains approximately 22% fat)

2 T. water
1 tsp. butter granules
12 oz. boneless, skinless
   chicken breast, sliced
   very thin
1/2 c. salsa

8 (6") flour tortillas, warmed
   per pkg. directions
1/2 c. "light" sour cream
1/2 c. "free" no-fat shredded
   Cheddar cheese
1 tomato, seeded & chopped
1 c. shredded lettuce

Put water and butter granules in hot skillet. Add chicken strips and cook 3 to 5 minutes, or until tender and browned. Add salsa and heat through. Divide meat mixture among 8 heated tortillas, putting meat mixture down the center. Top with sour cream and shredded cheese. Sprinkle with chopped tomato and shredded lettuce. Fold over from both sides.

Yield: 8 servings

Approximate Per Fajita:
Calories: 226
Fat: 5.4 g
Cholesterol: 35.1 mg

Carbohydrates: 26.5 g
Protein: 20.2 g
Sodium: 277 mg

Exchanges: 1 1/2 meat; 1 bread; 1 milk

If you have trouble threading a needle, push it through a sheet of white paper before threading--the eye will be easier to see.

Filled Chicken Salad Loaf

(Recipe contains approximately 16% fat)

4 whole chicken breasts,
   cooked, skinned, boned &
   cut in bite-sized pieces
2 T. finely-chopped onion
2 T. finely-chopped green
   pepper
2 T. finely-chopped celery
1 tomato, seeded & chopped
4 T. "free" no-fat Philadelphia
   cream cheese

1/4 c. "free" no-fat
   mayonnaise
1/4 tsp. garlic powder
2 T. boiling water
1 tsp. chicken bouillon
   granules
Curly lettuce leaves
1 round loaf pumpernickel
   unsliced bread

Put diced chicken, onion, green pepper, celery and tomato in mixing bowl and toss. Set aside. In a small mixing bowl. Blend cream cheese, mayonnaise and garlic powder. Dissolve bouillon in boiling water and add to cheese mixture. Beat until smooth. Add to chicken mixture and gently blend. Put bread on a cutting board and slice in 16 slices, being very careful not to slice the bread all the way through. Spread slices apart enough to spread every other slice with chicken spread. Line slices not spread with chicken salad, with curly lettuce. Shape with hands by pushing loaf back together to slight degree. Take to table on cutting board for a nice presentation. To serve, cut sandwiches the rest of the way through and put sandwich onto a serving plate.
Yield: 8 servings

Approximate Per Serving:
Calories: 323
Fat: 5.8 g
Cholesterol: 67.3 mg

Carbohydrates: 30.5 g
Protein: 33.6 g
Sodium: 281 mg

Exchanges: 3 meat; 2 bread; 1/4 milk

To make a throw-away dustpan for a messy cleanup,
cut a disposable foil pie pan in half.

Flounder on a Bun

(Recipe contains approximately 8% fat)

4 (3 oz.) flounder fillets
1/4 c. water
1 tsp. butter granules
1/8 tsp. salt
1/8 tsp. pepper
1/4 c. "free" no-fat
    mayonnaise

1 T. sweet pickle relish
1 T. finely-chopped onion
1/2 c. shredded cabbage
4 slices "free" no-fat American
    cheese
4 reduced-calorie whole
    wheat buns

Put water, butter granules, salt and pepper in a skillet and bring to boil. Add flounder fillets and simmer, turning once. Simmer until fish flakes easily—6 to 10 minutes. DO NOT OVERCOOK. Blend mayonnaise, relish and onion. Spread both sides of buns with mayonnaise mixture. Top with shredded cabbage and slice of cheese. Put flounder fillet on top of cheese and top with second half of bun.
Yield: 4 servings

Approximate Per Serving:
Calories: 229
Fat: 2.0 g
Cholesterol: 65 mg

Carbohydrates: 22.7 g
Protein: 35.2 g
Sodium: 549 mg

Exchanges: 3 meat; 1 bread

Like your fish sprinkled with lemon juice? Put lemon juice in small pepper shaker. Great for sprinkling fish or other foods.

Open-Faced Sloppy Joe's

(Recipe contains approximately 18% fat)

3/4 lb. ground round
1/2 c. chopped onions
2 cloves garlic, minced
1/4 c. green pepper
1 (8 oz.) can tomato sauce
1 (6 oz.) can tomato paste

1 tsp. vinegar
1/2 tsp. dry mustard
1/2 tsp. garlic powder
1/4 tsp. pepper
3 English muffins, split
& toasted

In a skillet, put ground round, onions, garlic and green pepper. Cook until pink disappears. Add remaining ingredients, except English muffins, and simmer until thick. Serve on top of toasted English muffins.
Yield: 6 servings

Approximate Per Serving:
Calories: 239
Fat: 4.7 g
Cholesterol: 40.0 mg

Carbohydrates: 22.2 g
Protein: 22.0 g
Sodium: 434 mg

Exchanges: 2 meat; 1 bread; 2 vegetable

Clean your leather bindings of your books with a lather made from saddle soap. Wipe dry with a soft clean cloth.

Open-Faced Veggie Sandwich

(Recipe contains approximately 4% fat)

4 English muffins, split & toasted
1 (8 oz.) pkg. "free" no-fat Philadelphia cream cheese
1/4 c. "free" no-fat ranch dressing
1/4 c. finely-chopped green onions
1/4 c. finely-chopped green pepper
1/4 c. chopped broccoli
1/4 c. chopped cauliflower
1/4 c. finely-chopped carrots
1/4 tsp. garlic powder

Toast English muffins and set aside. In a bowl, put softened cream cheese, ranch dressing, green onion, green pepper, broccoli, cauliflower, carrots and garlic powder. Blend well and pile on top of English muffin halves.
Yield: 8 servings

Approximate Per Serving:
Calories: 102
Fat: 0.5 g
Cholesterol: 5.0 mg
Carbohydrates: 16.0 g
Protein: 7.3 g
Sodium: 363 mg

Exchanges: 1/2 meat; 1 bread

Place a piece of double-faced tape underneath bookends to keep them from sliding out of place.

Pita Pizza

(Recipe contains approximately 9% fat)

4 sandwich-size pitas
   (see index)
1/4 c. tomato sauce
4 (1 oz.) slices cooked
   turkey breast

8 slices fresh tomato
1/8 tsp. salt
4 slices "free" American
   cheese

Spread one inner side of each pita with tomato sauce. On top of sauce, stack 1 slice turkey, 2 slices tomato (lightly salted, if desired), and one slice of cheese. Place pita in toaster oven or under the broiler, until cheese melts and sandwich is heated through.
Yield: 4 servings

Approximate Per Serving:
Calories: 246
Fat: 2.5 g
Cholesterol: 27.0 mg

Carbohydrates: 35.1 g
Protein: 28.8 g
Sodium: 935 mg

Exchanges: 1 meat; 1 bread; 1 milk; 1 vegetable; 1/4 fat

Hang a small whisk broom on a hook attached to an upright vacuum to brush out corners you can't get into with the machine.

Salmon and Cream Cheese on Bagel

(Recipe contains approximately 17% fat)

4 low-fat bagels, toasted
   (see index)
1/2 of 8 oz. ctn. "free"
   Philadelphia cream cheese
2 T. dill pickle relish

1 (7 1/2 oz.) can salmon,
   drained, skin discarded;
   bones mashed & stirred
   into flaked salmon (the
   bones in salmon provide a
   wealth of calcium)

Blend cream cheese and pickle relish and spread over bagel halves. Top with flaked salmon. Serve.
Yield: 8 servings

Approximate Per Serving:
Calories: 166
Fat: 3.2 g
Cholesterol: 11.9 mg

Carbohydrates: 20.3 g
Protein: 10.9 g
Sodium: 402 mg

Exchanges: 1 meat; 1 bread; 1/2 milk

*To vacuum fine dog hairs from your carpet spray it
first with water from a plant mister.*

Taco Deluxe

(Recipe contains approximately 11% fat)

6 flour tortillas, heated per
   pkg. directions
1/4 c. water
1 tsp. butter granules
1/2 c. finely-chopped onions
1/4 c. finely-chopped green
   pepper
1 clove garlic, minced
3/4 lb. ground turkey breast
1/4 lb. ground round
1/2 tsp. sodium-free
   seasoned salt (opt.)

1/2 tsp. garlic powder
1/4 tsp. pepper
1 pkg. taco mix
1 c. water
1 can dark red kidney beans,
   drained
1 c. "free" no-fat shredded
   Cheddar cheese
1 c. shredded lettuce
2 tomatoes, seeded & diced

In a skillet, put 1/4 cup water and butter granules. Bring to boil. Add onions, green pepper and garlic and sauté until moisture is absorbed. DO NOT BURN. Add ground meat, salt, garlic powder and pepper; cook until meat browns. Add taco mix and 1 cup of water. Stir and simmer 10 to 15 minutes. Stir in beans; heat through. Remove from stove. Divide meat mixture among tortillas, placing only on one-half of tortilla. Top with shredded cheese, shredded lettuce and diced tomato. Fold over and serve.
Yield: 6 servings

Approximate Per Serving:
Calories: 370
Fat: 4.7 g
Cholesterol: 60 mg

Carbohydrates: 41.9 g
Protein: 39.0 g
Sodium: 228 mg

Exchanges: 3 meat; 2 bread; 1 vegetable; 1 fat

When washing windows dry the inside of the window with up and down strokes; the outside of the window with side to side strokes. If any streaks show you will know which side needs extra wiping.

Three-Cheese Sandwich

(Recipe contains approximately 8% fat)

4 English muffins, halved
Cooking spray
2 tsp. butter granules
1/2 of 8 oz. ctn. "free"
　　Philadelphia cream cheese

1 T. finely-chopped green
　　pepper
4 slices "free" no-fat American
　　cheese, halved
1/2 c. no-fat shredded
　　mozzarella cheese

Spray each muffin half with cooking spray (3 seconds per muffin). Sprinkle with butter granules. Toast lightly (don't burn butter granules). Blend cream cheese and green pepper. Spread over muffin halves. Top with half-slice of American cheese and sprinkle with mozzarella cheese.
Yield: 8 servings

Approximate Per Serving:
Calories: 126
Fat: 1.1 g
Cholesterol: 6.1 mg

Carbohydrates: 17.0 g
Protein: 14.3 g
Sodium: 604 mg

Exchanges: 1 meat; 1 bread

Now is the time for all good men to come to the aid of their party.

Toasted Ham and Cheese on Bun

(Recipe contains approximately 9% fat)

1 c. very lean, chopped ham	4 slices "free" no-fat
2 T. pickle relish	American cheese
2 T. "free" no-fat mayonnaise	4 whole wheat, reduced-
	calorie buns, split

In a bowl, put chopped ham, relish and mayonnaise. Blend well. Cut cheese slices in half. Put 1/2 slice cheese on bottom half of bun. Spread 1/4 of ham salad over cheese and top with second half-slice of cheese. Put top of bun over cheese; wrap each sandwich with aluminum foil. Put on baking sheet and bake in 375° oven 10 to 15 minutes.

Yield: 4 servings

Approximate Per Serving:

Calories: 196	Carbohydrates: 21.0 g
Fat: 1.9 g	Protein: 25.8 g
Cholesterol: 32.5 mg	Sodium: 1,194 mg

(Sodium can reduced by buying a low-sodium ham.)

Exchanges: 2 meat; 1 bread; 1/4 fat

Before storing storm windows coat both sides with glass cleaner. In autum just polish the glass and install.

Tuna Salad Sandwich

(Recipe contains approximately 13% fat)

2 (6 1/2 oz.) cans white
   premium tuna, drained
2 T. chopped dill pickle
2 T. finely-chopped onion
1 c. frozen peas, cooked
   & cooled

1/4 c. "light" sour cream
1/4 tsp. garlic powder
12 slices "light" whole wheat
   bread
1 c. shredded lettuce

Put tuna, pickle, onion and peas in a small mixing bowl. Blend sour cream and garlic powder. Pour over tuna mixture and blend well. Spread 4 pieces of bread with tuna mixture and top with shredded lettuce. Top with second piece of bread and cut cornerwise into 4 pieces.
Yield: 4 sandwiches

Approximate Per Sandwich:
Calories: 226
Fat: 3.2 g
Cholesterol: 41.3 mg

Carbohydrates: 13.0 g
Protein: 26.9 g
Sodium: 311 mg

Exchanges: 2 meat; 1 1/2 bread

*A small soft brush moistened with furniture polish is a
great way to dust wicker furniture.*

Turkey-Beef Filled Pitas

(Recipe contains approximately 17% fat)

1/4 c. water
1 tsp. butter granules
1 med. onion, chopped
1 green pepper, finely chopped
1 lb. ground turkey breast
1/2 lb. ground round
2 sm. tomatoes, peeled, seeded
  & chopped fine

1/2 tsp. sodium-free
  seasoned salt
1/2 tsp. garlic powder
1/4 tsp. pepper
4 whole pitas, torn in half
  (see index)

Put water and butter granules in a skillet and bring to boil. Add onion and green pepper; sauté. Add ground turkey breast and ground round; brown until pink disappears. Add remaining ingredients, except pitas, and simmer 10 minutes. Divide meat mixture among 8 pita halves.

Yield: 8 servings

Approximate Per Serving:
Calories: 227
Fat: 4.2 g
Cholesterol: 84 mg

Carbohydrates: 17.7 g
Protein: 30.2 g
Sodium: 290 mg

Exchanges: 3 meat; 1 bread

When you have a small bottomed vase you can't get clean, fill it with water and drop a denture cleaning tablet into it.

Turkey Burgers

(Recipe contains approximately 12% fat)

3/4 lb. ground, raw turkey breast
1/2 c. dried bread crumbs
3 T. finely-chopped onion
2 T. catsup
1 T. Worcestershire sauce
2 tsp. soy sauce
3 to 4 drops Tabasco sauce
1/4 tsp. black pepper
1/4 tsp. salt (opt.)
Egg substitute to = 1 egg
1/4 c. water
1 tsp. butter granules
6 reduced-calorie buns

In a mixing bowl, put all of listed ingredients, except buns, water and butter granules, and blend well. Form into 6 patties and set aside. Put 1/4 cup water and 1 teaspoon butter granules in a skillet, bring to boil; add patties and cook until they are done and all moisture is absorbed. Water may be added, as needed, 1 tablespoon at a time.

Yield: 6 servings

Approximate Per Serving:
Calories: 189
Fat: 2.6 g
Cholesterol: 44.0 mg
Carbohydrates: 15.6 g
Protein: 19.6 g
Sodium: 412 mg

Exchanges: 2 meat; 1 bread

Waxing a natural brick fireplace makes it easier to keep clean.

Turkey Club Sandwich

(Recipe contains approximately 15% fat)

4 T. "free" mayonnaise	1 c. shredded lettuce
4 T. "free" Philadelphia cream cheese	4 tsp. bacon bits (prepared with soy)
4 slices "light" whole wheat bread, toasted	8 thin slices tomato
	8 (1 oz.) slices turkey breast

Blend mayonnaise and cream cheese. Spread on 4 pieces of toast. Top with lettuce, bacon bits, tomato and turkey breast. Cover with second slice of bread. Cut in fourths cornerwise.
Yield: 4 sandwiches

Approximate Per Sandwich:
Calories: 240   **Carbohydrates: 23.2 g**
Fat: 4.0 g   **Protein: 25.7 g**
Cholesterol: 46.5 mg   **Sodium: 633 mg**

Exchanges: 2 meat; 1 1/2 bread; 1 vegetable

Clean glass fireplace doors with a scrub pad designed for nonstick cookware. It cleans, but does not scratch.

Luncheon Meats

Nearly all luncheon meats are high in fat. However, there is some good news. A couple of manufacturers have come out with a fat-free luncheon meat in the thin-sliced variety.

Those packages that say 93% lean—96% lean—etc., are misleading. Check the fat content. You may be surprised to discover that they are teetering on the edge of 30% fat in content (some over—some a little under).

Where the consumer is thinking of total fat in the product, the manufacturer has played around with the terms and can explain away the misleading labeling, however, it does not represent the total percent of fat regarding the product per serving.

Buyer Beware: When checking luncheon meat labels for fat content, first, look at the total calories and then check the number of calories from fat. You can usually tell at a glance about how fat the product is. The calories and calories from fat are the closest to accurate. Use this figure --DON'T BE TRICKED BY THE MANUFACATURER!

The best low-fat luncheon meats are the thin-sliced meat. Stick to the deli sliced meats—they now come packaged.

I have discovered, however, that some of the thin-sliced meats, such as the Buddig brand and similar store brands, are much higher in fat content than I once believed. Most of these run 45% fat content and over. I have listed them on the chart so you can see the fat content.

Also, there are now low-fat hot dogs. They lack some in taste compared to the high-fat hot dogs, but are certainly better than doing without.

Another pitfall to luncheon meats is their high sodium content.

Study the chart on luncheon meats. I'm sure there are areas that will surprise you.

Another "watch-point" is the "light" labeled luncheon meats. Check them out carefully. Some are still very high in fat content. There are not too many "light" luncheon meats, but the one I checked was 72% fat—it is shown on the chart.

Luncheon Meat

Fat-Free Luncheon Meat

	Cal	Fat	Cho	Car	Pro	Sod	% of Fat
Deli Select **by Hillshire Farms** Oven Roasted Chicken Breast; 6 slices	50	0.0	15	1.0	11.0	690	0%
Smoked Chicken Breast; 6 slices	60	0.0	5	0.0	13.0	650	0%
Healthy Favorite **By Oscar Mayer** Turkey Breast 4 slices	40	0.0	15	2.0	8.0	610	0%
Chicken Breast 4 slices	40	0.0	25	1.0	9.0	620	0%
Smoked Turkey Breast; 4 slices	40	0.0	15	2.0	8.0	350	0%
Louis Rich Hickory Smoked Turkey 1 slice	25	0.0	10	1.0	4.0	300	0%

Luncheon Meat (continued)
Low-Fat Luncheon Meat

	Cal	Fat	Cho	Car	Pro	Sod	% of Fat
Carving Board by Louis Rich							
Ham, 2 slices	45	1.0	25	1.0	8.0	510	20%
Hickory Smoked Turkey Breast; 2 slices	40	0.5	20	0.0	9.0	560	11%
Oven-Roasted Turkey Breast; 6 slices	60	0.5	25	0.0	12.0	740	8%
Deli Select by Hillshire Farms							
Cajun-Style Ham 6 slices	60	1.5	25	0.0	10.0	760	23%
Corned Beef 6 slices	60	1.0	15	1.0	12.0	590	15%
Honey Ham 6 slices	60	1.5	20	2.0	10.0	600	23%
Oven-Roasted & Cured Beef; 6 slices	50	0.5	20	1.0	11.0	570	9%

Luncheon Meat (continued)

Low-Fat Luncheon Meat

	Cal	Fat	Cho	Car	Pro	Sod	% of Fat
Deli Select (continued)							
Roast Turkey; 6 slices	50	1.0	20	1.0	12.0	560	18%
Smoked Beef; 6 slices	60	1.0	15	1.0	12.0	530	15%
Low-Sodium Ham							
6 slices	60	1.5	20	1.0	11.0	480	23%
Thin-Sliced Meats by Oscar Mayer							
Boiled Ham							
4 slices	50	2.0	25	0.0	9.0	680	36%
Chicken Breast							
4 slices	60	1.0	25	2.0	10.0	740	15%
Roast Beef							
4 slices	60	1.5	25	1.0	11.0	530	23%
96% Fat-Free Honey Ham							
3 slices	70	2.5	30	2.0	10	760	32%
96% Fat-Free Smoked							
Ham; 3 slices	60	2.5	30	2.0	10	760	38%
96% Fat-Free Low-Sodium							
Ham	70	2.5	30	2.0	10	520	32%

Note: don't be fooled by the 96% fat-free labeling--it is misleading. Beware!!

Luncheon Meat (continued)

Low-Fat Luncheon Meat

	Cal	Fat	Cho	Car	Pro	Sod	% of Fat
"Light" Sliced Meat							
"Light" Bologna							
1 slice	35	1.0	15	1.0	5.0	380	27%
Note: It appears the only thing "Light" are the calories							
Hot Dogs							
Healthy Choice; 1	70	1.5	20	5.0	8.0	570	19%
Hormel Light & Lean; 1	45	1.0	10	3.0	5.0	560	20%
Buddig Thin Sliced							
Beef (2.5 oz. pkg.)	100	5.0	50	Tr.	14.0	1,020	45%
Chicken (2.5 oz. pkg.)	60	7.0	40	Tr.	12.0	680	
Corned Beef (2.5 oz. pkg.)	100	5.0	50	Tr.	14.0	950	45%
Ham (2.5 oz. pkg.)	120	5.0	50	Tr.	13.0	980	53%
Pastrami (2.5 oz. pkg.)	100	5.0	50	Tr.	14.0	750	45%
Turkey (2.5 oz. pkg.)	110	7.0	40	Tr.	12.0	710	57%

Luncheon Meat (continued)
Low-Fat Luncheon Meat

	Cal	Fat	Cho	Car	Pro	Sod	% of Fat
Healthy Choice							
97% Fat-Free Smoked Ham; 1 slice	70	2.0	30	1.0	13.0	560	26%
97% Fat-Free Smoked Turkey Breast; 1 slice	30	1.0	10	0.0	5.0	230	30%
97% Fat-Free Roast Beef. 1 slice	30	1.0	10	0.0	5.0	260	30%
97% Fat-Free Ham 1 slice	30	1.0	10	1.0	5.0	250	30%
97% Fat-Free Oven-Roasted Turkey Breast; 1 slice	35	1.0	15	1.0	6.0	270	26%

Note: In this group we have luncheon meat that is labeled "97%" fat-free. This is not a per serving figure of total fat. As you can see, the total fat runs in the neighborhood of 30%. Beware!!

Skillet &
Oven Meals

Skillet, Stove-Top and Oven Meals

In this book I decided to go for meals that are easy to prepare. I put in a chapter of "Skillet, Stove-Top and Oven Meals". Meals that can be prepared on top of the stove or in the oven.

I have also done something a little different. I have made up a chart with general directions for preparing such skillet meals as Hamburger Helper and Tuna Helper.

Be sure to read the section in the preface about box labeling on such foods as these. You'll be surprised by what you read.

In experimenting with these foods I have found that the margarine called for on the box is usually more than is actually needed. In some of the boxed mixes I have used a NO-FAT mayonnaise as a substitute for part of the margarine called for. In other box mixes I have found that cutting the margarine works fine.

In the box mixes that called for ground beef I have substituted 3/4 pound ground turkey breast and 1/4 pound ground round. The reason for this is, while visiting with some of my readers I have been surprised by the number that tell me their husbands and children will not accept ground turkey.

You will note that I do not use ground turkey. **I use ground turkey breast.** It is much purer in taste and much, much lower in fat. By mixing it with just a little ground round it takes on the beef taste. I'll bet if you don't tell your family that there is turkey in the meal they will never suspect. At least give it a try.

When I write my cookbooks it is not without being aware of the need for easy foods in the busy world in which we live. For this reason I have included some convenience box foods in the book. Enjoy!

Use a melon-baller to form appetizer-size meatballs. If onions have been used in meatballs, dip the baller into cold water occasionally to prevent sticking.

Skillet and Stove-Top Meals

Beef

Beef Burgundy with Rice

(Recipe contains approximately 16% fat)

5 med. onions, diced &
　separated into rings
1/4 c. water
1 tsp. butter granules
1 tsp. canola oil
1 lb round steak, all visible
　fat removed & cut into
　small pieces
2 T. flour

1/2 tsp. sodium-free seasoned
　salt
1/4 tsp. pepper
1/2 c. beef stock, can use
　canned
1 c. red wine (can use bouillon)
1/2 lb. fresh mushrooms,
　sliced
3 c. hot, cooked brown rice

In a heavy-bottomed skillet, put water and butter granules and bring to boil. Add onions and sauté until tender. Remove onions from skillet and set aside. Put oil in skillet, add beef and brown. Sprinkle browned beef with flour, salt and pepper. Stir in stock and red wine, stirring to blend. Simmer 2 1/2 to 3 hours, adding more bouillon, if needed. Return onions to skillet and add mushrooms. Cook 30 minutes longer (add more liquid if needed). Serve over rice.

Yield: 6 servings

Approximate Per Serving:
Calories: 341
Fat: 6.1 g
Cholesterol: 53 mg

Carbohydrates: 38.7 g
Protein: 27.2 g
Sodium: 354 mg

Exchanges: 3 meat; 1 bread; 2 vegetable; 1 fat

To thicken soup add instant rice or mashed potatoes.

Cheesy Italian Pasta Skillet

(Recipe contains approximately 14% fat)

1 lg. onion, diced
1 lb. ground round
1 (16 oz.) can tomato sauce
2 oz. tomato paste
1 (16 oz.) can cream-style
   corn
1 tsp. basil

1/2 tsp. garlic powder
2 c. water
1 (8 oz.) pkg. eggless noodles
1/2 c. "free" no-fat shredded
   Cheddar cheese
1 (8 oz.) ctn. "free" cream
   cheese

In a large, heavy-bottomed skillet, brown onions and ground round. Drain off any rendered fat. Add tomato sauce, tomato paste, corn, basil and garlic powder. Add 2 cups water and noodles. Cover and simmer 20 minutes, or until noodles are tender. Add shredded cheese and stir in cream cheese by the teaspoonfuls. Cook until cheeses are melted, stirring constantly.
Yield: 8 servings

Approximate Per Serving:
Calories: 355
Fat: 5.4 g
Cholesterol: 46 mg

Carbohydrates: 39.3 g
Protein: 26.3 g
Sodium: 689 mg

Exchanges: 3 meat; 1 1/2 bread; 1 milk

When making stock with bones wrap them in cheesecloth.
Makes them easy to remove from stock.

Cheesy Skillet Lasagna

(Recipe contains approximately 13% fat)

1/2 lb. ground round
1/2 lb. ground turkey breast
1 med. onion, chopped
1 (15 oz.) can tomato sauce
1 tsp. oregano
1/4 tsp. garlic powder
2 c. low-fat cottage cheese, puréed

Egg substitute to = 1 egg
1/2 tsp. sodium-free seasoned salt
1/4 tsp. pepper
10 lasagna noodles, cooked
1 c. "free" no-fat shredded mozzarella cheese

In a large, deep skillet, cook beef and onion over medium heat. Drain off any rendered fat. Blend tomato sauce, oregano and garlic powder. Reserve 1/3 of sauce and add remainder to meat mixture. Heat through. Remove from heat. Put half of beef mixture in a bowl and set aside. Combine puréed cottage cheese, egg substitute, salt and pepper. blend. Spoon 1/2 of cottage cheese mixture over meat mixture in skillet. Top with 5 lasagna noodles and sprinkle with 1/2 of cheese. Layer remaining meat mixture, top with cheese and 5 lasagna noodles. Spread reserved tomato sauce over noodles. Cook over low heat, until heated through and cheese has melted. **Yield: 10 servings**

Approximate Per Serving:
Calories: 331
Fat: 4.9 g
Cholesterol: 49 mg

Carbohydrates: 13.6 g
Protein: 39.5 g
Sodium: 547 mg

Exchanges: 2 meat; 1 bread; 1 1/2 milk; 1 vegetable

Try a little dill in tomato soup. Peps it up.

Easy Beef Skillet

(Recipe contains approximately 21% fat)

3/4 lb. ground round
1 med. onion, chopped
1 (16 oz.) can tomatoes,
    chopped & undrained
2 c. water
6 oz. uncooked eggless noodles
1 T. chili powder
1/2 tsp. garlic powder

1/4 tsp. seasoned salt
1/4 tsp. pepper
1 (8 oz.) can whole kernel
    corn, drained
1 (4 oz.) can sliced mushrooms,
    drained
2 T. grated Parmesan cheese

Brown ground round and onions in deep, heavy-bottomed skillet. Drain off any rendered fat. Add tomatoes, water, noodles, chili powder, garlic powder, seasoned salt and pepper. Cover and bring to boil. Reduce heat and simmer 30 minutes. Add corn and mushrooms and heat through. Sprinkle with Parmesan cheese.
Yield: 6 servings

Approximate Per Serving:
Calories: 283
Fat: 6.5 g
Cholesterol: 41 mg

Carbohydrates: 34.0 g
Protein: 30.5 g
Sodium: 434 mg

Exchanges: 2 meat; 1 1/2 bread; 1 vegetable; 1 fat

An empty milk carton stuffed with newspaper makes an excellent starter for fireplaces. Stuff with newspaper; poke holes into all sides and light.

Easy Beef Stroganoff

(Recipe contains approximately 29% fat)

3/4 lb. ground round
1/4 c. chopped onions
1 clove garlic, minced
1 recipe casserole cream soup
   mix (see index)

1/4 c. skim milk
1/2 c. "light" dairy sour cream
2 c. hot, cooked noodles
Minced parsley

In a heavy-bottomed skillet, brown beef, onions and garlic. Drain off any rendered fat. Blend together prepared soup mix and milk until smooth. Add to meat mixture, stirring to blend. Reduce heat and gently blend in sour cream. Serve over noodles sprinkled with parsley.
Yield: 4 servings

Approximate Per Serving:
Calories: 344
Fat: 10.9 g
Cholesterol: 61 mg

Carbohydrates: 24.8 g
Protein: 35.9 g
Sodium: 880 mg

Exchanges: 3 meat; 2 bread; 1/2 milk

Keep a small squeegee in the shower to wipe clean the walls and glass doors. Children love to do it and it keeps the glass and ceramic tiles shining.

Skillet Beef and Macaroni
(Recipe contains approximately 12% fat)

1/2 lb. ground round	1 (8 oz.) can tomato sauce
1/2 lb. ground turkey breast	1 (16 oz.) can stewed tomatoes
1/2 c. minced onion	1 (16 oz.) can beef broth
8 oz. uncooked macaroni	1/4 tsp. seasoned salt
1/2 c. chopped green pepper	1/4 tsp. pepper

Brown ground round in a heavy-bottomed skillet. Add onion, macaroni and green pepper. Stir until macaroni has turned yellow. Add tomato sauce and stewed tomatoes. Blend well. Add beef broth, salt and pepper. Blend. Cover and simmer about 25 minutes, or until macaroni is tender. If needed, add more water. Stir several times during cooking.
Yield: 8 servings

Approximate Per Serving:
Calories: 232
Fat: 3.2 g
Cholesterol: 42 mg
Carbohydrates: 25.1 g
Protein: 23.3 g
Sodium: 495 mg

Exchanges: 2 meat; 1 bread; 1 vegetable; 3/4 fat

After cleaning ceramic tile and grout, apply a thin film of furniture polish to prevent mildew and to discourage soap film.

Skillet Chili

(Recipe contains approximately 15% fat)

1 onion, chopped
1/4 c. water
1 tsp. butter granules
1/2 lb. ground round
1/2 lb. ground turkey breast
1 c. water
1/2 tsp. garlic powder

1 1/2 tsp. chili powder
1/4 tsp. salt
1 (28 oz.) can tomatoes
1 (8 oz.) can tomato sauce
1 (16 oz.) can dark red kidney
   beans

Put 1/4 cup water and butter granules into a large skillet and bring to boil. Add onions and sauté until moisture is absorbed. Add ground round and brown. Add remaining ingredients. Bring mixture to boil; reduce heat and simmer 35 to 40 minutes, stirring often. **Yield: 10 servings**

Approximate Per Serving:
Calories: 155
Fat: 2.5 g
Cholesterol: 34.0 mg

Carbohydrates: 14.4 g
Protein: 21.1 g
Sodium: 270 mg

Exchanges: 2 meat; 2 vegetable

A quick way to clean and shine chrome fixture in kitchen and bathroom is to spray with vinegar and wipe to a shine.

Spanish Rice

(Recipe contains approximately 15% fat)

1/4 c. water	2 c. cooked brown rice
1 tsp. butter granules	1 (6 oz.) can tomato paste
1 med. onion, chopped	1 pkg. taco mix
3 ribs celery, chopped	1 c. water
1 clove garlic, minced	1/2 tsp. garlic powder
1 bell pepper, chopped	1/4 tsp. pepper
3/4 lb. ground round	

Put water and butter granules in skillet and bring to boil. Add onions, celery, garlic and green pepper. Sauté until tender. Add ground beef and brown until pink disappears. Add rice. Stir in tomato paste, taco mix, water, garlic powder and pepper. Cook several minutes until water has been absorbed.

Yield: 8 servings

Approximate Per Serving:

Calories: 212	**Carbohydrates: 20.8 g**
Fat: 3.6 g	**Protein: 17.8 g**
Cholesterol: 30 mg	**Sodium: 570 mg**

Exchanges: 1 1/2 meat; 1 1/2 bread; 1 vegetable

Put your pastry board across the washbowl before cleaning out your medicine cabinet. This makes a handy table to hold bottles and jars while you clean the cabinet.

Pasta Skillet Meals

Refreshing Spaghetti
(Recipe contains approximately 21% fat)

6 tomatoes, skinned &
    chopped
1/2 lb. spaghetti, cooked,
    drained & hot
1 green pepper, diced
1/2 c. chopped green onions
1/4 c. chopped ripe olives

1/2 tsp. garlic salt
1/4 tsp. pepper
Juice of 1/2 lemon
Olive oil cooking spray
1/4 c. chopped, fresh parsley
2 T. Parmesan cheese

In a skillet, put tomatoes and heat through, stirring until heated. Add hot spaghetti, green pepper, onion, olives, salt, pepper and lemon juice. Blend. Spray mixture with olive oil cooking spray for 6 seconds. Put in serving dish. Sprinkle with parsley and Parmesan cheese.

Yield: 8 servings

Approximate Per Serving:
Calories: 165
Fat: 3.8 g
Cholesterol: 1.0 mg

Carbohydrates: 31.9 g
Protein: 5.4 g
Sodium: 178 mg

Exchanges: 2 bread; 1 vegetable

Cover a large oatmeal box with decorative paper and use it to hold extra rolls of toilet paper.

Skillet Pasta and Vegetables

(Recipe contains approximately 16% fat)

6 oz. spaghetti, cooked &
    drained
1/4 c. water
1 tsp. butter granules
1 c. broccoli flowerets
1 c. thinly-sliced carrots
1 c. sliced zucchini

1/4 c. sliced onions
1 sm. green pepper, seeded &
    cut in strips
1/2 c. sliced mushrooms
1 tomato, cut into 8 wedges
2 oz. grated fresh Parmesan
1 T. fresh parsley, minced

Put water and butter granules in a skillet and bring to boil. Add broccoli, carrots, zucchini and onions. Sauté over medium heat 4 minutes. Add green pepper and mushrooms. Sauté an additional 4 minutes. Add tomatoes and pasta and cook until heated through. Sprinkle with Parmesan and parsley; toss and serve.
Yield: 6 servings

Approximate Per Serving:
Calories: 164
Fat: 3.0 g
Cholesterol: 2.7 mg

Carbohydrates: 27.2 g
Protein: 10.5 g
Sodium: 59 mg

Exchanges: 1 bread; 2 vegetable; 1/2 milk

*If you wrap a little adhesive tape around the wire where
it rests to hang a picture it will not slip.*

Spaghetti Sauce from a Jar

When we think of spaghetti sauce we think of vegetables, herbs and seasoning. A low-fat food.

However, when you get into the commercial types of spaghetti sauce, you run into a river of fat. Some spaghetti sauces are very high in fat and most are much higher than one might think.

This leads me to believe that the vegetables are sautéed in a fat base, thus leading to the fat in the sauce.

When choosing a commercial spaghetti sauce, it is best to stick to the "light" sauces. The only problem with this is, in the small city where I live, I was only able to find one light sauce.

I found some sauces that were under 30% fat and have included them on a chart. Prepare them by following the General Instructions.

General Instructions for Spaghetti Sauce

Cook an 8 ounce package spaghetti, according to package directions; drain; spray lightly with olive oil flavored cooking spray and set aside, keeping warm. Heat 3 cups of sauce according to jar directions. Divide spaghetti among six plates; top with 1/2 cup heated sauce; sprinkle with one teaspoon grated Parmesan cheese.

Hunts Homestyle with Mushrooms
(Approximate 23% fat)   Serves 6

Approximately Per Serving:

Follow General	**Calories**	215	**Carbohydrates**	35.0 g
Instructions	**Fat**	5.4 g	**Protein**	6.7 g
	Cholesterol	1.3 mg	**Sodium**	634 mg

Exchanges: 3 bread; 1 vegetable

Hunts Old Country   Serves 6
(Approximate 19% fat)

Approximately Per Serving:

Follow General	**Calories**	235	**Carbohydrates**	41.0 g
Instructions	**Fat**	4.9 g	**Protein**	6.7 g
	Cholesterol	1.3 mg	**Sodium**	604 mg

Exchanges: 3 bread; 1 vegetable

Prego Meat Flavored   Serves 6
(Aproximate 25% fat)

Approximately Per Serving:

Follow General	**Calories**	315	**Carbohydrates**	51.0 g
Instructions	**Fat**	8.9 g	**Protein**	7.7 g
	Cholesterol	1.3 mg	**Sodium**	744 mg

Exchanges: 3 bread; 2 vegetable; 1 1/2 fat

Prego Traditional Serves 6
(Approximate 26% fat)

Approximately Per Serving:

Follow General	**Calories**	305	**Carbohydrates**	50.0 g
Instructions	**Fat**	8.9 g	**Protein**	6.7 g
	Cholesterol	1.3 mg	**Sodium**	684 mg

Exchanges: 3 bread; 1 vegetable; 1 1/2 fat

Ragu Chunky Serves 6
(Approximate 23% fat)

Approximately Per Serving:

Follow General	**Calories**	275	**Carbohydrates**	47.0 g
Instructions	**Fat**	6.9 g	**Protein**	6.7 g
	Cholesterol	1.3 mg	**Sodium**	604 mg

Exchanges: 3 bread; 3 vegetable; 2 fat

Ragu Chunky Garden Style Serves 6
(Approximate 23% fat)

Approximately Per Serving:

Follow General	**Calories**	275	**Carbohydrates**	46.0 g
Instructions	**Fat**	6.9 g	**Protein**	6.7 g
	Cholesterol	1.3 mg	**Sodium**	614 mg

Exchanges: 3 bread; 1 vegetable; 1 fat

Ragu "Light" Serves 6
(Approximate 13% fat)

Approximately Per Serving:

Follow General	**Calories**	205	**Carbohydrates**	39.0 g
Instructions	**Fat**	2.9 g	**Protein**	6.7 g
	Cholesterol	1.3 mg	**Sodium**	454 mg

Exchanges: 2 bread; 2 vegetable

Ragu Thick and Hearty Serves 6
(Approximate 23% fat)

Approximately Per Serving:

Follow General	**Calories**	285	**Carbohydrates**	47.0 g
Instructions	**Fat**	7.4 g	**Protein**	8.7 g
	Cholesterol	1.3 mg	**Sodium**	608 mg

Exchanges: 3 bread; 1 vegetable; 1 fat

Poultry Skillet Meals

Chicken and Rice
with Orange Sauce

(Recipe contains approximately 13% fat)

5 1/4 c. water
1 c. uncooked brown rice
2 tsp. chicken bouillon granules
6 boneless, skinned chicken
   breast fillets, 3 oz. each
1/2 tsp. garlic powder
1 bay leaf
1/4 tsp. pepper
2 c. unsweetened orange juice

2 T. cornstarch
1 tsp. grated orange rind
1 tsp. butter granules
2 c. diagonally-sliced celery
1 lg. green pepper, seeded &
   cut into strips
1 lg. red pepper, seeded & cut
   into strips

Put 2 1/2 cups water, rice and bouillon in a medium saucepan and bring to boil. Cover; reduce heat and simmer 50 minutes, or until liquid is all absorbed and rice is tender. Put 2 1/2 cups water in a second saucepan and add chicken, garlic salt, bay leaf and pepper. Simmer 30 minutes, or until chicken is tender. In a small saucepan, blend orange juice, cornstarch and orange rind. Cook until thick, stirring constantly. Put 1/4 cup water and butter granules in a skillet and bring to boil. Add celery and red and green pepper. Sauté until liquid has been absorbed. Add rice, chicken and orange sauce, and blend.
Yield: 6 servings

Approximate Per Serving:
Calories: 331
Fat: 4.6 g
Cholesterol: 66 mg

Carbohydrates: 42.5 g
Protein: 32.4 g
Sodium: 271 mg

Exchanges: 3 meat; 1 bread; 1/2 vegetable; 1 fruit; 1 fat

An empty egg carton stores golf balls easily and neatly.

Italian Noodle Stew

(Recipe contains approximately 17% fat)

1 lb. turkey sausage (see index)	2 beef bouillon cubes
1/2 c. chopped onion	1 tsp. oregano
1/2 c. chopped celery	1/4 tsp. basil
1/4 c. chopped green pepper	1 (16 oz.) can Italian green
1 (16 oz.) can tomatoes,	beans
undrained & chopped	1 (7 oz.) pkg. eggless noodles
2 c. boiling water	

In a heavy-bottomed skillet, brown turkey sausage, onion, celery and green pepper. Add tomatoes and juice. Dissolve bouillon in boiling water and add. Add remaining ingredients and simmer until noodles are tender (10 to 15 minutes). Add more water, if needed.

Yield: 8 servings

Approximate Per Serving:
Calories: 229

Fat: 4.3 g

Cholesterol: 46 mg

Carbohydrates: 23.9 g

Protein: 23.0 g

Sodium: 398 mg

Exchanges: 2 meat; 1 bread; 2 vegetable

You can prevent ugly picture marks on your walls by sticking a thumbtack in the corner on the back of the frame. It should stick out about 1/8-inch.

Oriental Gingered Turkey with Rice

(Recipe contains approximately 7% fat)

1 c. brown rice	1 c. orange juice
1/4 c. water	2 T. "light" soy sauce
1 tsp. butter granules	1/2 tsp. ground ginger
12 oz. turkey breast, cut into thin strips	Dash of black pepper
1 sm. carrots, sliced thin	2 c. cauliflower flowerets
	1 T. cornstarch

Put water and butter granules in heavy-bottomed skillet and bring to boil. Add turkey strips and carrots. Cook, tossing often. When tender, remove from skillet with slotted spoon and set aside. Blend 1/2 cup orange juice, soy sauce, ginger and pepper. Put in skillet with cauliflower and bring to boil. Reduce heat; cover and simmer 2 minutes. Combine remaining juice with cornstarch, stirring until smooth. Stir mixture into cauliflower and simmer until thick and bubbly. Stir in turkey, carrots and rice; heat through.
Yield: 4 servings

Approximate Per Serving:

Calories: 371	Carbohydrates: 19.0 g
Fat: 2.8 g	Protein: 33.5 g
Cholesterol: 66 mg	Sodium: 833 mg

Exchanges: 3 meat; 2 bread; 1 vegetable; 1 fruit

Liquor cartons are perfect for storing Christmas ornaments.
The carboard dividers separate and protect.

Sausage Skillet

(Recipe contains approximately 14% fat)

3/4 lb. homestyle sausage
  (see index)
1 c. brown rice
3/4 c. chopped celery

1 med. onion, chopped
1 (10 1/2 oz.) can chicken rice
  soup

Put sausage into skillet and brown. Drain off rendered fat. Add rice, celery and onion. Drain broth from soup and add enough water to make 2 cups liquid. Add liquid and drained soup. Blend. Bring to boil. Cover and simmer, stirring occasionally, for 30 to 35 minutes, or until rice is tender and liquid is absorbed. More water can be added, if needed.
Yield: 6 servings

Approximate Per Serving:
Calories: 245
Fat: 3.7 g
Cholesterol: 49.3 mg

Carbohydrates: 29.3 g
Protein: 20.1 g
Sodium: 215 mg

Exchanges: 2 meat; 1 bread; 1 vegetable; 1 fat

*Paint top and bottom step of basement stairs
with flourescent paint. Prevents accidents.*

Sausage with Curly Noodles

(Recipe contains approximately 15% fat)

1/4 c. water
1 tsp. butter granules
1/4 c. chopped onion
1/4 c. chopped green pepper
3/4 lb. turkey sausage
  (see index)
1 (7 oz.) pkg. curly noodles,
  uncooked

1 (16 oz.) can tomatoes,
  chopped (use juice)
1 (8 oz.) can whole kernel
  corn, undrained
2 tsp. beef bouillon granules
1/4 tsp. pepper
1/4 tsp. garlic powder

Put water and butter granules in skillet and bring to boil. Add onions and green pepper; sauté. Add turkey sausage and brown. Add remaining ingredients and simmer until noodles are tender, 10 to 15 minutes.
Yield: 6 servings

Approximate Per Serving:
Calories: 279
Fat: 4.8 g
Cholesterol: 46 mg

Carbohydrates: 35.2 g
Protein: 24.4 g
Sodium: 340 mg

Exchanges: 2 meat; 2 bread; 1 vegetable

When spraying houseplants, hold an opened umbrella behind the plant to keep the fine mist from settling on walls and furniture.

Skillet Chicken and Noodles

(Recipe contains approximately 16% fat)

3/4 lb. skinless, boneless
   chicken breast, cut in bite-
   sized pieces
1/4 c. water
1 tsp. butter granules
2 c. sliced, fresh mushrooms
1/2 c. chopped celery
1/2 c. chopped green pepper

1 clove garlic, minced
2 c. chicken stock, can use
   canned
1 bay leaf
1/4 tsp. garlic salt
1/4 tsp. pepper
3 c. cooked, med., eggless
   noodles

Put water and butter granules in a heavy-bottomed skillet and bring to boil. Add chicken and cook until tender and browned. Remove from skillet with slotted spoon and set aside. Add mushrooms, celery, green pepper and garlic to skillet. Sauté, adding a little water, if needed. Add stock, bay leaf, garlic salt and pepper. Cover and simmer about 1 hour, or until stock has reduced by half. Remove bay leaf. Add cooked noodles and chicken. Simmer, uncovered, until heated through.
Yield: 6 servings

Approximate Per Serving:
Calories: 235
Fat: 4.1 g
Cholesterol: 44 mg

Carbohydrates: 23.6 g
Protein: 25.7 g
Sodium: 433 mg

Exchanges: 2 meat; 1 bread; 1 vegetable; 1/2 fat

A shoehorn makes a good trowel for transplanting small houseplants.

Zucchini, Chicken and Pasta

(Recipe contains approximately 19% fat)

8 (3 oz.) boneless, skinless
   chicken breast fillets
1/4 tsp. salt
1/4 tsp. pepper
1/4 c. water
1 tsp. butter granules
1/4 c. chopped onion

1 clove garlic, minced
1 c. sliced zucchini
1 (16 oz.) can tomato sauce
1 lb. fresh mushrooms, sliced
1 (8 oz.) pkg. spaghetti,
   cooked
2 T. grated Parmesan cheese

Season chicken breasts with salt and pepper and put under broiler for 15 to 20 minutes, turning once. In a skillet, put water and butter granules. Bring to boil. Sauté onion and garlic until tender. Add zucchini, tomato sauce and mushrooms. Cook until zucchini is cooked, 3 or 4 minutes. Put cooked spaghetti on large serving plate and pour sauce over it. Sprinkle with Parmesan cheese and put chicken breasts around edge of spaghetti.
Yield: 8 servings

Approximate Per Serving:
Calories: 299
Fat: 6.2 g
Cholesterol: 66 mg

Carbohydrates: 26.3 g
Protein: 34.2 g
Sodium: 548 mg

Exchanges: 3 meat; 1 bread; 1 vegetable; 1 fat

*Put a layer of gravel on top of the soil in a window box to keep
rain from spattering dirt on your windows.*

Pork Skillet Meals

Pork Chops and Rice in a Skillet

(Recipe contains approximately 27% fat)

4 (3 oz.) boneless pork chops,
  all visible fat removed
10-second spray of cooking
  spray
3 c. boiling water
3 bouillon cubes

1 c. chopped celery
1/2 c. carrots, sliced thin
1/4 c. chopped green onion
1/4 tsp. pepper
1 c. uncooked brown rice

In a heavy-bottom skillet, sprayed with cooking spray, brown chops. Remove from pan and add boiling water and bouillon cubes. Dissolve cubes. Add celery, carrots, green onion, salt and pepper. Simmer 5 minutes. Sprinkle rice over top and put chops on top of rice. Cover and simmer 45 minutes, or until rice is tender. Add more water, if needed.

Yield: 4 servings

Approximate Per Serving:
Calories: 418
Fat: 12.6 g
Cholesterol: 75 mg

Carbohydrates: 41.3 g
Protein: 30.3 g
Sodium: 821 mg

Exchanges: 3 meat, 2 bread, 1 vegetable, 2 fat

Keep a toothbrush at the kitchen sink. You will be surprised how useful it is in cleaning hard-to-get at objects such as beaters, graters, etc.

Pork Tenderloin and Noodle Skillet

(Recipe contains approximately 25% fat)

12 oz. pork tenderloin, all
    visible fat removed; cubed
1/4 c. water
1 tsp. butter granules
1 c. diced celery
8 oz. thin, eggless noodles,
    cooked

1 (16 oz.) can whole kernel
    corn, drained
1 diced green pepper
1 can mushrooms, drained &
    diced
Recipe for 2 cans casserole
    soup mix (see index)

Put water and butter granules in skillet and bring to boil. Add cubed pork tenderloin and brown. Add celery and simmer pork and celery for 30 minutes, or until tender. Add a little more water, if needed. Add remaining ingredients and simmer 20 to 30 minutes, covered, stirring often. Add more water, if needed.
Yield: 6 servings

Approximate Per Serving:
Calories: 361
Fat: 10.0 g
Cholesterol: 60 mg

Carbohydrates: 44.7 g
Protein: 26.3 g
Sodium: 708 mg

Exchanges: 2 meat; 2 bread; 1/2 milk; 1 vegetable; 1 fat

When your hands are badly stained from gardening, add a teaspoon of sugar to the soapy water you wash them in. Helps hands clean faster.

Seafood and Fish

Shrimp Paella

(Recipe contains approximately 7% fat)

1 c. brown rice, uncooked
1 tsp. chicken bouillon granules
1/2 tsp. garlic powder
1/4 tsp. saffron
Dash of pepper

8 oz. cooked, frozen shrimp,
   thawed & warmed
1 tomato, seeded & chopped
1 c. cooked chicken breast, cut
   into bite-sized pieces

Cook rice per package directions, adding bouillon, garlic powder, saffron and pepper to cooking water. To cooked rice, add remaining ingredients and toss to blend.
Yield: 4 servings

Approximate Per Serving:
Calories: 296
Fat: 2.4 g
Cholesterol: 117 mg

Carbohydrates: 40.0 g
Protein: 28.0 g
Sodium: 358 mg

Exchanges: 3 meat; 1 1/2 bread; 1 vegetable

*To prevent drains from clogging, once a month pour a handful of
bicarbonate of soda in drain followed by 1/2 cup vinegar.
Let them work a few minutes, then rinse well with hot water.*

Shrimp with Noodles

(Recipe contains approximately 9% fat)

1 (8 oz.) pkg. eggless noodles, cooked	1/4 tsp. basil
3 c. frozen California Mix	1/4 tsp. pepper
2 T. water	1/4 tsp. garlic powder
1 tsp. butter granules	1/4 tsp. seasoned salt
1 (1 lb.) pkg. frozen, cooked shrimp	1 (8 oz.) ctn. "free" cream cheese

Cook pasta per package directions, omitting salt. Cook California Mix per package directions. In a skillet, put water and butter granules. Add shrimp and toss until liquid is absorbed. Add noodles, California Mix, basil, pepper, garlic powder and seasoned salt. Stir in cream cheese, tossing until cheese melts and blends in. Serve hot.

Yield: 6 servings

Approximate Per Serving:

Calories: 286	Carbohydrates: 32.9 g
Fat: 2.9 g	Protein: 31.9 g
Cholesterol: 123 mg	Sodium: 472 mg

Exchanges: 3 meat; 1 1/2 bread; 1 vegetable

When two glasses stick together, dip the bottom one in hot water and pour ice water into the top glass. The glasses will come apart easily.

Skillet Macaroni and Tuna

(Recipe contains approximately 7% fat)

1 c. uncooked, med. shell
   macaroni
Cooking spray
2 T. water
1 tsp. butter granules
1/2 c. minced onion
1/2 c. minced green pepper
1 T. tub margarine

2 T. flour
1 1/2 c. skim milk
2 T. cheese granules
2 (6 1/2 oz.) cans water-
   packed tuna, drained
1/4 tsp. garlic powder
1/4 tsp. pepper

Cook macaroni per package directions. Drain and spray lightly with cooking spray, tossing to coat. Set aside. In a large, heavy-bottomed skillet, put water and butter granules and bring to boil. Add onion and green pepper; sauté until tender and moisture has been absorbed. Remove from skillet and set aside. Melt margarine in skillet and add flour, stirring as you cook, for 2 minutes. Slowly add milk, whisking until smooth. Cook over medium heat until smooth and bubbly. Add cheese granules. Stir in onion mixture, macaroni, tuna, garlic powder and pepper. Simmer until thick.
Yield: 6 servings

Approximate Per Serving:
Calories: 244
Fat: 2 g
Cholesterol: 36.7 mg

Carbohydrates: 11.1 g
Protein: 25.3 g
Sodium: 234 mg

Exchanges: 2 meat; 1 bread; 1/2 milk; 1/2 fat

To clean copper mix equal amounts of salt and vinegar and scrub away.

Stove-Top Shrimp Jambalaya

(Recipe contains approximately 11% fat)

1/4 c. water
1 tsp. butter granules
1/2 c. finely-chopped onion
1 green pepper, chopped fine
1 clove garlic, minced
1 (16 oz.) can tomato sauce
2 drops Tabasco

1/4 tsp. seasoned salt
1/4 tsp. garlic powder
1/4 tsp. black pepper
3 c. cooked brown rice
1 1/2 lb. cooked shrimp (can use frozen)

Put water and butter granules in a large, heavy-bottomed skillet and bring to boil. Add onions, green pepper and garlic; sauté until tender. Stir in tomato sauce, Tabasco, seasoned salt, garlic powder and pepper. Add cooked rice and shrimp. Simmer until liquid is absorbed.
Yield: 8 servings

Approximate Per Serving:
Calories: 214
Fat: 2.6 g
Cholesterol: 131 mg

Carbohydrates: 26.8 g
Protein: 29.9 g
Sodium: 595 mg

Exchanges: 3 meat; 1 vegetable; 1/2 fat

To insure good air circulation in the oven, stagger cake pans and pie plates so one is not directly over the other.

Skillet Dinners from a Box

We all like the convenience of using a quick mix to make a skillet dinner. The key to doing this is to keep the fat down. It is best to not make it a habit of using the ones with cheese in them, as they are higher in saturated fat. The real pitfall to these mixes, however, is the sodium. Most mixes are high in sodium content.

General Instructions

Substitute 3/4 pound ground turkey breast and 1/4 pound ground round for the ground beef called for in the package directions. Blend the turkey breast and the ground round together before browning. Brown meat and follow package directions.

Hamburger Helper

Beef Taco   Serves 5
(Approximate 16% fat)

Approximately Per Serving:

Follow General Instructions				
	Calories	300	**Carbohydrates**	28.0 g
	Fat	5.3 g	**Protein**	34.1 g
	Cholesterol	69 mg	**Sodium**	890

Exchanges: 2 1/2 meat; 2 bread; 1/2 fat

❖

Beef Stew   Serves 6
(Approximate 12% fat)

Approximately Per Serving:

Follow General Instructions				
	Calories	235	**Carbohydrates**	23.0 g
	Fat	3.2 g	**Protein**	27.3 g
	Cholesterol	57 mg	**Sodium**	798 mg

Exchanges: 2 meat; 1 bread; 1 vegetable; 3/4 fat

❖

Chili Mac Serves 5
(Approximate 13% fat)

Approximately Per Serving:

Follow General Instructions	**Calories**	290	**Carbohydrates**	30.0 g
	Fat	4.2 g	**Protein**	32.7 g
	Cholesterol	69 mg	**Sodium**	890

Exchanges: 3 meat; 1 bread; 1/2 vegetable; 1 fat

❖

Italian Ragatori Serves 5
(Approximate 13% fat)

Approximately Per Serving:

Follow General Instructions	**Calories**	290	**Carbohydrates**	30.0 g
	Fat	4.2 g	**Protein**	33.1 g
	Cholesterol	69 mg	**Sodium**	850 mg

Exchanges: 3 meat; 1 bread; 1 vegetable; 1 fat

❖

Mushroom and Wild Rice Serves 5
(Approximate 16% fat)

Approximately Per Serving:

Follow General Instructions	**Calories**	320	**Carbohydrates**	33.0 g
	Fat	5.7 g	**Protein**	33.1 g
	Cholesterol	69 mg	**Sodium**	950 mg

Exchanges: 3 meat; 1 bread; 1 vegetable; 1 fat

❖

Salisbury Steak Serves 5
(Approximate 16% fat)

Approximately Per Serving:

Follow General Instructions	**Calories**	300	**Carbohydrates**	30.0 g
	Fat	5.2 g	**Protein**	34.1g
	Cholesterol	69 mg	**Sodium**	1,126 mg

Exchanges: 3 meat; 1 bread; 1 vegetable; 1 fat

Tuna Helper
General Instructions for Tuna Helper

I like to pay the extra and use the water-packed white tuna, however, if your family is satisfied with the water-packed light tuna, by all means use it. When preparing the Tuna Helper, use only 1 tablespoon of tub margarine (not to exceed 6 grams of fat per tablespoon), plus 1 tablespoon of no-fat mayonnaise. Add 1 teaspoon of butter granules and use only skim milk when preparing. With these exceptions, follow package directions.

Au Gratin   Serves 5
(Approximate 19% fat)

Approximately Per Serving:

Follow General Instructions	**Calories**	272	**Carbohydrates**	31.0 g
	Fat	5.7 g	**Protein**	15.7 g
	Cholesterol	21 mg	**Sodium**	890 mg

Exchanges: 1 meat; 2 bread; 1/2 milk; 1 fat

❖

Cheesey Noodles   Serves 5
(Approximate 20% fat)

Approximately Per Serving:

Follow General Instructions	**Calories**	260	**Carbohydrates**	31.4 g
	Fat	5.7 g	**Protein**	19.7 g
	Cholesterol	22 mg	**Sodium**	902 mg

Exchanges: 1 meat; 2 bread; 1/4 milk; 1 fat

❖

Creamy Broccoli   Serves 5
(Approximate 18% fat)

Approximately Per Serving:

Follow General Instructions	**Calories**	290	**Carbohydrates**	37.6 g
	Fat	5.7 g	**Protein**	20.7 g
	Cholesterol	22 mg	**Sodium**	912 mg

Exchanges: 1 meat; 2 bread; 1/2 milk; 1 fat

❖

Creamy Noodle   Serves 5
(Approximate 12% fat)

Approximately Per Serving:

Follow General	**Calories**	281	**Carbohydrates**	11.9 g
Instructions	**Fat**	3.7 g	**Protein**	8.4 g
	Cholesterol	40 mg	**Sodium**	882 mg

Exchanges: 1 meat; 2 bread;1/2 milk; 1 fat

❖

Fettucini Alfredo   Serves 4
(Approximate 19% fat)

Approximately Per Serving:

Follow General	**Calories**	315	**Carbohydrates**	38.0 g
Instructions	**Fat**	6.7 g	**Protein**	25.1 g
	Cholesterol	27 mg	**Sodium**	1,054 mg

Exchanges: 1 meat; 2 bread; 1 milk; 1 fat

❖

Garden Cheddar   Serves 5
(Approximate 18% fat)

Approximately Per Serving

Follow General	**Calories**	291	**Carbohydrates**	37.4 g
Instructions	**Fat**	5.7 g	**Protein**	21.7 g
	Cholesterol	22 mg	**Sodium**	1,032 mg

Exchanges: 1 meat; 2 bread; 1/2 milk; 1 fat

❖

Tetrazzini   Serves 4
(Approximate 17% fat)

Approximately Per Serving:

Follow General	**Calories**	278	**Carbohydrates**	34.3 g
Instructions	**Fat**	5.1 g	**Protein**	24.0 g
	Cholesterol	26 mg	**Sodium**	934 mg

Exchanges: 1 meat; 2 bread; 1/2 milk; 1 fat

Oven Meals

Beef

Beef, Eggplant and Zucchini Casserole

(Recipe contains approximately 21% fat)

1/4 c. water
1 tsp. butter granules
3/4 c. thinly-sliced onions
1 clove garlic, minced
1/2 lb. ground round
1/2 lb. ground turkey breast
2 green peppers, seeded & cut in strips

3 c. peeled, seeded & cubed eggplant
2 1/2 c. sliced young zucchini
2 c. fresh tomatoes, peeled, seeded & diced
1/2 tsp. seasoned salt
1/4 tsp. pepper

Put water and butter granules in a skillet and bring to boil. Add onions and garlic and sauté until tender. Add ground meat and brown until pink disappears. In a mixing bowl, blend peppers, eggplant, zucchini and tomatoes. Add meat mixture. Blend. Stir in salt and pepper. Pour into a 9x13-inch baking dish that has been sprayed with cooking spray. Cover and bake in 325° preheated oven for 30 minutes. Uncover and bake 10 to 15 minutes longer, or until most of moisture has been absorbed.
Yield: 8 servings

Approximate Per Serving:
Calories: 130
Fat: 3.0 g
Cholesterol: 42 mg

Carbohydrates: 11.9 g
Protein: 20.2 g
Sodium: 223 mg

Exchanges: 2 meat; 1/2 vegetable

Beef and Potato Casserole

(Recipe contains approximately 20% fat)

4 med. red potatoes, sliced
2 med. onions, sliced thin &
   separated into rings
3/4 lb. ground round
1 can tomato soup

1 tsp. butter granules
1/2 tsp. sodium-free
   seasoned salt
1/4 tsp. pepper
1 c. water

In a 9-inch square casserole, sprayed with cooking spray, put sliced potatoes. Add onions and crumble raw ground round over top. Spoon soup over layers. Sprinkle with butter granules, salt and pepper. Pour water over top. Cover and bake in 350° preheated oven 1 1/2 hours. Uncover the last 15 minutes of baking.
Yield: 4 servings

Approximate Per Serving:
Calories: 305
Fat: 6.9 g
Cholesterol: 60 mg

Carbohydrates: 30.8 g
Protein: 29.5 g
Sodium: 208 mg

Exchanges: 3 meat; 1 bread; 1 vegetable; 1 fat

Soften hardened brown sugar in the microwave by placing an open box of brown sugar in the oven with 1 cup hot water. MIcrowave on HIGH for 1 1/2 to 2 minutes for 1/2 pound; 2 to 3 minutes for a pound.

Cabbage and Beef Casserole

(Recipe contains approximately 25% fat)

1/4 lb. ground round	1/4 tsp. salt
1/2 lb. ground turkey breast	1/8 tsp. pepper
1/4 c. finely-chopped onion	1/8 tsp. cinnamon
1 (16 oz.) can tomato sauce	4 c. shredded cabbage

Brown meat and onions. Drain off any rendered fat. Add tomato sauce, salt, pepper and cinnamon; blend well. In a 2-quart casserole, that has been sprayed with cooking spray, put 2 cups cabbage, and top with 1/2 cup of meat sauce. Add remaining cabbage, topped with remaining meat sauce. Bake, covered, in a 350° preheated oven for 45 minutes.

Yield: 4 servings

Approximate Per Serving:

Calories: 198	**Carbohydrates: 13.8 g**
Fat: 3.6 g	**Protein: 29.7 g**
Cholesterol: 64 mg	**Sodium: 650 mg**

Exchanges: 3 meat; 1 1/2 vegetable

A woodenpick or two inserted through a cabbage wedge will hold the leaves together during cooking.

Cabbage Roll Casserole

(Recipe contains approximately 22% fat)

2 T. water
1/2 tsp. butter granules
1 lg. onion, chopped
1/2 lb. ground round
1 lb. ground turkey breast
1/2 tsp. pepper
1 lg. head cabbage, shredded

1/2 c. brown rice, uncooked
1 can tomato soup
1 (6 oz.) can tomato paste
2 T. brown sugar
3/4 c. water
1/4 c. vinegar

Put water and butter granules in a skillet and bring to boil. Add onions and cook 1 minute. Add meat, 1/2 teaspoon salt and 1/4 teaspoon pepper. Brown until pink disappears. Put half of chopped cabbage in a 9x13-inch baking dish, that has been sprayed with cooking spray. Add rice to meat mixture. Blend. Pour meat mixture over chopped cabbage. Put remaining chopped cabbage over meat mixture. In a small mixing bowl, blend remaining ingredients and pour over casserole. Cover with foil and bake in 350° preheated oven for 1 1/2 hours.
Yield: 8 servings

Approximate Per Serving:
Calories: 263
Fat: 4.3 g
Cholesterol: 64mg

Carbohydrates: 22.7 g
Protein: 30.6 g
Sodium: 367 mg

Exchanges: 3 meat; 1/2 bread; 1 vegetable; 1 fat

Add a bit of sugar to milk to prevent it from scorching--do not swirl.

Cottage-Beef Casserole

(Recipe contains approximately 16% fat)

1/2 lb. ground round
1/2 lb. ground turkey breast
1 med. onion, chopped
1/4 tsp. sodium-free
   seasoned salt
1/4 tsp. pepper
1 (16 oz.) can tomato sauce
1 c. low-fat cottage cheese

1 (8 oz.) ctn. "free" no-fat
   Philadelphia cream cheese
1/4 c. "light" sour cream
1/2 c. chopped green pepper
1/3 c. chopped green onion
   (include some green)
1 (8 oz.) pkg. eggless noodles,
   cooked & drained

In a skillet, combine ground meat and onions. Cook until pink leaves beef. Add salt, pepper and tomato sauce. Simmer 15 minutes. Blend cottage cheese, cream cheese, sour cream, green pepper and green onion. Set aside. In a 9x13-inch casserole, sprayed with cooking spray, put 1/2 of cooked noodles in bottom of casserole. Top with half of cheese mixture. Add remaining noodles and top with remaining cheese mixture. Pour meat mixture over top. Cover and bake in 350° preheated oven 30 minutes. Uncover and bake 15 minutes.
Yield: 8 servings

Approximate Per Serving:
Calories: 313
Fat: 5.5 g
Cholesterol: 31 mg

Carbohydrates: 30.7 g
Protein: 32.3 g
Sodium: 717 mg

Exchanges: 2 meat; 1 bread; 1 milk; 1/2 vegetable; 1 fat

Store almost empty jars of jam, mayonnaise, mustard, etc. on their side. Much easier to scrape out the last little bit.

Iowa Hash

(Recipe contains approximately 18% fat)

1/4 c. water	1/2 c. brown rice
1 tsp. butter granules	1/2 tsp. chili powder
1 lg. onion, chopped	1/2 tsp. sodium-free
1 green pepper, chopped	seasoned salt
3/4 lb. ground round	1/2 tsp. garlic powder
1 (16 oz.) can tomato sauce	1/2 to 1 tsp. pepper

Put water and butter granules in skillet and bring to boil. Add onion and green pepper; sauté until tender. Add ground round and brown. Add remaining ingredients and blend. Pour into a casserole dish, that has been sprayed with cooking spray, and bake, covered, in a 375° preheated oven to 45 minutes, or until rice is tender.
Yield: 4 servings

Approximate Per Serving:

Calories: 297	Carbohydrates: 33.2 g
Fat: 5.9 g	Protein: 29.5 g
Cholesterol: 60 mg	Sodium: 718 mg

Exchanges: 3 meat; 1 bread; 1 vegetable; 1 fat

A punch-type can opener makes a good shrimp cleaner and deveiner.

Mexican Casserole

(Recipe contains approximate 10% fat)

1/4 lb. ground round
1/2 lb. ground turkey breast
1 c. chopped onions
1 c. chopped celery
1 clove garlic, minced
1 1/2 T. Worcestershire sauce
1 tsp. chili powder

1 (16 oz.) can dark red
  kidney beans
1 (16 oz.) can creamed corn
1 (8 oz.) can tomato sauce
6 corn tortillas
6 slices "free" no-fat American
  cheese

In a large skillet, brown ground meat. Drain off any rendered fat. Add remaining ingredients, except tortilla and cheese slices. Spray a deep, round casserole with cooking spray. Put 1 tortilla in casserole and top with about 1 cup meat mixture. Repeat layers until tortillas and meat mixture have been used up. Pour remaining meat mixture over top. Put cheese slices on top. Bake, uncovered, in 350° preheated oven for 30 minutes.
Yield: 6 servings

Approximate Per Serving:
Calories: 367
Fat: 4.0 g
Cholesterol: 48 mg

Carbohydrates: 51.2 g
Protein: 42.2 g
Sodium: 910 mg

Exchanges: 2 meat; 2 bread; 1/2 milk; 1 1/2 vegetable; 1 fat

Use leftover low-fat onion soup dip for topping for baked potatoes.

Mexican Lasagna

(Recipe contains approximately 21% fat)

1 lb. ground round	2 1/2 c. picante sauce
2 tsp. oregano	2 1/2 c. water
3/4 tsp. garlic powder	1 c. "light" sour cream
1/4 tsp. salt	1 (8 oz.) ctn. "free" no-fat
1 tsp. cumin	cream cheese
1 (16 oz.) can dark red	3/4 c. chopped green onion
kidney beans	10 ripe olives, chopped
8 lasagna noodles, uncooked	

In a heavy-bottomed skillet, brown meat with oregano, garlic powder, salt and cumin. Mash kidney beans, using a little juice to make a smooth paste. Stir mashed beans into meat. Blend well. Put 4 noodles on bottom of 9x13-inch casserole, that has been sprayed with cooking spray. Top with half of meat mixture. Layer remaining 4 noodles and top with remaining meat mixture. Combine picante sauce and water; pour over casserole. Cover and bake in 350° preheated oven for 1 1/2 hours, or until noodles are tender. Remove from oven. Blend sour cream and cream cheese and drizzle over casserole. Blend chopped green onion and olives; sprinkle over top of casserole.

Yield: 8 servings

Approximate Per Serving:

Calories: 413	**Carbohydrates: 42.2 g**
Fat: 9.8 g	**Protein: 30.3 g**
Cholesterol: 65 mg	**Sodium: 565 mg**

Exchanges: 3 meat; 2 bread, 1 milk; 1 vegetable

Crushed dill seeds give homemade potato salad great flavor.

Swiss Steak with Mashed Potatoes

(Recipe contains approximately 24% fat)

8 med., red potatoes, peeled, diced & boiled
1 (8 oz.) ctn. "free" cream cheese
2 tsp. butter granules
1/2 tsp. garlic powder
1 T. canola oil
1 1/2 lb. round steak, all visible fat removed, cut into 8 serving pieces
1 T. dry mustard
1/2 c. enriched all-purpose flour
1/4 tsp. seasoned salt
1/4 tsp. pepper
1 c. thinly-sliced onions, separated into rings
1/2 c. diced carrots
1 (16 oz.) can tomatoes, chopped (include juice)
1 T. Worcestershire sauce

Drain potatoes and put back on stove for 2 minutes to allow to dry. Shake pan several times. Put in mixing bowl. Add cream cheese, butter granules and garlic salt. Beat with electric mixer until smooth. Spread potatoes evenly over bottom of 9x13-inch baking dish, that has been sprayed with cooking spray. Set aside. Heat oil in skillet. Combine mustard and flour. With the edge of saucer, pound mixture into meat pieces; pounding flour into both sides of meat. Season one side with seasoned salt and pepper and brown in oil. Put meat on top of potatoes. Combine remaining ingredients and pour over top of meat. Cover and bake in 325° preheated oven for 1 1/2 hours, or until meat is tender.
Yield: 8 servings

Approximate Per Serving:
Calories: 335
Fat: 8.8 g
Cholesterol: 65 mg
Carbohydrates: 29.0 g
Protein: 34.4 g
Sodium: 525 mg

Exchanges: 3 meat; 1 bread; 1/2 milk; 1 vegetable; 1/2 fat

For a nice change in flavor, add a dash of cinnamon to squash, turnips beets or baked beans.

Taco Pie in Potato Shell

(Recipe contains approximate 12% fat)

1 pkg. taco seasoning mix
2 c. mashed potatoes, prepared
   with skim milk and 1 tsp.
   butter granules
1/2 lb. ground round
1/2 lb. ground turkey breast
1/2 c. chopped onion

1 (16 oz.) can dark red kidney
   beans, mashed
1/2 c. bottled barbecue sauce
1/4 c. water
1/4 c. "free" no-fat shredded
   Cheddar cheese
1 c. shredded lettuce
1 med. tomato, chopped

To mashed potatoes, blend in 2 tablespoons taco seasoning mix. Put potatoes into 10-inch pie plate, covering bottom and side. In a skillet, cook meat and onion. Drain off any rendered fat. Stir in mashed beans, barbecue sauce, water and remaining dry taco mix. Cook until bubbly. Pour into potato crust. Bake, uncovered, in a 350° preheated oven 30 to 35 minutes. Remove from oven and top with cheese, lettuce and tomato.
Yield: 6 servings

Approximate Per Serving:
Calories: 333
Fat: 4.5 g
Cholesterol: 58 mg

Carbohydrates: 37.3 g
Protein: 36.1 g
Sodium: 937 mg

Exchanges: 2 1/2 meat; 1 bread; 2 vegetable; 1 milk

*Corn silks come off easier if held under water while genlty
rubbing with brush. A paper towel works well also.*

Tortilla Pie

(Recipe contains approximately 10% fat)

5 (6") flour tortillas
1/4 lb. ground round
1/2 lb. ground turkey breast
1 (4 oz.) can green chilies,
    drained & chopped
1 sm. onion, chopped
6 slices "free" no-fat
    American cheese, diced

Egg substitute to = 3 eggs
1/2 c. evaporated skim milk
3 T. enriched all-purpose flour
1/2 tsp. baking powder
1/2 tsp. chili powder
1/2 tsp. garlic powder

Spray the bottom of a 9-inch pie plate with cooking spray. Line pie plate with tortillas. In a large, heavy-bottomed skillet, brown ground meat over medium heat. Drain off any rendered fat. To meat, add chilies, onion and cheese. Spoon into pie plate onto tortillas. In a mixing bowl, put remaining ingredients and blend well. Pour over meat mixture. Bake in 350° preheated oven for 45 minutes, or until set.
Yield: 6 servings

Approximate Per Serving:
Calories: 376
Fat: 4.0 g
Cholesterol: 48 mg

Carbohydrates: 30.7 g
Protein: 38 g
Sodium: 661 mg

Exchanges: 3 meat; 2 bread; 1 vegetable

To put attractive scalloped edges on thin cucumber slices for salad, run the tines of a fork lengthwise over the peeled cucumber, then slice as usual.

Vegetable-Beef Meat Loaf with Vegetables

(Recipe contains approximately 16% fat)

1/4 c. water
1 tsp. butter granules
4 c. firmly-packed cabbage
1 med. onion, chopped
1 c. firmly-packed shredded
   carrots
2 cloves garlic, minced
1/2 lb. ground round
Egg substitute to = 1 egg
1 egg white
1/2 c. bread crumbs

1/2 tsp. dried basil
1/2 tsp. salt
1/4 tsp. pepper
1/4 c. skim milk
2 T. vinegar
1 c. firmly-packed, grated
   potatoes
2 lg. red potatoes, peeled &
   quartered
12 baby carrots

Put water and butter granules in skillet and bring to boil. Add cabbage and onion and cook over medium heat until moisture is absorbed (about 10 minutes). Remove from heat and cool. Combine carrots, garlic, beef, egg substitute, egg white, crumbs, basil, salt, pepper, milk, vinegar and grated potatoes. Blend well. Blend in cooked cabbage. Shape into 8-inch loaf and put in shallow baking pan. Put quartered potatoes and carrots around meat loaf. Cover and bake in 350° preheated oven 30 minutes. Uncover and bake an additional 30 minutes.
Yield: 4 servings

Approximate Per Serving:
Calories: 269
Fat: 4.7 g
Cholesterol: 40 mg

Carbohydrates: 25.8 g
Protein: 28.5 g
Sodium: 391 mg

Exchanges: 2 meat; 1 bread; 2 vegetable; 1/2 milk

To dissolve frozen orange juice, use a potato masher instead of a spoon.

Pasta Oven Meals

Baked Pasta with Cheese and Tomato

(Recipe contains approximately 14% fat)

1/4 c. water
1 tsp. butter granules
1 c. chopped onion
2 cloves garlic, minced
1/4 c. chopped green pepper
2 c. peeled, seeded & chopped
    fresh tomatoes
1 tsp. dried oregano
    (2 T. fresh)
1 tsp. dried sweet basil, or
    2 T. fresh

1/2 tsp. salt
1/4 tsp. sugar
1/4 tsp. pepper
16 oz. macaroni, cooked
Cooking spray
1/2 c. fresh, grated Parmesan
    cheese
1 1/2 c. puréed low-fat cottage
    cheese

In a heavy-bottomed skillet, put water and butter granules. Bring to boil. Add onions, garlic and green pepper; sauté until tender and moisture has been absorbed. Add tomatoes, oregano, basil, salt, sugar and pepper. Heat through and remove from stove. Spray hot, cooked macaroni with cooking spray. Add Parmesan cheese and toss. Spray a 9x13-inch baking dish with cooking spray. Put 1/3 of macaroni in dish and top with 1/2 cup puréed cottage cheese and 1/3 cup tomato sauce. Repeat layers until ingredients are all used. Bake in 375° oven 25 to 30 minutes, or until bubbly. **Yield: 8 servings**

Approximate Per Serving:
Calories: 291
Fat: 4.5 g
Cholesterol: 5.6 mg

Carbohydrates: 46.1 g
Protein: 17.7 g
Sodium: 227 mg

Exchanges: 1 meat; 2 bread; 1 milk; 1 vegetable

Vegetable Manicotti

(Recipe contains approximately 14% fat)

8 manicotti shells
1 (10 oz.) pkg. frozen,
  chopped spinach
1 sm. onion, chopped
1 tsp. chicken bouillon
  granules
1/2 tsp. garlic powder
1/4 tsp. basil
1/2 tsp. oregano

1 1/2 c. low-fat cream-style
  cottage cheese
Egg substitute to = 2 eggs
1/4 c. grated Parmesan cheese
1 (8 oz.) can tomato sauce
1 c. "free" no-fat shredded
  mozzarella cheese
2 tsp. chopped parsley

Cook manicotti shells per package directions. Drain and set aside. In a mixing bowl, put thawed spinach (all of moisture squeezed out), onion, bouillon, garlic powder, basil, oregano, cottage cheese, egg substitute and Parmesan cheese. Blend. Stuff mixture into shells and put stuffed shells in a 9x13-inch baking dish, that has been sprayed with cooking spray. Pour tomato sauce over shells. Sprinkle with mozzarella cheese and parsley. Cover and cook in 350° preheated oven for 25 minutes.

Yield: 8 servings

Approximate Per Serving:
Calories: 164
Fat: 2.5 g
Cholesterol: 5.9 mg

Carbohydrates: 27.7 g
Protein: 17.6 g
Sodium: 348 mg

Exchanges: 1 bread; 1 milk; 1/2 vegetable

*Wash seedless grapes, put them in a plastic freezer container
and freeze them. Great treat frozen--kids love them.*

Poultry Oven Meals

Baked Chicken Hash
(Recipe contains approximately 17% fat)

3/4 c. skim milk, scalded
1 1/2 c. bread crumbs from
   reduced-calorie bread
2 tsp. butter granules
2 c. cooked, diced chicken
   breast

1/2 c. chopped onion
1/2 c. chopped celery
1/4 tsp. seasoned salt
1 tsp. poultry seasoning
1/4 tsp. pepper
Egg substitute to = 2 eggs

Pour hot milk over bread crumbs and add butter granules. Stir. Set aside for 5 minutes. In a large mixing bowl, blend chicken, onion, celery, salt, poultry seasoning and pepper. Stir egg substitute into crumb mixture. Stir crumb mixture into chicken mixture. Blend. Pour into 1-quart casserole that has been sprayed with cooking spray. Bake in a 350° preheated oven 35 to 40 minutes
Yield: 4 servings

Approximate Per Serving:
Calories: 188
Fat: 3.6 g
Cholesterol: 61 mg

Carbohydrates: 10.0 g
Protein: 24.6 g
Sodium: 367 mg

Exchanges: 2 meat; 1 bread

Put honey in small plastic freezer containers and freeze to prevent sugaring. It also thaws out in a short time.

Chicken and Dressing with Mushrooms

(Recipe contains approximately 20% fat)

1 1/2 lb. boneless, skinless chicken breast	1 tsp. butter granules
6 c. water	1/2 c. chopped celery
4 chicken bouillon cubes	1/2 c. chopped onion
1 bay leaf	1 c. sliced mushrooms
4 c. chicken stock	1 tsp. sage
14 slices reduced-calorie bread, cut in cubes	1/2 tsp. seasoned salt
1/4 c. water	1/2 tsp. garlic powder
	1/4 tsp. pepper

In a saucepan, put chicken breasts and add water, bouillon and bay leaf. Bring to boil. Cover and simmer until chicken is tender, 30 to 45 minutes. Cut in bite-sized pieces and put in mixing bowl. Add remaining ingredients and blend well. Pour into a 9x13-inch baking dish sprayed with cooking spray. Cover and bake in 350° preheated oven 45 minutes. Bake, uncovered, the last 15 minutes.
Yield: 8 servings

Approximate Per Serving:

Calories: 232	Carbohydrates: 12.9 g
Fat: 5.1 g	Protein: 29.7 g
Cholesterol: 66 mg	Sodium: 341 mg

Exchanges: 3 meat; 1 bread

If a cookie recipe suggests shaping the dough into balls, try using a melon ball scoop instead of rolling the dough in your hands.

Chicken Casserole
with Pasta and Rice

(Recipe contains approximately 12% fat)

3 whole chicken breasts, cook-
    ed, bones & skin removed,
    & cut in bite-sized pieces
2 c. fresh broccoli, steamed
    2 minutes
1 (8 oz.) pkg. eggless noodles,
    cooked
2 c. soft reduced-calorie
    bread crumbs

1 c. cooked brown rice
Egg substitute to = 4 eggs
1 recipe casserole soup mix to =
    1 can cream soup, prepared
    (see index)
2 c. chicken stock
2 c. evaporated skim milk

Combine cooked chicken, broccoli, noodles, bread crumbs and cooked rice. Blend and put in a 9x13-inch baking dish, that has been sprayed with cooking spray. In a mixing bowl, blend egg substitute, casserole soup mix, stock and milk. Pour over top of chicken mixture. Cover and bake in 350° preheated oven for at least 1 hour, or until set.

Yield: 8 servings

Approximate Per Serving:
Calories: 443
Fat: 5.8 g
Cholesterol: 54 mg

Carbohydrates: 34.8 g
Protein: 37.8 g
Sodium: 463 mg

Exchanges: 3 meat; 3 bread; 1 milk

For a cookie kids will love, brush with corn syrup and sprinkle with any flavor gelatin.

Chicken-Spaghetti Casserole

(Recipe contains approximately 21% fat)

1/4 c. water
1 tsp. butter granules
3/4 lb. skinless, boneless
   chicken breast, cut in
   bite-sized pieces
1/3 c. chopped onion
1/4 c. chopped celery
1/4 c. chopped green onion
1 clove garlic, minced
1 (16 oz.) can tomatoes &
   juice, chopped
1 T. diet margarine

1/2 tsp. sodium-free
   seasoned salt
1/4 tsp. pepper
1 T. enriched all-purpose flour
2 T. skim milk
1/2 c. boiling water
1 tsp. chicken bouillon
   granules
4 oz. spaghetti, cooked
1/2 c. shredded no-fat
   Cheddar cheese

Put water and butter granules in a skillet and bring to boil. Add chicken and sauté until tender, 10 to 12 minutes. Remove from skillet with slotted spoon and set aside. Put onion, celery, green pepper and garlic in skillet and sauté (add a little water, if needed). Add tomatoes and blend. Remove from heat and set aside. In a saucepan, melt margarine with salt and pepper. Add flour, blend well and cook two minutes, stirring constantly. Add milk and blend. Dissolve bouillon in hot water and stir into saucepan. Put tomato mixture back on stove and stir in sauce. Add cooked spaghetti and chicken. Blend; pour into 1 1/2-quart casserole that has been sprayed with cooking spray. Top with cheese. Cover and bake in 350° preheated oven 20 minutes. Uncover and bake 5 minutes.
Yield: 4 servings

Approximate Per Serving:
Calories: 351
Fat: 8.2 g
Cholesterol: 69 mg

Carbohydrates: 31.0 g
Protein: 37.0 g
Sodium: 428 mg

Exchanges: 3 meat; 1 bread; 1 milk; 1 vegetable; 1/4 fat

When cutting bar cookies use a pizza cutter. Works great.

Chili a'la Mashed Potatoes

(Recipe contains approximately 9% fat)

1/4 c. water
1 tsp. butter granules
1 sm. onion, chopped
1/2 green pepper, chopped
3/4 lb. ground turkey breast
1 (16 oz.) can dark red kidney
   beans

1 (16 oz.) can tomatoes, chopped
   (include juice)
1 tsp. chili powder
1/2 tsp. cumin
1/4 tsp. pepper
2 c. mashed potatoes prepared
   with butter granules &
   skim milk

Put water and butter granules in a skillet and bring to boil. Add onion and green pepper; sauté until most of water is absorbed. Add ground turkey breast and brown. Add remaining ingredients, except potatoes, and simmer 5 minutes. Pour into baking dish and top with dollops of mashed potatoes. Bake in 350° preheated oven for 30 minutes.
Yield: 4 servings

Approximate Per Serving:
Calories: 372
Fat: 3.7 g
Cholesterol: 66 mg

Carbohydrates: 49.0 g
Protein: 39.1 g
Sodium: 646 mg

Exchanges: 3 meat; 1 1/2 bread; 2 vegetables; 1 fat

*Before wrapping a freshly frosted cake in plastic, freeze it first--
the wrapping will not stick to the frosting then.*

Chinese Chicken Rolls
with Carrots and Rice

(Recipe contains approximately 14% fat)

4 (3 oz.) boneless, skinless
   chicken breast fillets
4 (2") lengths green onion
2 cloves garlic, minced
1/2 tsp. grated fresh gingerroot
1/4 tsp. salt
1/4 tsp. pepper

1/4 c. soy sauce
1/4 c. water
1/2 c. dry sherry (can use
   chicken stock)
1/2 tsp. ground ginger
12 baby carrots
4 c. cooked brown rice

Pound chicken breasts lightly between two pieces of wax paper to flatten. On the boned side of each breast, put 2-inch length green onion, garlic, gingerroot, salt and pepper. Starting at the short end, roll up jellyroll fashion and tie with kitchen string or fasten with a toothpick. In a small bowl, combine soy sauce, dry sherry and ground ginger. Put chicken in mixture and marinate overnight in the refrigerator. Drain chicken rolls and reserve marinade. Put chicken rolls in a baking dish that has been sprayed with cooking spray. Put carrots around chicken rolls and spoon several spoonfuls marinade over chicken rolls and carrots. Bake in 350° preheated oven 45 minutes. Serve over rice.
Yield: 4 servings

Approximate Per Serving:
Calories: 324
Fat: 5.2 g
Cholesterol: 66 mg

Carbohydrates: 32.0 g
Protein: 60.0 g
Sodium: 889 mg

Exchanges: 3 meat; 1 bread; 1 vegetable

*If you have an ice bucket that you are not using store cookies in it.
They will stay fresh and crisp.*

Seafood and Fish Oven Meals

Baked Flounder with Vegetables

(Recipe contains approximately 10% fat)

6 med. red potatoes, parboiled
  to crisp-tender & quartered
18 baby carrots, parboiled to
  crisp-tender
1/4 c. boiling water
1/2 tsp. chicken bouillon
  granules

6 (3 oz.) flounder fillets
10-second spray of cooking
  spray
1/2 tsp. salt
1/8 tsp. pepper
1/2 tsp. Italian seasoning

In a 9x13-inch baking dish, sprayed a 2-second spray with cooking spray, arrange potatoes and carrots. Dissolve bouillon granules in water and pour over vegetables. Lay flounder fillets on top of vegetables and spray 8 seconds with cooking spray. Sprinkle flounder with salt, pepper and Italian seasoning. Cover with foil and bake in 350° preheated oven 20 to 25 minutes, or until fish is done and flakes easily. DO NOT OVERCOOK.
Yield: 6 servings

Approximate Per Serving:
Calories: 206
Fat: 2.4 g
Cholesterol: 60 mg

Carbohydrates: 23.4 g
Protein: 20.8 g
Sodium: 295 mg

Exchanges: 3 meat; 2 vegetable

Use a pipe cleaner to clean cake decorating tube.

Crab and Potato Casserole

(Recipe contains approximately 9% fat)

6 med., red potatoes, peeled & sliced thin	1/4 c. finely-chopped onion
1/4 tsp. pepper	2 T. chopped parsley
2 (6 oz.) cans crabmeat, sorted	1 T. finely-chopped green pepper
1 tsp. butter granules	1/2 tsp. dried mustard
1 c. fine cracker crumbs	1/3 c. milk
1/4 c. finely-chopped celery	1/2 c. skim milk

Spray a 9x13-inch casserole with cooking spray and spread sliced potatoes over bottom. Evenly sprinkle with pepper. Top with crab and sprinkle with butter granules. In a large mixing bowl, blend remaining ingredients. Pour over crab and spread evenly. Bake in 350° preheated oven 30 to 35 minutes.
Yield: 6 servings

Approximate Per Serving:
Calories: 183   **Carbohydrates: 26.7 g**
Fat: 1.9 g   **Protein: 12.9 g**
Cholesterol: 58 mg   **Sodium: 716 mg**

Exchanges: 2 meat; 1 bread

Heated maple syrup is great on frozen yogurt or fat-free ice cream.

Salmon Balls with Carrots and Potatoes

(Recipe contains approximately 20% fat)

1 (15 1/2 oz.) can salmon, skin removed & discarded; bones mashed & put with flaked salmon
1 c. soft whole wheat reduced-calorie bread crumbs
Egg substitute to = 2 eggs
1/4 c. minced onion
2 T. finely-chopped green pepper

2 T. lemon juice
1/4 tsp. pepper
1/4 tsp. seasoned salt
6 med., red potatoes, boiled in skins until tender
18 baby carrots, boiled until crisp-tender
Cooking spray
1 T. butter granules

In a mixing bowl, put salmon, bread crumbs, egg substitute, onion, green pepper, lemon, pepper and salt. Blend well. Form into 24 balls. Place salmon balls in a 9x13-inch baking dish, that has been sprayed with cooking spray. Peel potatoes and cut in half. Place around salmon balls. Put carrots around salmon balls. Spray potatoes and carrots with cooking spray and sprinkle with butter granules. Bake, uncovered, in a 350° preheated oven for 25 to 30 minutes, or until salmon balls are browned and done.
Yield: 6 servings

Approximate Per Serving:
Calories: 264
Fat: 5.8 g
Cholesterol: 26 mg

Carbohydrates: 21.2 g
Protein: 21.2 g
Sodium: 495 mg

Exchanges: 3 meat; 1 bread; 1 vegetable

Make your own ice cream sandwiches--spread softened frozen yogurt or fat-free ice cream between two graham crackers.

Salmon, Potato and Corn Scallop

(Recipe contains approximately 18% fat)

1 (16 oz.) can red salmon, skin discarded, bones mashed & stirred into flaked salmon
1 (16 oz.) can cream-style corn
1 c. evaporated skim milk
4 med. red potatoes, diced (peel, if desired)

Egg substitute to = 3 eggs
2 doz. crackers, rolled into fine crumbs
1/2 tsp. sodium-free seasoned salt
1/4 tsp. pepper

In a large mixing bowl, blend all ingredients. Pour into a 9x13-inch baking dish, that has been sprayed with cooking spray. Bake in 350° preheated oven for 1 hour.
Yield: 6 servings

Approximate Per Serving:
Calories: 356
Fat: 7.2 g
Cholesterol: 32 mg

Carbohydrates: 40.3 g
Protein: 23.5 g
Sodium: 817 mg

Exchanges: 2 1/2 meat; 2 bread; 1 milk

When a cookie recipe directs you to drop dough from spoon, drop from knife instead--works great.

Tuna Lasagna

(Recipe contains approximately 10% fat)

1/4 c. water
2 tsp. butter granules
1/3 c. chopped onion
1 c. chopped celery
1/2 c. flour
4 c. skim milk
1/4 tsp. salt
1/4 tsp. pepper
1 (8 oz.) pkg. lasagna noodles, cooked

2 (6 1/2 oz.) cans good-grade white tuna
1 c. "free" no-fat shredded Cheddar cheese
Cooking spray
1 T. tub margarine
1 c. reduced-calorie bread crumbs

Put water and 1 teaspoon butter granules in skillet and bring to boil. Add onion and celery and sauté until tender. Stir in flour and cook 2 minutes, stirring constantly. Gradually whisk in milk. Cook, stirring, until thick. DO NOT BOIL. Stir in salt and pepper and 1 teaspoon butter granules. Remove from stove. In a 9x13-inch baking dish, that has been sprayed with cooking spray, alternate layers of noodles, sauce, tuna and cheese until ingredients are used up. Put margarine in skillet and add bread crumbs. Cook until crumbs are browned. Sprinkle over casserole. Bake, covered, in 350° preheated oven for 30 to 40 minutes. Uncover and bake 5 minutes longer.

Yield: 6 servings

Approximate Per Serving:
Calories: 407
Fat: 4.3 g
Cholesterol: 43 mg

Carbohydrates: 48..9 g
Protein: 47.5 g
Sodium: 565 mg

Exchanges: 3 meat; 1 1/2 bread; 1 milk; 1 vegetable; 1/2 fat

Notes &
Recipes

Side Dishes -
Vegetables, Fruit, Pasta & Grains

Side-Dishes

So often when we think of side-dishes, we think of vegetables. This, however, is not the case. We need vegetable side dishes, but we also need fruit side-dishes. And what about pasta, rice and grains. They are certainly an important part of the diet.

When planning side-dishes, choose from the different categories. This does not mean to forget the vegetables. We need 3 to 5 servings of vegetables a day.

But we also need fruit and starch. Using the side-dish section of this book, along with the salad section, is a good way to balance out a meal.

Vegetables

Asparagus

Steamed Fresh Asparagus
(Recipe contains approximately 27% fat)

2 lb. fresh asparagus, washed	1/4 tsp. salt
1/2 c. boiling water	1/8 tsp. pepper
Cooking spray	1 tsp. butter granules

Snap off lower part of stalks at joint where they break easily. Divide the asparagus into 3 bunches and tie with white kitchen string. Put asparagus in bottom of a double boiler, standing up the bunches of asparagus. Add water to the pan. Invert top of double boiler to use as lid. Cook over medium-high heat about 12 minutes, or until asparagus is tender. Drain. Put on serving platter. Spray 4 seconds with cooking spray, then sprinkle with salt, pepper and butter granules.
Yield: 6 servings

Approximate Per Serving:
Calories: 27	Carbohydrates: 4.3 g
Fat: 0.8 g	Protein: 2.5 g
Cholesterol: 0.0 mg	Sodium: 123 mg

Exchanges: 1 vegetable

Stir-Fried Asparagus

(Recipe contains approximately 23% fat)

2 lb. fresh asparagus	1 T. "light" soy sauce
Cooking spray	1 T. water

Wash asparagus and snap off bottom. Cut diagonally into 1/2-inch pieces. Spray wok or iron skillet with cooking spray and add asparagus. Stir around for 2 to 3 minutes. Blend soy sauce and water and pour into wok or skillet. Cover with tight lid. Cook 3 to 5 minutes, or until tender. Shake pan several times to prevent burning.
Yield: 6 servings

Approximate Per Serving:
Calories: 27
Fat: 0.7 g
Cholesterol: 0.0 mg

Carbohydrates: 4.3 g
Protein: 2.8 g
Sodium: 114 mg

Exchanges: 1 vegetable

Beans

Canned Green Beans

(Recipe contains approximately 7% fat)

2 cans cut green beans	1/4 tsp. minced garlic
1/4 c. water	1/2 tsp. garlic powder
1 tsp. butter granules	1/8 tsp. pepper
2 T. finely-chopped onion	

Put water and butter granules in a saucepan and bring to boil. Add onion and garlic; sauté. DO NOT BURN. Add beans, garlic powder and pepper. Simmer 20 minutes.
Yield: 6 servings

Approximate Per Serving:
Calories: 25
Fat: 0.2 g
Cholesterol: 0.0 mg

Carbohydrates: 7.3 g
Protein: 1.8 g
Sodium: 406 mg

Exchanges: 1 vegetable

Baked Fresh Green Beans

(Recipe contains approximately 20% fat)

1 lb. fresh green beans	1/2 tsp. garlic powder
2 med. onions, peeled & diced	1/4 tsp. seasoned salt
1 lg. green pepper, seeded &	1/8 tsp. pepper
diced	1 tsp. butter granules
8-second spray of cooking spray	

Snap ends off beans, then snap beans in half. Wash well. Spray a 1 1/2-quart casserole with cooking spray. Put 1/3 of beans in bottom and top with 1/2 of onions and 1/2 green pepper. Repeat layers. Top with last 1/3 of green beans. As vegetables are layered, spray lightly with cooking spray and sprinkle with garlic powder, salt, pepper and butter granules. Bake, covered, in a 350° preheated oven for 1 hour.

Yield: 6 servings

Approximate Per Serving:

Calories: 50	**Carbohydrates: 16. 3 g**
Fat: 1.1 g	**Protein: 3.8 g**
Cholesterol: 0.0 mg	**Sodium: 100 mg**

Exchanges: 2 vegetable

When making sugar cookies use presweetened drink mix on cookies instead of sugar. Kids love them.

Green Bean Sauté

(Recipe contains approximately 3% fat)

1 can whole green beans, drained	1 green pepper, diced
1/4 c. water	1 med. onion, diced
1 tsp. butter granules	2 carrots, grated
1/2 lb. fresh mushrooms, sliced	1/4 tsp. garlic salt
	1/4 tsp. pepper

Drain green beans and set aside. Put water and butter granules in a large, heavy-bottomed skillet and bring to boil. Add mushrooms, green pepper, onion and carrots. Sauté 5 minutes. Add green beans, garlic salt and pepper. Cook 10 to 15 minutes, or until liquid is absorbed.

Yield: 8 servings

Approximate Per Serving:
Calories: 28
Fat: 0.1 g
Cholesterol: 0.0 mg

Carbohydrates: 5.2 g
Protein: 2.6 g
Sodium: 103 mg

Exchanges: 1 vegetable

Fresh Green Beans

(Recipe contains approximately 2% fat)

1 lb. fresh green beans	1/4 c. finely-chopped onion
Water, to cover	1/4 tsp. minced garlic
1/4 c. water	1/2 tsp. garlic powder
1 tsp. butter granules	1/8 tsp. pepper

Snap ends from beans, then snap in half. Wash well. In a saucepan, put 1/4 cup water and butter granules. Sauté onions until moisture has been absorbed. Add beans, garlic, garlic salt and pepper. Cover with water. Cook beans to desired degree of doneness.

Yield: 4 servings

Approximate Per Serving:
Calories: 40
Fat: 0.1 g
Cholesterol: 0.0 mg

Carbohydrates: 5.4 g
Protein: 2.1 g
Sodium: 47 mg

Exchanges: 1 1/2 vegetable

Green Beans with Tomatoes

(Recipe contains approximately 12% fat)

1/4 c. water
1 tsp. butter granules
1 T. finely-diced green
  pepper
2 T. finely-diced onion

1 (16 oz.) can cut green beans
1/4 tsp. minced garlic
1 (16 oz.) can tomatoes & juice,
  chopped
1/8 tsp. pepper

Put water and butter granules in a saucepan and bring to boil. Add green pepper, onion and garlic. Sauté. DO NOT BURN. Add green beans, tomatoes and pepper. Simmer 20 minutes.
Yield: 6 servings

Approximate Per Serving:
Calories: 30
Fat: 0.4 g
Cholesterol: 0.0 mg

Carbohydrates: 7.3 g
Protein: 1.6 g
Sodium: 338 mg

Exchanges: 1 vegetable

NOTE: To lower sodium, use low-sodium canned tomatoes.

A dash of mace gives cherry pie a great flavor.

Barbecued Beans and Corn

(Recipe contains approximately 8% fat)

1 T. water
1/4 tsp. butter granules
1 T. finely-chopped onion
1 T. finely-chopped green
  pepper
1/4 c. tomato sauce
3 T. vinegar
2 tsp. brown sugar
1 T. Worcestershire sauce

2 tsp. prepared mustard
1/2 tsp. chili powder
1/4 tsp. garlic salt
1/8 tsp. pepper
1 (16 oz.) can Great Northern
  beans, drained
1 (16 oz.) can whole kernel
  corn, drained

Put water and butter granules in skillet and bring to boil. Add onion and green pepper; sauté until tender. Add tomato sauce and blend. Add vinegar, brown sugar, Worcestershire sauce, mustard, chili powder, salt and pepper. Simmer 5 minutes. Stir in beans and corn. Cover. Reduce heat and simmer 10 minutes.
Yield: 8 servings

Approximate Per Serving:
Calories: 105
Fat: 0.9 g
Cholesterol: 0.0 mg

Carbohydrates: 22.4 g
Protein: 4.8 g
Sodium: 316 mg

Exchanges: 1 1/2 bread

To give pie crust a sheen, remove from oven when almost baked and brush top with white vinegar--put back in oven for a few minutes. You won't taste the vinegar.

Canned Great Northern Beans

(Recipe contains approximately 5% fat)

1 (16 oz.) can Great Northern
  beans
1/2 tsp. vinegar

1/2 tsp. butter granules
1/8 tsp. pepper

Pour beans into saucepan and add remaining ingredients. Simmer until heated through. Drain and serve.
Yield: 4 servings

Approximate Per Serving:
Calories: 104
Fat: 0.6 g
Cholesterol: 0.0 mg ˙

Carbohydrates: 20.8 g
Protein: 7.0 g
Sodium: 29 mg

Exchanges: 1 1/2 bread

Dried Great Northern (or Navy) Beans

(Recipe contains approximately 5% fat)

1 c. dried Great Northern
  (or navy) beans
Water to cover by 4"
1/4 tsp. seasoned salt

1/2 tsp. garlic powder
1/4 tsp. pepper
1/2 c. finely-chopped onion
2 tsp. vinegar

Wash and sort beans. Put in saucepan with remaining ingredients. Bring to boil. Reduce heat and simmer 2 to 2 1/2 hours, or until beans are tender. Drain and serve.
Yield: 4 servings

Approximate Per Serving:
Calories: 162
Fat: 0.9 g
Cholesterol: 0.0 mg

Carbohydrates: 31.9 g
Protein: 11.2 g
Sodium: 145 mg

Exchanges: 2 bread; 1 vegetable

Beets

Canned Beets

(Recipe contains approximately 3% fat)

1 can diced beets
1 tsp. butter granules

1/8 tsp. pepper

Put beets in saucepan and bring to boil. Simmer 5 minutes. Drain. Add butter granules and pepper, stirring until butter granules dissolve.
Yield: 4 servings

Approximate Per Serving:
Calories: 30
Fat: 0.1 g
Cholesterol: 0.0 mg

Carbohydrates: 6.5 g
Protein: 1.0 g
Sodium: 278 mg

Exchanges: 1 vegetable

Canned Beets in Gelatin

(Recipe contains approximately 4% fat)

1 (16 oz.) can diced beets & juice
1 (3 oz.) pkg. sugar-free lemon
   gelatin

1 c. boiling water
1 tsp. lemon juice
Dash of cinnamon

Dissolve gelatin in 1 cup boiling water. Add beets and juice. Cool to room temperature. Add lemon juice and cinnamon. Cover and refrigerate until set. Stir when partially set.
Yield: 6 servings

Approximate Per Serving:
Calories: 24
Fat: 0.1 g
Cholesterol: 0.0 mg

Carbohydrates: 4.0 g
Protein: 2.0 g
Sodium: 161 mg

Exchanges: 1 vegetable

Harvard Beets

(Recipe contains approximately 2% fat)

2 cans sliced beets, drained
12 pkt. Equal sweetener or
   sweetener of choice to =
   1/2 c. sugar

1 T. cornstarch
1/2 c. vinegar
1 tsp. butter granules

Put cornstarch and vinegar (and sugar, if using) in a saucepan and cook until clear and thickened. Remove from stove and add sweetener (if using). Add butter granules. Stir until dissolved. Add beets. Serve hot.
Yield: 8 servings

Approximate Per Serving:
Calories: 40
Fat: 0.1 g
Cholesterol: 0.0 mg

Carbohydrates: 8.0 g
Protein: 1.0 g
Sodium: 256 mg

Exchanges: 1 1/2 vegetable

For fluffier meringue add 1/4 teaspoon white vinegar before whipping.

Broccoli

Broccoli with Cheese Sauce

(Recipe contains approximately 3% fat)

2 lb. fresh broccoli
1/4 c. milk
1/2 c. no-fat shredded
   Cheddar cheese

1/4 tsp. sodium-free
   seasoned salt
1/8 tsp. pepper

Remove leaves and tough part of stalks and separate into flowerets. Put in large pan of cold water and soak 10 minutes. Drain well. Put 1-inch water in 2-quart pan. Add broccoli and cover tightly. Bring to boil. Lower heat and cook 8 to 10 minutes, or until barely tender. Put milk, cheese, salt and pepper in a saucepan and cook over medium heat, stirring constantly, until cheese melts. Remove broccoli from stove and drain well. Add cheese sauce. Blend. Put in serving dish.

Yield: 4 servings

Approximate Per Serving:
Calories: 61
Fat: 0.2 g
Cholesterol: 2.3 mg

Carbohydrates: 3.0 g
Protein: 8.5 g
Sodium: 178 mg

Exchanges: 1 vegetable; 1/2 milk

*Add a little milk to the water when cooking
cauliflower and it will remain white.*

Fresh Broccoli

(Recipe contains approximately 3% fat)

2 lb. fresh broccoli (broccoli should be green, with no yellow)	1/4 tsp. sodium-free seasoned salt 1 tsp. butter granules

Remove leaves and tough part of stalks. Separate into flowerets. Put in large pan of cold water and soak 10 minutes. Drain well. Put 1-inch water in a 2-quart pan. Add broccoli and cover tightly. Bring to boil; lower heat. Cook 8 to 10 minutes or until barely tender. Remove from pan with slotted spoon. Sprinkle with butter granules and salt.

Yield: 4 servings

Approximate Per Serving:
Calories: 27　　　　　　**Carbohydrates: 5.5 g**
Fat: 0.1 g　　　　　　　**Protein: 3.0 g**
Cholesterol: 0.0 mg　　　**Sodium: 68 mg**

Exchanges: 1 vegetable

To prevent sticking, rinse the saucepan with cold water
before putting milk in it to heat.

Brussels Sprouts

Fresh Brussels Sprouts

(Recipe contains approximately 9% fat)

1 lb. Brussels sprouts	1 tsp. butter granules
Water	

Remove any wilted leaves from Brussels sprouts. Cut off stem. Put in cold water and soak 10 minutes. Bring a pan of water to a gentle boil. Drop Brussels sprouts into water and simmer, uncovered, until tender, about 10 minutes—DO NOT OVERCOOK. Remove from pan with slotted spoon, into a serving dish. Sprinkle with butter granules, tossing until granules dissolve. If desired, sprinkle with a little lemon juice for a little tang.
Yield: 6 servings

Approximate Per Serving:
Calories: 20
Fat: 0.2 g
Cholesterol: 0.0 mg

Carbohydrates: 3.7 g
Protein: 2.3 g
Sodium: 35 mg

Exchanges: 1 vegetable

Beets require less cooking time when vinegar has been added to the cooking water. Add 1 tablespoon of vinegar to a quart of beets.

Mushrooms and Brussels Sprouts

(Recipe contains approximately 6% fat)

12 oz. sm. Brussels sprouts	1 c. sliced mushrooms
1/4 c. water	1/4 tsp. sodium-free
1 tsp. butter granules	seasoned salt
1/2 c. chopped onion	1/4 tsp. black pepper

Bring a kettle of water to boil. Cook Brussels sprouts for 15 minutes, or until almost tender. Drain and set aside. Put 1/4 cup water and butter granules in a skillet and bring to boil. Add onion and sauté 1 minute. Add mushrooms and cook 3 minutes. Stir in salt and pepper. Add sprouts and cook until tender and moisture is absorbed.

Yield: 4 servings

Approximate Per Serving:

Calories: 28	Carbohydrates: 6.5 g
Fat: 0.2 g	Protein: 3.3 g
Cholesterol: 0.0 mg	Sodium: 54 mg

Exchanges: 1 vegetable

Cook beets with their skins on to help them retain color and flavor.

Stir-Fried Brussels Sprouts

(Recipe contains approximately 28% fat)

1 lb. fresh Brussels sprouts	2 T. hot water
4-second spray of cooking spray	1 tsp. butter granules
	1 T. water
1/2 tsp. canola oil	1 T. "light" soy sauce

Remove wilted leaves and cut off tough stems. Heat a wok or iron skillet over medium heat until hot. Spray with cooking spray and add oil. Add Brussels sprouts and toss in oil to coat, 1 to 2 minutes. Dissolve butter granules in hot water and add to sprouts. Cook, uncovered, tossing often for 4 minutes. Blend 1 tablespoon water and soy and add to skillet. Cover with tight lid and cook 5 to 7 minutes, or until tender. DO NOT OVERCOOK. Shake skillet several times during cooking process to prevent burning. Put in serving dish.
Yield: 4 servings

Approximate Per Serving:
Calories: 42
Fat: 1.3 g
Cholesterol: 0.0 mg
Carbohydrates: 6.0 g
Protein: 4.0 g
Sodium: 218 mg

Exchanges: 1 vegetable; 1/4 fat

To keep food from spattering, invert a metal colander over the pan, allowing steam to escape.

Cabbage

Boiled Cabbage Wedges

(Recipe contains only a trace of fat)

1 (2 lb.) head cabbage
Water
1/4 tsp. salt

1/8 tsp. pepper
1 tsp. butter granules

Remove loose leaves from head of cabbage and cut off rough part of core. Cut head into 6 wedges. Put 1-inch water in 2-quart saucepan and bring to boil. Add cabbage wedges. Reduce heat and simmer, uncovered, until tender, but still crisp. Remove from pan with slotted spoon allowing each wedge to drain well before putting into serving dish. Sprinkle with salt, pepper and butter granules
Yield: 6 servings

Approximate Per Serving:
Calories: 31
Fat: Trace
Cholesterol: 0.0 mg

Carbohydrates: 4.3 g
Protein: 1.0 g
Sodium: 130 mg

Exchanges: 1 vegetable

Boil vinegar in a brand new frying pan to keep things from sticking to it.

Fried Cabbage

(Recipe contains approximately 8% fat)

6 c. shredded cabbage	1/4 tsp. salt
1/4 c. water	1/4 tsp. pepper
2 tsp. butter granules	

Put water and butter granules in large skillet and bring to boil. Add cabbage and toss. Add salt and pepper and simmer, stirring often, until cabbage is tender. DO NOT OVERCOOK.
Yield: 6 servings

Approximate Per Serving:

Calories: 33	Carbohydrates: 7.7 g
Fat: 0.3 g	Protein: 1.0 g
Cholesterol: 0.0 mg	Sodium: 178 mg

Exchanges: 1 vegetable

German Red Cabbage and Apples

(Recipe contains approximately 11% fat)

4 c. shredded cabbage	1 T. water
1/2 tsp. salt	1 tsp. butter granules
1/8 tsp. pepper	1 sm. onion, chopped
2 tsp. sugar	2 apples, peeled & sliced
1/2 c. vinegar	3/4 c. hot water

Put cabbage in bowl. Add salt, pepper, sugar and vinegar. Weight down with plate. Refrigerate and allow to stand overnight. Put 1 tablespoon water and butter granules in a large skillet and bring to boil. Sauté onions. Add cabbage and apples. Cook 5 minutes. Add hot water and steam, covered, until tender.
Yield: 8 servings

Approximate Per Serving:

Calories 40	Carbohydrates: 10.1 g
Fat: 0.5 g	Protein: 0.8 g
Cholesterol: 0.0 mg	Sodium: 231 mg

Exchanges: 1 vegetable; 1/2 fruit

Sweet and Sour Red Cabbage

(Recipe contains approximately 5% fat)

1/4 c. water
1 tsp. butter granules
8 c. shredded red cabbage
4 cloves garlic, minced
Cooking spray
3/4 c. cider vinegar
3 T. "light" soy sauce

1 c. raisins
3 T. honey
1 tsp. ground ginger
1/2 tsp. white pepper
4 tsp. cornstarch
2 T. cold water

In a heavy-bottomed skillet, put water and butter granules and bring to boil. Add cabbage and garlic and sauté, stirring often until cabbage is coated. As you stir cabbage, spray with cooking spray (three 3-second sprays). To skillet, add vinegar, soy, raisins, honey, ginger and pepper. Cook over medium heat, stirring, for 10 minutes or until cabbage is tender. Blend cornstarch and cold water. Stir into cabbage mixture, tossing to coat, and cooking until liquid is slightly thickened. Serve immediately.

Yield: 8 servings

Approximate Per Serving:
Calories: 105
Fat: 0.6 g
Cholesterol: 0.0 mg

Carbohydrates: 21.5 g
Protein: 4.6 g
Sodium: 263 mg

Exchanges: 2 vegetable; 1 1/2 fruit

*Put frozen bread loaves in a clean brown paper bag and place for
5 minutes in a 325° oven to thaw completely.*

Carrots

Baked Carrot Sticks
(Recipe contains approximately 16% fat)

1 (1 lb.) pkg. carrots, cleaned
   & cut into 3" strips
Cooking spray
1/4 c. boiling water

2 tsp. sugar
2 tsp. butter granules
1 tsp. parsley flakes

Spray a 9x9-inch baking dish with cooking spray. Put carrots sticks in dish and sprinkle with sugar, butter granules and parsley flakes. Cover and bake in 400° preheated oven for 45 minutes.
Yield: 6 servings

Approximate Per Serving:
Calories: 29
Fat: 0.5 g
Cholesterol: 0.0 mg

Carbohydrates: 2.5 g
Protein: 3.1 mg
Sodium: 247 mg

Exchanges: 1 vegetable

To quickly crack open a large amount of nuts, put them in a bag and genlty hammer until they are cracked open. Then remove nutmeats with a pick.

Buttered Carrots

(Recipe contains approximately 2% fat)

2 c. diced carrots
1/2 c. canned beef stock
1/4 tsp. sodium-free
   seasoned salt

1/8 tsp. pepper
1 tsp. butter granules

Put stock in 2-quart saucepan and bring to boil. Add carrots, cover and simmer until tender, about 20 to 30 minutes. Remove from heat and drain. Add salt, pepper and butter granules, tossing until granules are dissolved. Put in serving dish.
Yield: 4 servings

Approximate Per Serving:
Calories: 45
Fat: 0.1 g
Cholesterol: 0.0 mg

Carbohydrates: 1.8 g
Protein: 6.6 g
Sodium: 162 mg

Exchanges: 2 vegetable

Cauliflower

Fresh Cauliflower

(Recipe contains only a trace of fat)

1 (2 lb.) head cauliflower
Water
1/4 tsp. salt

1/8 tsp. pepper
1 tsp. butter granules

Trim leaves and core from head and break into flowerets. Put 1/4-inch water in a 2-quart saucepan. Add cauliflower. Bring to boil, cover and reduce heat; simmer 8 to 10 minutes or until crisp-tender. Drain. Add salt, pepper and butter granules. Toss to blend. Put in serving dish.
Yield: 4 servings

Approximate Per Serving:
Calories: 26
Fat: Trace
Cholesterol: 0.0 mg

Carbohydrates: 6.5 g
Protein: 1.5 g
Sodium: 191 mg

Exchanges: 1 vegetable

Cauliflower Head with Cheese

(Recipe contains approximately 7% fat)

1 (3 lb.) head cauliflower
Water
1/4 tsp. salt

1 tsp. butter granules
1/2 c. no-fat shredded
   Cheddar cheese

Trim off leaves and round part of core. Put in pan of cold water and soak 10 minutes. Drain well. Put 1-inch water in 2-quart saucepan and bring to boil. Put cauliflower head in pan, head-side-up; partially cover, reduce heat and simmer about 12 minutes. Stalk should be barely done. Drain very well. Put on serving plate. Sprinkle with salt, butter granules and cheese. Serve immediately. **Yield: 6 servings**

Approximate Per Serving:
Calories: 39
Fat: 0.3 g
Cholesterol: 1.5 mg

Carbohydrates: 6.3 g
Protein: 4.3 g
Sodium: 224 mg

Exchanges: 1 vegetable; 1/4 milk

If nuts are stale, place them in the oven at 250°F and leave them there for 5 or 10 minutes. The heat will revive them.

Celery

Celery in Lemony Mustard Sauce

(Recipe contains approximately 4% fat)

3 c. celery, sliced diagonally	1 T. lemon juice
1 c. thin-sliced carrots	1 T. Dijon mustard
1 can water chestnuts, sliced	1/4 tsp. garlic powder
3 T. "free" no-fat mayonnaise	1/4 tsp. pepper

Cook celery and carrots in small amount of water until tender (8 to 10 minutes). Drain. Return vegetables to saucepan. Add water chestnuts. Blend remaining ingredients. Pour sauce over vegetables and heat through.
Yield: 6 servings

Approximate Per Serving:
Calories: 42
Fat: 0.2 g
Cholesterol: 0.0 mg

Carbohydrates: 5.5 g
Protein: 2.8 g
Sodium: 152 mg

Exchanges: 1 1/2 vegetable

Rinse the pan with cold water before scalding milk and it will be much easier to clean.

Corn

Canned Corn

(Recipe contains approximately 5% fat)

1 can whole kernel corn   1/8 tsp. pepper
1 tsp. butter granules

Put all ingredients in saucepan and heat until heated through.
Yield: 4 servings

Approximate Per Serving:
Calories 85   Carbohydrates: 23.5 g
Fat: 0.5 g   Protein: 2.5 g
Cholesterol: 0.0 mg   Sodium: 410 mg

Exchanges: 1 1/4 bread

Corn on the Cob

(Recipe contains approximately 9% fat)

6 med. ears of corn, shucked   1 T. hot water
     & cleaned   1 tsp. butter granules
Boiling water to cover

Bring pot of water to boil. Put corn in boiling water. Bring to boil
and boil corn 3 to 4 minutes, depending on maturity of corn.
Remove from water with slotted spoon. Blend 1 tablespoon water
and butter granules. Brush ears with mixture and put on serving
plate.
Yield: 6 servings

Approximate Per Serving:
Calories: 96   Carbohydrates: 19.3 g
Fat: 1.0 g   Protein: 3.0 g
Cholesterol: 0.0 mg   Sodium: 43 mg

Exchanges: 1 1/2 bread

Fresh Corn Off the Cob

(Recipe contains approximately 10% fat)

6 med. ears of corn (1 3/4"x5"), shucked & cleaned	1 tsp. butter granules
2 T. water	1/4 tsp. salt
	1/8 tsp. pepper

Cut corn from cob and put in small saucepan. Add remaining ingredients and bring to boil. Reduce heat and simmer 3 to 5 minutes, or until most of liquid is absorbed.
Yield: 6 servings

Approximate Per Serving:
Calories: 86   **Carbohydrates: 19.3 g**
Fat: 1.0 g   **Protein: 3.0 g**
Cholesterol: 0.0 mg   **Sodium: 132 mg**

Exchanges: 1 1/4 bread

Scalloped Corn

(Recipe contains approximately 9% fat)

2 c. fresh or frozen corn	1 tsp. butter granules
Egg substitute to = 2 eggs	3/4 c. evaporated skim milk
1/8 tsp. pepper	Cooking spray

Put all ingredients in a mixing bowl and blend. Pour into small baking dish, that has been sprayed with cooking spray. Bake in 325° preheated oven for 30 minutes.
Yield: 4 servings

Approximate Per Serving:
Calories: 154   **Carbohydrates: 29.2 g**
Fat: 1.5 g   **Protein: 7.6 g**
Cholesterol: 1.7 mg   **Sodium: 458 mg**

Exchanges: 1 1/2 bread; 1/2 milk

Cucumbers

Pickled Cucumbers and Onions

(Recipe contains approximately 8% fat)

2 med.-sized cucumbers,
washed & sliced
1 med. onion, sliced thin &
separated into rings

Water, to cover
1/4 c. "light" soy sauce
2 T. vinegar

Put cucumbers and onions in bowl and add water just to cover. Add soy and vinegar. Put in refrigerator and allow to stand several hours. **Yield: 4 servings**

Approximate Per Serving:
Calories: 44
Fat: 0.4 g
Cholesterol: 0.0 mg

Carbohydrates: 10.0 g
Protein: 3.4 g
Sodium: 673 mg

Exchanges: 2 vegetable

Sautéed Cucumbers

(Recipe contains approximately 8% fat)

1/4 c. water
1/2 tsp. butter granules
2 c. peeled & diced
cucumbers

1/2 tsp. salt
1/4 tsp. pepper
1 green onion, chopped
(use green, also)

Put water and butter granules in a skillet and bring to boil. Add cucumbers, salt and pepper. Sauté until moisture is absorbed. Put in serving dish and sprinkle with chopped onion. **Yield: 4 servings**

Approximate Per Serving:
Calories: 22
Fat: 0.2 g
Cholesterol: 0.0 mg

Carbohydrates: 5.2 g
Protein: 0.9 g
Sodium: 298 mg

Exchanges: 1 vegetable

Eggplant

Eggplant Parmesan
(Recipe contains approximately 12% fat)

1 lg. eggplant	2 c. Italian tomato sauce
Egg substitute to = 2 eggs	1/2 c. "free" no-fat shredded
1 c. cracker crumbs	mozzarella cheese
Cooking spray	1 T. grated Parmesan cheese

Slice unpeeled eggplant crosswise. Dip slices into egg substitute, then dredge in crumbs. Spray skillet with cooking spray and brown eggplant on both sides. Put 1/3 of sauce in 9x9-inch baking dish and top with half of eggplant slices. Top with 1/3 of sauce, half of mozzarella cheese. Repeat layers and top with Parmesan cheese. Bake in 350° preheated oven 30 minutes.
Yield: 8 servings

Approximate Per Serving:

Calories: 68	Carbohydrates: 10.3 g
Fat: 0.9 g	Protein: 4.8 g
Cholesterol: 1.6 mg	Sodium: 349 mg

Exchanges: 1 vegetable; 1/2 bread

*A wedge of lemon cooked with onion or cabbage
will absorb the cooking odors.*

Louisiana Eggplant

(Recipe contains approximately 23% fat)

1 lg. eggplant
1/4 tsp. marjoram
4 green onions, finely
   chopped, include tops
1 (16 oz.) can tomatoes,
   chopped
1/4 tsp. pepper

1 can condensed tomato soup,
   undiluted
1 T. minced parsley
1 c. seasoned bread crumbs
   (see index)
1 tsp. butter granules

Peel eggplant and cut into 1/2-inch slices. Sprinkle with salt; stack, cover and let stand 20 minutes. Wipe salt from slices and cook in a little water for 5 minutes. Drain eggplant and put in shallow 2-quart baking dish, that has been sprayed with cooking spray. In a saucepan, put marjoram, green onion, tomatoes, pepper, soup and parsley. Blend. Pour over eggplant. Top with bread crumbs and sprinkle butter granules over top. Bake in 350° preheated oven 15 minutes.

Yield: 6 servings

Approximate Per Serving:
Calories: 91
Fat: 2.3 g
Cholesterol: 0.0 mg

Carbohydrates: 18.0 g
Protein: 2.8 g
Sodium: 572 mg

Exchanges: 2 vegetable, 1/4 milk, 1/2 fat

When peeling an onion, cut the bottom off first so the juice will go down and not bother the eyes; or, refrigerate them before chopping.

Mushrooms

Sautéed Mushrooms
(Recipe contains approximately 8% fat)

1/4 c. water
1 tsp. butter granules
1/2 tsp. lemon juice

1 lb. firm, white mushrooms,
   thinly sliced
1/4 tsp. salt
1/4 tsp. pepper

Put water and butter granules in a skillet. Add lemon juice. Bring to boil. Add mushrooms and toss to coat. Add salt and pepper and cook over medium-high heat until done, and moisture is absorbed. **Yield: 4 servings**

Approximate Per Serving:
Calories: 32
Fat: 0.3 g
Cholesterol: 0.0 mg

Carbohydrates: 2.0 g
Protein: 0.5 g
Sodium: 180 mg

Exchanges: 1 vegetable

*To prevent boiled potatoes from turning black,
add a small amount of cream of tartar.*

Stir-Fried Mushrooms

(Recipe contains approximately 23% fat)

1 lb. fresh mushrooms,
  cleaned & sliced
Cooking spray
2 T. hot water
1 tsp. butter granules

1/8 tsp. salt
1/8 tsp. pepper
1 T. "light" soy sauce
1 T. water

Spray skillet with cooking spray. Add mushrooms and spray mushrooms. Blend water and butter granules and add to skillet. Add salt and pepper. Cook, uncovered, over high heat, until liquid is absorbed. Blend soy sauce and water; add to skillet. Cover and cook 2 to 3 minutes.
Yield: 4 servings

Approximate Per Serving:
Calories: 43
Fat: 1.1 g
Cholesterol: 0.0 mg

Carbohydrates: 2.5 g
Protein: 1.0 g
Sodium: 278 mg

Exchanges: 1 1/2 vegetable

Keep a container labeled "For Soup" in the freezer. Each time there is just a small amount of vegetable leftover from a meal, add it to the "soup" container. Later, add to a pot of soup without wasting vegetables.

Onions

Caramel Onions

(Recipe contains approximately 2% fat)

3 lg. onions, sliced thin &
    separated into rings
1/4 c. water
1 tsp. butter granules

1/4 tsp. salt
Artificial brown sugar sweet-
    ener to = 2 T. brown sugar
2 T. vinegar

Prepare onions and set aside. Heat skillet and add water and butter granules. Bring to boil. Add onions and salt. Toss to coat. Cook until tender, about 10 minutes, stirring often. Blend sweetener (or sugar) and vinegar. Pour over onions and cook 3 to 5 minutes, or until caramelized.
Yield: 6 servings

Approximate Per Serving:
Calories: 44
Fat: 0.1 g
Cholesterol: 0.0 mg

Carbohydrates: 32.1 g
Protein: 1.3 g
Sodium: 138 mg

Exchanges: 2 vegetable

Use rice instead of potatoes for vegetable stew that you plan to freeze. Use 1/4 to 1/ 2 cup of rice, depending upon the amount of liquid that you have.

Cheesy Onions

Recipe contains approximately 6% fat)

3 lg. onions, sliced thin &
   separated into rings
2-second spray of cooking
   spray

1/4 c. water
1 tsp. butter granules
1/4 tsp. salt
1 T. cheese granules

Spray skillet with cooking spray. Put water and butter granules in skillet and bring to boil. Add onions and toss. Stir in salt and cook until onions are tender, and most of liquid has been absorbed. Remove from stove and stir in cheese granules.
Yield: 6 servings

Approximate Per Serving:
Calories: 43
Fat: 0.3 g
Cholesterol: 0.0 mg

Carbohydrates: 9.3 g
Protein: 1.3 g
Sodium: 220 mg

Exchanges: 2 vegetable

Sautéed Onions

(Recipe contains approximately 3% fat)

2 lg. onions, peeled, sliced thin
   & separated into rings
1/4 c. water

1 tsp. butter granules
1/4 tsp. salt
1/8 tsp. pepper

Prepare onions and set aside. Put water and butter granules in skillet and bring to boil. Add onions. Sprinkle with salt and pepper; sauté until tender, stirring often.
Yield: 4 servings

Approximate Per Serving:
Calories: 30
Fat: 0.1 g
Cholesterol: 0.0 mg

Carbohydrates: 6.5 g
Protein: 1.0 g
Sodium: 187 mg

Exchanges: 1 vegetable

Peas

Canned Peas

(Recipe contains approximately (5% fat)

1 can quality peas
1 tsp. butter granules
1/4 tsp. seasoned salt

1/4 tsp. garlic powder
1/8 tsp. pepper

Put all ingredients in a saucepan and stir. Heat over medium heat to boiling point. DO NOT BOIL. Drain and serve hot.
Yield: 4 servings

Approximate Per Serving:
Calories: 77
Fat: 0.4 g
Cholesterol: 0.0 mg

Carbohydrates: 11.0 g
Protein: 4.0 g
Sodium: 325 mg

Exchanges: 1 bread

Fresh Green Peas

(Recipe contains approximately 5% fat)

2 c. hulled peas, about 1 1/4 to
   1 1/2 lb.)
1/2 c. canned beef stock
1/4 tsp. lemon juice (helps
   hold color)

Pinch of sugar
1/8 tsp. pepper
1 tsp. butter granules

Put stock, lemon juice and peas in pan and stir. Add sugar and pepper; cover and simmer 7 to 10 minutes, or until peas are tender. DO NOT OVERCOOK. Drain, and add butter granules; tossing until dissolved. Serve hot.
Yield: 4 servings

Approximate Per Serving:
Calories: 69
Fat: 0.4 g
Cholesterol: 0.0 mg

Carbohydrates: 10.8 g
Protein: 4.6 g
Sodium: 110 mg

Exchanges: 1 bread

Peas in Cheese Sauce

(Recipe contains approximately 3% fat)

2 c. frozen peas, cooked per   2 T. skim milk
    pkg. directions & drained   1/8 tsp. pepper
1/2 c. no-fat Cheddar cheese

Put cheese and milk in saucepan and heat over low heat until melted, stirring constantly. Add pepper. Pour over cooked peas and blend.

Yield: 4 servings

Approximate Per Serving:
Calories: 89   **Carbohydrates: 11.9 g**
Fat: 0.3 g   **Protein: 8.8 g**
Cholesterol: 2.4 mg   **Sodium: 291 mg**

Exchanges: 1 bread; 1/4 milk

When cooking cabbage, place a small tin cup or can half full of vinegar on the stove near the cabbage, and it will absorb all odor from it.

Potatoes

Baked New Potato Rosettes

(Recipe contains approximately 20% fat)

16 sm., new potatoes
Cooking spray
1 T. tub margarine

4 T. "free" no-fat
   Philadelphia cream cheese
2 tsp. sour cream granules
1 T. chopped parsley

Scrub skins of new potatoes. Spray with cooking oil. Put in shallow baking dish and bake in 400° preheated oven for 20 to 30 minutes, or until tender. With a sharp knife, cut an X into each potato. Squeeze potato, gently, until potato looks like a rosette. Blend margarine and cream cheese and put 1/4 teaspoon of mixture on top of each potato. Sprinkle with sour cream granules and parsley.

Yield: 4 servings

Approximate Per Serving:
Calories 123
Fat: 2.7 g
Cholesterol: 3.0 mg

Carbohydrates: 18.9 g
Protein: 4.0 g
Sodium: 189

Exchanges: 1 1/2 bread; 1/2 fat

Potatoes soaked in salt water for 20 minutes before baking will bake more rapidly.

Baked Potatoes O'Brien

(Recipe contains approximately 3% fat)

6 med., boiled potatoes,
   peeled & diced
1 green pepper, seeded
   & diced
1 med. onion, diced
1 T. flour

1/2 tsp. salt
1/4 tsp. pepper
Cooking spray
1 c. hot skim milk
1/2 c. no-fat shredded
   Cheddar cheese

In a mixing bowl, blend potatoes, green pepper, onion, flour, salt and pepper. Pour into baking dish, sprayed with cooking spray. Pour hot milk over potato mixture. Sprinkle cheese over top. Cover and bake in 350° preheated oven for 30 minutes.
Yield: 6 servings

Approximate Per Serving:
Calories: 122
Fat: 0.4 g
Cholesterol: 2.2 mg

Carbohydrates: 23.4 g
Protein: 7.1 g
Sodium: 215 mg

Exchanges: 1 bread; 1 vegetable; 1/4 milk

Fresh tomatoes keep longer if stored in the refrigerator with stems down.

Browned Canned Potatoes

(Recipe contains approximately 14% fat)

2 cans canned potatoes,
    drained & halved
12-second spray of cooking
    spray

1/4 tsp. salt
1/8 tsp. pepper

Prepare potatoes. Heat skillet and spray a 4-second spray with cooking spray. Add potatoes. Spray potatoes a 4-second spray. Cover with tight lid and cook over medium heat, stirring often, for 5 minutes. Spray a second 4-second spray. Cover and cook until potatoes reach desired degree of brownness.
Yield: 4 servings

Approximate Per Serving:
Calories: 88
Fat: 1.4 g
Cholesterol: 0.0 mg

Carbohydrates: 16.9 g
Protein: 2.2 g
Sodium: 136 mg

Exchanges: 1 1/4 bread

Overcooked potatoes can become soggy when the milk is added.
Sprinkle with dry powdered milk for the fluffiest mashed potatoes ever.

Buttery Potato Cakes

(Recipe contains approximately 18% fat)

2 c. coarsely-grated, boiled
   & peeled potatoes
Egg substitute to = 1 egg
1/2 tsp. salt

1/4 tsp. pepper
2- to 6-second spray of
   cooking spray
1 tsp. butter granules

In a mixing bowl, blend potatoes, egg substitute, salt and pepper. Spray an 8-inch heavy-bottomed skillet with cooking spray. Sprinkle with 1/2 teaspoon butter granules and add half of potato mixture, spreading it into a flat cake. Cook over medium heat for about 3 minutes, or until nicely browned. Spray top (a 3-second spray) and turn. Brown second side. Put on plate and keep warm. Cook second potato cake in same manner.

Yield: 4 servings

Approximate Per Serving:
Calories: 86
Fat: 1.7 g
Cholesterol: 0.0 mg

Carbohydrates: 13.5 g
Protein: 2.4 g
Sodium: 194 mg

Exchanges: 1 bread; 1/4 fat

To hurry up baked potatoes, boil in salted water for 10 minutes, then place in a very hot oven. Or, cut potatoes in half and place them face down on a baking sheet in the oven to make the baking time shorter.

Cheesy Scalloped Potatoes Au Gratin

(Recipe contains approximately 3% fat)

8 med., red potatoes, scrubbed & sliced thin (peel, if desired)
1/2 c. finely-minced onion
Cooking spray to = 6 seconds

1 c. "free" no-fat shredded Cheddar cheese
1/4 tsp. salt
1/4 tsp. pepper
1 can evaporated skim milk

Spray a shallow baking dish with cooking spray and put a layer of sliced potatoes in bottom. Spray 2 seconds with cooking spray; sprinkle with salt and pepper and part of onion and cheese. Repeat layers until ingredients are used up. Pour milk into corner and bake in a 350° preheated oven for 1 1/2 to 2 hours, or until potatoes are done, and most of milk is absorbed.

Yield: 8 servings

Approximate Per Serving:
Calories: 143
Fat: 0.4 g
Cholesterol: 1.7 mg

Carbohydrates: 24.8 g
Protein: 6.7 g
Sodium: 236 mg

Exchanges: 1 1/2 bread; 1/2 milk

Save some of the water in which the potatoes were boiled - add to some powdered milk and use when mashing. This restores some of the nutrients that were lost in the cooking process.

Great Low-Fat
Mashed Potatoes

(Recipe contains approximately 1% fat)

6 med., red potatoes
2 tsp. butter granules
1/4 tsp. baking powder
1/4 tsp. garlic powder

1/2 tsp. salt
1/8 tsp. white pepper
1/2 c. (more if needed) warm
  skim milk

Peel, dice and boil potatoes until tender. Drain well. Return potatoes to stove, covered, and allow to dry out for 1 to 2 minutes. Shake pan a couple of times to prevent burning. Put potatoes through a coarse sieve or ricer. Return potatoes to pan and cook potatoes over low heat, stirring with a wooden spoon, until they are very smooth. Add butter granules, baking powder, garlic powder, salt and pepper. Stir in milk, just a little at a time, until creamy and fluffy.

Yield: 6 servings

Approximate Per Serving:
Calories: 86
Fat: 0.1 g
Cholesterol: 0.3 mg

Carbohydrates: 18.1 g
Protein: 2.7 g
Sodium: 257 mg

Exchanges: 1 bread; 1/4 milk

If fresh vegetables are wilted or blemished, pick off the brown edges. Sprinkle with cool water, wrap in towel and refrigerate for an hour or so.

Herbed Potatoes

(Recipe contains approximately 6% fat)

6 c. diced potatoes, parboiled
    for 5 minutes
8-second spray of cooking
    spray
1 onion, diced
1 c. celery, minced

1/2 c. parsley flakes
1/2 tsp. salt
1/4 tsp. pepper
1 tsp. butter granules
1 tsp. poultry seasoning

Put drained potatoes in a shallow baking dish, that has been sprayed with cooking spray. Spray potatoes with cooking spray, tossing lightly as potatoes are sprayed. Blend remaining ingredients and sprinkle over potatoes. Bake in 375° preheated oven for 30 to 35 minutes, or until potatoes are brown and tender.

Yield: 8 servings

Approximate Per Serving:
Calories: 76
Fat: 0.5 g
Cholesterol: 0.0 mg

Carbohydrates: 14.2 g
Protein: 5.9 g
Sodium: 166 mg

Exchanges: 1 bread

---

*Perk up soggy lettuce by adding lemon juice to a bowl of cold
water and soak for an hour in the refrigerator.*

Low-Fat American Fries

(Recipe contains approximately 13% fat)

4 med. potatoes, sliced 1/8"
  thick
12-second spray of cooking
  spray

1/4 tsp. salt
1/8 tsp. pepper

Slice potatoes, peeling if desired. Spray baking sheet with a 6-second spray of cooking spray. Spread potato slices out on baking sheet in a single layer. Spray potatoes with a 6-second spray and sprinkle with salt and pepper. Bake in 400° preheated oven for 30 to 40 minutes, or to desired degree of brownness.

Yield: 4 servings

Approximate Per Serving:
Calories: 91
Fat: 1.3 g
Cholesterol: 0.0 mg

Carbohydrates: 16.4 g
Protein: 2.0 g
Sodium: 141 mg

Exchanges: 1 1/4 bread

Low-Fat French Fries

(Recipe contains approximately 11% fat)

4 lg. baking potatoes
12-second spray of cooking
  spray

1/4 tsp. pepper
1/2 tsp. salt

Peel potatoes (if desired) and slice potatoes lengthwise and then into French fries (or cut with French-fry cutter). Line a baking sheet with foil and spray 4 seconds with cooking spray. Spread fries out onto baking sheet in single layer and spray with cooking spray for 8 seconds. Sprinkle with salt and pepper. Bake in 400° preheated oven for 30 to 40 minutes, or until done, and the desired degree of brownness.

Yield: 6 servings

Approximate Per Serving:
Calories: 84
Fat: 1.0 g
Cholesterol: 0.0 mg

Carbohydrates: 10.9 g
Protein: 1.3 g
Sodium: 181 mg

Exchanges: 1 1/4 bread

Low-Fat Fried Potatoes

(Recipe contains approximately 4% fat)

4 med. potatoes, sliced thin   1/8 tsp. salt
Cooking spray (total 12 seconds) 1/8 tsp. pepper

Heat skillet over medium heat until hot. Spray with cooking spray (3 seconds). Put layer of potatoes in skillet and sprinkle with pepper and half of salt. Spray potatoes lightly with cooking spray. Add remaining potatoes and spray with cooking spray; sprinkle with salt. Cover with tight lid and cook over medium heat, turning often. Halfway through, spray potatoes lightly. Cook until tender and browned.
Yield: 4 servings

Approximate Per Serving:
Calories: 88   **Carbohydrates: 16.4 g**
Fat: 0.4 g   **Protein: 2.0 g**
Cholesterol: 0.0 mg   **Sodium: 72 mg**

Exchanges: 1 1/4 bread

Note: Use however many potatoes are needed, adding a 3-second spray for each potato added.

---

*Lettuce and celery will crisp up fast if you place it in a pan of
cold water and add a few sliced potatoes.*

Low-Fat Western Fries

(Recipe contains approximately 1% fat)

6 med. baking potatoes (be sure
   skins are new & edible)
2 T. barbecue sauce
1 tsp. A-1 steak sauce

1 tsp. sodium-free seasoning
   salt
Pepper, to taste
Cooking spray

Boil potatoes in skins until crisp-tender. Remove from water and cool. Refrigerate for at least 2 hours. Cut potatoes into 4 to 6 wedges, depending on size desired. Put aluminum foil on baking sheet and spray with cooking spray. Place potato wedges on cookie sheet, skin-side down, and brush with mixture of barbecue sauce and A-1 sauce. Sprinkle with seasoned salt and pepper. Bake in 400° preheated oven for 25 to 30 minutes, or until potatoes are nicely browned. Turn once during cooking.

Yield: 6 servings

Approximate Per Serving:
Calories: 82
Fat: 0.1 g
Cholesterol: 0.0 mg

Carbohydrates: 18.0 g
Protein: 2.0 g
Sodium: 62 mg

Exchanges: 1 1/4 bread

If vegetables are overdone, put the pot in a pan of cold water.
Let it stand from 15 minutes to 1/2 hour without scraping pan.

Microwave Potatoes and Carrots

(Recipe contains approximately 2% fat)

4 med. potatoes, cut in 4 slices each	1/2 tsp. beef bouillon granules
2 lg. carrots, cut in 1/2" slices	1/8 tsp. pepper
1/4 c. boiling water	1/8 tsp. salt

Prepare potatoes and carrots and arrange on large plate. Dissolve bouillon in hot water. Spoon over vegetables. Sprinkle with pepper and salt. Cover with plastic wrap and cook in microwave on FULL POWER 8 to 10 minutes, or until tender.
Yield: 4 servings

Approximate Per Serving:
Calories: 94
Fat: 0.2 g
Cholesterol: 0.0 mg

Carbohydrates: 16.9 g
Protein: 5.1 g
Sodium: 141 mg

Exchanges: 1 bread; 1 vegetable

By lining the crisper section of your refrigerator with newspaper and wrapping vegetables with it, moisture will be absorbed and your vegetables will stay fresher longer.

Potato-Cabbage Casserole

(Recipe contains approximately 2% fat)

5 red potatoes, peeled & diced
3/4 c. warm skim milk
3 1/2 tsp. butter granules
4 c. shredded cabbage

2 T. water
1/3 c. finely-chopped onion
6 slices "free" no-fat American
   cheese

In a saucepan, cover diced potatoes with water and boil 20 minutes, or until tender. Drain potatoes, then return to stove, covered, and cook over low heat several minutes to dry out potatoes. Shake several times to prevent burning. Add 3 teaspoons butter granules and warm milk to potatoes and blend well. In a saucepan of boiling water, boil cabbage for 5 minutes. Drain very well and stir into potatoes. Put 2 tablespoons water and 1/2 teaspoon butter granules in a skillet and bring to boil. Add onion and sauté 3 to 4 minutes. Add to potato mixture. Season with salt and pepper. Pour into shallow baking dish. Lay cheese slices over top. Put under broiler 2 to 3 minutes, or until cheese melts.
Yield: 6 servings

Approximate Per Serving:
Calories: 137
Fat: 0.3 g
Cholesterol: 5.5 mg

Carbohydrates: 23.7 g
Protein: 18.4 g
Sodium: 563 mg

Exchanges: 1 bread; 1/2 milk; 1 vegetable

Store leftover corn, peas, green beans, carrots, celery, potatoes and onions in a container in the freezer. Add to other ingredients when making stew.

Potato Casserole

(Recipe contains approximately 12% fat)

10 med., red potatoes, peeled
   & diced
1 sm. onion, chopped
2 med. carrots, sliced thin
1 (8 oz.) ctn. "free"
   Philadelphia cream cheese

1 c. buttermilk
1/2 tsp. garlic salt
1/2 (8 oz.) ctn. "light"
   sour cream

Boil potatoes, onion and carrots in water until tender. Drain. Return to stove, covered, and over low heat, cook 5 minutes to allow to dry out. Shake often to prevent burning. Remove from stove and mash; add remaining ingredients and blend well. Pour into baking dish, that has been sprayed with cooking spray, and bake in 350° oven for 30 minutes. These will keep in the refrigerator for up to two weeks. If refrigerated, bake 45 minutes.
Yield: 10 servings

Approximate Per Serving:
Calories: 143
Fat: 1.9 g
Cholesterol: 12.9 mg

Carbohydrates: 20.6 g
Protein: 7.8 g
Sodium: 234 mg

Exchanges: 1 bread; 1 milk

Onions, broccoli and Brussels sprouts will cook faster if you make an X-shaped cut at the base of the vegetables.

Refrigerator Potatoes

(Recipe contains approximately 15% fat)

5 lb. red potatoes, peeled &
diced
1 (8 oz.) pkg. "free" no-fat
Philadelphia cream cheese
1 c. "light" sour cream
2 tsp. onion salt
1 tsp. white pepper
1 T. butter granules

Boil potatoes until tender, 20 to 25 minutes. Drain. Return to stove, covered, and cook over low heat for 3 to 4 minutes to dry out. Shake pan several times to prevent burning. Add remaining ingredients and beat until smooth and creamy. If needed, add just a little skim milk. Cool to room temperature. Put in covered storage container and refrigerate. Use as needed. Will keep in refrigerator for 2 weeks.

To Use: Put amount of potatoes needed in a baking dish that has been sprayed with cooking spray. Lightly spray top of potatoes with cooking spray. Bake, covered, in a 350° preheated oven for 30 to 45 minutes. If preferred, can be heated through in microwave.
Yield: 20 servings

Approximate Per Serving:
Calories: 105
Fat: 1.7 g
Cholesterol: 10.0 mg
Carbohydrates: 16.6 mg
Protein: 3.8 g
Sodium: 320 mg

Exchanges: 1 bread; 1/2 milk

*A ball of nylon net cleans and smooths
cucumbers when making pickles.*

Potatoes From a Box

We all like quick convenience food on busy days. You can use boxed potatoes if you cut the fat. Just keep in mind that the ones containing cheese are higher in saturated fat than the others. If you want to cut more fat here, add 1 tablespoon of cheese granules to one of the non-cheese mixes.

General Instructions

When preparing any of the box potatoes use only 1 tablespoon of tub margarine (not to exceed 6 grams of fat per tablespoon) plus 1 teaspoon of butter granules. When less margarine is used, it is sometimes necessary to stir or watch the preparation of the product more closely. Use skim milk and if recipe calls for an egg, use egg substitute. With these exceptions follow package directions.

Betty Crocker Brand

Cheddar and Sour Cream   Serves 5
(Approximate 19% fat)

Approximately Per Serving:

Follow General Instructions				
Calories	141	**Carbohydrates**	26.5 g
Fat	2.9 g	**Protein**	2.8 g
Cholesterol	1.0 mg	**Sodium**	649 mg

Exchanges: 1 1/2 bread; 1 fat

❖

Home-Style Skin On   Serves 5
(Approximate 27% fat)

Approximately Per Serving:

Follow General Instructions				
Calories	114	**Carbohydrates**	19.4 g
Fat	3.4 g	**Protein**	2.0 g
Cholesterol	---	**Sodium**	508 mg

Exchanges: 1 bread; 1 fat

❖

Julienne Potatoes Serves 6
(Approximate 18% fat)

Approximately Per Serving:

Follow General	**Calories**	111	**Carbohydrates**	19.4 g
Instructions	**Fat**	2.2 g	**Protein**	3.1 g
	Cholesterol	0.5 g	**Sodium**	624 mg

Exchanges: 1 bread; 1 fat

❖

Smokey Cheddar Potatoes Serves 5
(Approximate 18% fat)

Approximately Per Serving:

Follow General	**Calories**	125	**Carbohydrates**	23.0 g
Instructions	**Fat**	2.5 g	**Protein**	3.1 g
	Cholesterol	0.6 mg	**Sodium**	615 mg

Exchanges: 1 bread; 1 fat

❖

Sour Cream and Chives Serves 5
(Approximate 21% fat)

Approximately Per Serving:

Follow General	**Calories**	127	**Carbohydrates**	23.2 g
Instructions	**Fat**	3.0 g	**Protein**	3.3 g
	Cholesterol	0.5 mg	**Sodium**	557 mg

Exchanges: 1 bread; 1 fat

❖

Three Cheese Potatoes Serves 5
(Approximate 22% fat)

Approximately Per Serving:

Follow General	**Calories**	119	**Carbohydrates**	26.4 g
Instructions	**Fat**	2.9 g	**Protein**	3.0 g
	Cholesterol	0.7 mg	**Sodium**	714 mg

Exchanges: 1 bread; 1 fat

❖

Twice Baked Sour Cream and Chives
(Approximate 25% fat)   Serves 5
                        Approximately Per Serving:

Follow General	**Calories**	131	**Carbohydrates**	18.8 g
Instructions	**Fat**	3.6 g	**Protein**	3.9 g
	Cholesterol	0.5 mg	**Sodium**	529 mg

Exchanges: 1 bread; 1/4 milk; 1 fat

❖

White Cheddar Potatoes   Serves 5
(Approximate 27% fat)
                        Approximately Per Serving:

Follow General	**Calories**	129	**Carbohydrates**	22.2 g
Instructions	**Fat**	3.8 g	**Protein**	2.6 g
	Cholesterol	0.3 mg	**Sodium**	646 mg

Exchanges: 1 bread; 1/4 milk; 1 fat

Hungry Jack Brand

Creamy Scalloped   Serves 6
(Approximate 26% fat)
                        Approximately Per Serving:

Follow General	**Calories**	111	**Carbohydrates**	20.7 g
Instructions	**Fat**	3.2 g	**Protein**	2.9 g
	Cholesterol	0.5 mg	**Sodium**	462 mg

Exchanges: 1 bread; 1 fat

❖

Skin on Au Gratin   Serves 6
(Approximate 16% fat)

Approximately Per Serving:

Follow General	**Calories**	121	**Carbohydrates**	21.7 g
Instructions	**Fat**	2.2 g	**Protein**	2.9 g
	Cholesterol	0.5 mg	**Sodium**	572 mg

Exchanges: 1 bread; 1 fat

❖

Skin on Cheesy Scalloped   Serves 6
(Approximate 16% fat)

Approximately Per Serving:

Follow General	**Calories**	121	**Carbohydrates**	21.7 g
Instructions	**Fat**	2.7 g	**Protein**	2.9 g
	Cholesterol	0.5 mg	**Sodium**	582 mg

Exchanges: 1 bread; 1 fat

❖

Sour Cream and Chives   Serves 6
(Approximate 20% fat)

Approximately Per Serving:

Follow General	**Calories**	121	**Carbohydrates**	21.7 g
Instructions	**Fat**	2.7 g	**Protein**	2.9 g
	Cholesterol	0.5 mg	**Sodium**	502 mg

Exchanges: 1 bread; 1 fat

Spinach

Canned Spinach

(Recipe contains approximately 12% fat)

1 can spinach
1 T. vinegar
1/4 tsp. garlic salt
1/4 tsp. pepper

Egg substitute to = 1 egg,
   scrambled & chopped
1 boiled egg, yolk discarded,
   white chopped
2 tsp. bacon bits

In a saucepan, put spinach, vinegar, salt and pepper. Stir and heat until hot. Drain and put in serving dish. Sprinkle scrambled, chopped egg substitute, chopped egg white and bacon bits over top.
Yield: 4 servings

Approximate Per Serving:
Calories: 51
Fat: 0.7 g
Cholesterol: 0.0 mg

Carbohydrates: 4.2 g
Protein: 5.2 g
Sodium: 557 mg

Exchanges: 1/2 milk; 1/2 vegetable

Save the juice from canned tomatoes in ice cube trays. When frozen, store in plastic bags in freezer for cooking use or for tomato drinks.

Fresh Spinach

(Recipe contains approximately 21% fat)

1 1/4 lb. fresh spinach	1/4 tsp. minced garlic
4 c. water	Cooking spray
1 tsp. butter granules	1/4 tsp. salt
2 T. finely-chopped green pepper	1/8 tsp. pepper
2 T. finely-chopped onion	1 tsp. lemon juice

Wash and pick through spinach, removing tough stems. Shake off water and set aside. In a skillet, put water and butter granules. Add green pepper, onion and garlic. Sauté 2 to 3 minutes, stirring often. Spray spinach with cooking spray (8-second spray), tossing as you spray. Add to skillet. Cover and cook over high heat 1 minute. Reduce heat and simmer 5 to 6 minutes. Remove from stove and chop as desired. Add salt, pepper and lemon juice.
Yield: 4 servings

Approximate Per Serving:

Calories: 38	**Carbohydrates: 4.9 g**
Fat: .09 g	**Protein: 3.1 g**
Cholesterol: 0.0 mg	**Sodium: 186 mg**

Exchanges: 1 1/2 vegetable

A small amount of hot, not boiling, milk added a little at a time to mashed potatoes will make them light and fluffy.

Spinach Casserole

(Recipe contains approximately 17% fat)

3 (10 oz.) pkg. frozen,
   chopped spinach
1 c. buttermilk

2 tsp. sour cream granules
1 pkg. dry onion soup mix

Cook spinach per package directions. Drain and squeeze as dry as possible. Blend buttermilk, sour cream granules, soup mix and salt. Add spinach and blend. Pour into a 1 1/2-quart baking dish, that has been sprayed with cooking spray. Bake in 325° preheated oven 20 minutes, or until heated through.

Yield: 8 servings

Approximate Per Serving:
Calories: 59
Fat: 1.1 g
Cholesterol: 1.4 mg

Carbohydrates: 6.8 g
Protein: 2.9 g
Sodium: 422 mg

Exchanges: 1 vegetable; 1/2 milk

Sweet potatoes will not turn dark if put in salted water (5 teaspoons to 1 quart of water) immediately after peeling.

Squash

Baked Summer Squash

(Recipe contains approximately 4% fat)

3 c. cubed summer squash
   (zucchini, crookneck,
   yellow, etc.)
1/4 c. evaporated skim milk
1 tsp. butter granules

1/4 tsp. salt
1/8 tsp. pepper
Dash of nutmeg
Cooking spray

In a mixing bowl, put all ingredients and blend. Pour into baking dish, that has been sprayed with cooking spray. Cover and bake in 350° preheated oven 30 minutes, or until tender.
Yield: 4 servings

Approximate Per Serving:
Calories: 41
Fat: 0.2 g
Cholesterol: 0.6 mg

Carbohydrates: 8.3 g
Protein: 2.7 g
Sodium: 58 mg

Exchanges: 1 1/2 vegetable

Sunlight doesn't ripen tomatoes. It's the warmth that makes them ripen. So find a warm spot near the stove or dishwasher where they can get a little heat.

Baked Winter Squash

(Recipe contains approximately 7% fat)

2 acorn squash
Cooking spray
2 tsp. butter granules

1/4 tsp. salt
1/8 tsp. pepper

Halve and seed squash. Place on a baking sheet. Spray squash halves with cooking spray (1 second each) and sprinkle with butter granules, salt and pepper. Bake in a 375° preheated oven for 45 minutes to 1 hour, or until tender.
Yield: 4 servings

Approximate Per Serving:
Calories: 80
Fat: 0.6 g
Cholesterol: 0.0 mg

Carbohydrates: 16.0 g
Protein: 1.7 g
Sodium: 92 mg

Exchanges: 3 vegetable

Steamed Summer Squash

(Recipe contains approximately 26% fat)

2 c. cubed summer squash
  (zucchini, crookneck,
  yellow, etc.)
2 T. water

1 tsp. butter granules
1/4 tsp. salt
1/8 tsp. pepper
4 tsp. grated Parmesan cheese

Put water and butter granules in skillet and bring to boil. Add squash, salt and pepper. Cover. Reduce heat and simmer 5 to 6 minutes. Shake pan a couple of times to prevent squash from burning. Remove lid and simmer 3 minutes longer. Remove from skillet and put in serving dish. Sprinkle with Parmesan cheese.
Yield: 4 servings

Approximate Per Serving:
Calories: 28
Fat: 0.8 g
Cholesterol: 1.3 mg

Carbohydrates: 4.5 g
Protein: 1.7 g
Sodium: 210 mg

Exchanges: 1 vegetable

Summer Squash Treat

(Recipe contains approximately 7% fat)

1/4 c. water	3 green onions, sliced
1 tsp. butter granules	1 c. cherry tomatoes, halved
1 clove garlic, minced	1 tsp. garlic powder
1 sm. green pepper, seeded & cut into strips	1/2 tsp. parsley
2 c. diced yellow squash	1/4 tsp. dried oregano
2 c. sliced zucchini squash	1/4 tsp. salt
	1/4 tsp. pepper

Put water and butter granules in a skillet and bring to boil. Add garlic and sauté 1 minute. Add green pepper and yellow and zucchini squash. Cook about 5 minutes. Add onion, tomatoes and seasoning. Blend. Cover and cook 1 minute, or until vegetables are crisp-tender and tomatoes are heated through.
Yield: 6 servings

Approximate Per Serving:
Calories: 55   **Carbohydrates: 14.9 g**
Fat: 0.4 g   **Protein: 2.5 g**
Cholesterol: 0.0 mg   **Sodium: 123 mg**

Exchanges: 2 vegetable

To improve the flavor of inexpensive tomato juice, pour a 46-ounce can of it into a refrigerator jar and add one chopped green onion and a cut-up stalk of celery.

Zucchini Chips

(Recipe contains approximately 16% fat)

3 med. zucchini, sliced 1/4"
   thick
Egg substitute to = 1 egg
2 T. "free" no-fat Italian
   dressing
1/2 c. fine cracker crumbs

2 T. flour
2 T. grated Parmesan cheese
1/4 tsp. pepper
1/4 tsp. garlic salt
Cooking spray
1 T. butter granules

Blend well, egg substitute and Italian dressing. In a second bowl, blend cracker crumbs, flour, Parmesan cheese, pepper and garlic salt. Dip zucchini in egg mixture and then in cracker mixture. Place onto baking sheet, that has been sprayed with cooking spray. Allow to remain on baking sheet 15 minutes, then spray zucchini with cooking spray and sprinkle with butter granules. Bake in 475° oven for 5 minutes. Turn. Spray with cooking spray and cook second side for 5 minutes.

Yield: 6 servings

Approximate Per Serving:
Calories: 69
Fat: 1.2 g
Cholesterol: 1.3 mg

Carbohydrates: 11.1 g
Protein: 3.6 g
Sodium: 120 mg

Exchanges: 1 vegetable; 1/2 bread

Peel and quarter onions. Place one layer deep in a pan and freeze. Quickly pack in bags or containers while frozen. Use as needed, chopping onions while frozen with a sharp knife.

Zucchini with Tomatoes

(Recipe contains approximately 7% fat)

1/4 c. water
1 tsp. butter granules
2 med. zucchini, sliced
2 med. tomatoes, seeded &
   chopped

1/4 tsp. salt
1/2 tsp. garlic powder
1/4 tsp. dried basil

Put water and butter granules in a skillet and bring to boil. Add zucchini and sauté 3 minutes or until crisp-tender. Add tomatoes, salt, garlic powder and basil. Toss to blend.
Yield: 6 servings

Approximate Per Serving:
Calories: 41
Fat: 0.3 g
Cholesterol: 0.0 mg

Carbohydrates: 6.3 g
Protein: 1.3 g
Sodium: 121 mg

Exchanges: 1 1/2 vegetable

Size of a tomato does not indicate quality. Look for firm, unblemished tomatoes with good color. If you're buying them to eat another day, select pale pink ones and ripen them at home. Tiny cherry tomatoes are very perishable and should be used at once.

Tomatoes

Baked Stuffed Tomatoes
(Recipe contains approximately 9% fat)

8 med. tomatoes
2 T. water
1/2 tsp. butter granules
6 green onions, chopped fine
3 T. chopped parsley

1 1/2 c. bread crumbs, made
   from Italian bread
1 T. Worcestershire sauce
1/4 tsp. salt
1/4 tsp. pepper

Dip tomatoes in boiling water for 2 to 3 seconds and remove skins. Hollow out center of each tomato, reserving pulp. Lightly salt inside each tomato, if desired. Put 2 tablespoons water and butter granules in skillet and bring to boil. Sauté onion, parsley and tomato pulp. Add bread crumbs, Worcestershire sauce and seasoning. If a little dry, add a bit of water. Stuff mixture into tomatoes. Bake in 350° oven for 20 minutes, or until heated through.
Yield: 8 servings

Approximate Per Serving:
Calories: 95
Fat: 0.9 g
Cholesterol: 0.0 mg
Carbohydrates: 17.8 g
Protein: 3.4 g
Sodium: 200 mg

Exchanges: 1 bread; 1 vegetable

Stained hands from vegetables during canning season can be cured by rubbing your hands with a sliced potato.

Canned Tomatoes

(Recipe contains approximately 8% fat)

2 T. water
1 tsp. butter granules
1/4 green pepper, finely
    chopped
1/4 c. onion, finely chopped

1/4 tsp. minced garlic
1 (16 oz.) can tomatoes & juice,
    chopped coarsely
1/4 tsp. salt
1/8 tsp. pepper

Put water and butter granules in a skillet and bring to boil. Add green pepper, onion and garlic; sauté until liquid is absorbed. Add remaining ingredients and simmer 5 minutes.
Yield: 4 servings

Approximate Per Serving:
Calories: 32
Fat: 0.3 g
Cholesterol: 0.0 mg

Carbohydrates: 6.3 g
Protein: 1.1 g
Sodium: 375 mg

Exchanges: 1 vegetable

Cherry Tomato Sauté

(Recipe contains approximately 10% fat)

1 T. water
1 tsp. butter granules
20 cherry tomatoes, washed

1 tsp. Worcestershire sauce
1/4 tsp. salt
1/4 tsp. pepper

In a heavy-bottomed skillet, put water and butter granules and bring to boil. Add tomatoes and cook 3 minutes over medium-high heat. Add Worcestershire sauce, salt and pepper. Blend, tossing and cooking for 1 minute. Serve immediately.
Yield: 4 servings

Approximate Per Serving:
Calories: 28
Fat: 0.3 g
Cholesterol: 0.0 mg

Carbohydrates: 6.4 g
Protein: 1.8 g
Sodium: 204 mg

Exchanges: 1 vegetable

Scalloped Tomatoes

(Recipe contains approximately 10% fat)

2 T. water
1/2 tsp. butter granules
1 c. diced celery
1/2 c. chopped onion
1 T. flour
1 T. sugar
1/4 tsp. salt

1/2 tsp. basil
1 (28 oz.) can tomatoes,
   drained & chopped
3 slices "light" bread, toasted
   & cut into 1" cubes
1 T. Parmesan cheese

Put water and butter granules in a skillet and bring to boil. Add celery and onion and sauté until tender. Combine flour, sugar, salt and basil. Blend with celery and onions. Add tomatoes and cook, stirring until mixture thickens and bubbles. Stir in half of bread. Pour into 1 1/2-quart baking dish that has been sprayed with cooking spray. Bake in 350° preheated oven 30 minutes. Remove from stove. Top with remaining bread cubes and sprinkle with cheese.

Yield: 6 servings

Approximate Per Serving:
Calories: 78
Fat: 0.9 g
Cholesterol: 0.7 mg

Carbohydrates: 13.4 g
Protein: 3.1 g
Sodium: 392 mg

Exchanges: 1 1/2 vegetable; 1/2 bread

If a cracked dish is boiled for 45 minutes in sweet milk, the crack will be so welded together that it will hardly be visible, and will be so strong it will stand the same usage as before.

Stewed Creamy Tomatoes

(Recipe contains approximately 7% fat)

4 lg. tomatoes, peeled, seeded & halved
1/4 c. water
1 tsp. butter granules
1/4 tsp. sugar

1/4 c. chopped onion
1/4 c. chopped green pepper
1/4 tsp. salt
Dash of black pepper
1 c. evaporated skim milk

In a large skillet, put water, butter buds and sugar. Bring to boil. Add onion and green pepper; sauté 2 minutes. Add tomatoes, salt and pepper. Cover and cook over low heat, for 5 minutes. Remove tomatoes from skillet with slotted spoon onto a serving plate. Add milk and cook over high heat until reduced by half. Pour over tomatoes.

Yield: 4 servings

Approximate Per Serving:
Calories: 92
Fat: 0.7 g
Cholesterol: 2.3 mg

Carbohydrates: 16.8 g
Protein: 6.8 g
Sodium: 214 mg

Exchanges: 1 vegetable; 3/4 milk

*Occasionally throw a little salt on burning logs
to keep the chimney clean.*

Turnips

Cooked Fresh Turnips
(Recipe contains approximately 8% fat)

1 lb. young tender turnips	1/2 tsp. sugar
1/2 c. water	1 tsp. butter
1/4 tsp. salt	1 tsp. chopped parsley

Peel and slice turnips. Put water, salt and sugar in a saucepan. Add turnips; cover and simmer 15 to 20 minutes. Do not allow to boil dry. Add more water as needed. Drain and add butter granules, tossing gently until granules dissolve. Pour into serving dish and sprinkle with parsley.
Yield: 4 servings

Approximate Per Serving:
Calories: 33
Fat: 0.3 g
Cholesterol: 0.0 mg
Carbohydrates: 8.8 g
Protein: 1.0 g
Sodium: 196 mg

Exchanges: 1 vegetable

You can make your own liquid soap by shaving bar soap into a dish, then covering it with water and putting it in the microwave oven. In less than a minute the soup dissolves into a liquid.

Miscellaneous Vegetables

Marinated Vegetables
(Recipe contains approximately 11% fat)

5 lg. ripe tomatoes, peeled
   & quartered
1 med. green pepper, seeded
   & cut in strips
1 med. onion, sliced thin &
   separated into rings
3/4 c. cider vinegar

Artificial sweetener of choice
   to = 4 1/2 T. sugar
1 1/2 tsp. celery seed
1 1/2 tsp. mustard seed
1/4 tsp. salt
1 med. cucumber, peeled &
   sliced thin

Put tomatoes in hot water for 2 seconds before peeling. Quarter peeled tomatoes and put in large mixing bowl. Add green peppers and onion rings. In a small saucepan, put vinegar, sweetener, celery seeds, mustard seed and salt. Bring to boil and boil 1 minute. Pour hot mixture over vegetables and allow to cool to room temperature. Add cucumbers and chill several hours. Drain before serving.
Yield: 8 servings

Approximate Per Serving:
Calories: 51
Fat: 0.6 g
Cholesterol: 0.0 mg

Carbohydrates: 10.8 g
Protein: 2.0 g
Sodium: 78 mg

Exchanges: 2 vegetable

Relishes
(Recipe contains only a trace of fat)

PICK TWO:
3 celery sticks
3 carrot sticks
4 radishes
3 cauliflower flowerets
3 broccoli flowerets

3 green onions
3 green pepper sticks
2 turnip slices
6 cucumber slices

Exchanges: 1 vegetable

Stir-Fried California Mix

(Recipe contains approximately 30% fat)

2 c. frozen California Mix
Cooking spray
1/2 tsp. canola oil
3 T. hot water

1/4 tsp. beef bouillon granules
1/2 tsp. butter granules
1 T. "light" soy sauce

Spray wok or iron skillet (can use any heavy-bottomed skillet) with cooking spray. Add canola oil. Heat. Add vegetables and stir around to coat. Blend 2 tablespoons hot water and beef granules. Add to skillet and toss until moisture is absorbed (3 to 4 minutes). Mix soy sauce and 1 tablespoon water. Add to skillet. Cover with tight lid and simmer 4 to 5 minutes, or until vegetables are tender. Shake pan a couple of times to prevent burning.
Yield: 4 servings

Approximate Per Serving:
Calories: 36
Fat: 1.2 g
Cholesterol: 0.0 mg

Carbohydrates: 8.6 g
Protein: 2.6 g
Sodium: 266 mg

Exchanges: 1 vegetable; 1/4 fat

To remove a broken light bulb from a socket, insert a large cork into the socket and turn it out.

Stir-Fried Fresh Vegetable Medley
(Recipe contains approximately 24% fat)

Cooking spray
1/2 tsp. canola oil
1 c. cauliflower flowerets
1 c. broccoli flowerets
1 sm. carrot, sliced thin
1/2 green pepper, cut in strips
1/2 c. sliced celery

1/2 med. onion, coarsely
 chopped
3 T. hot water
1/4 tsp. chicken bouillon
 granules
1 T. "light" soy sauce

Heat wok or iron skillet until very hot. Spray with cooking spray and add oil. Add vegetables and toss to coat. Blend 2 tablespoons hot water and bouillon granules. Pour into skillet and toss vegetables 3 to 4 minutes. Blend soy sauce and 1 tablespoon water. Add to skillet. Cover with tight lid and simmer 4 to 5 minutes, or until vegetables are crisp-tender. Shake skillet a couple times to prevent burning.
Yield: 6 servings

Approximate Per Serving:
Calories: 34
Fat: 0.9 g
Cholesterol: 0.0 mg

Carbohydrates: 6.0 g
Protein: 3.3 g
Sodium: 174 mg

Exchanges: 1 vegetable; 1/4 fat

Did you know that you can stop a door hinge from creaking by rubbing it with a lead pencil?

Fruit Side-Dishes

Buttery-Maple Apple Rings
(Recipe contains approximately 5% fat)

4 lg. Granny Smith apples,
   cored & sliced into thin
   rings
3 T. "light" maple syrup

1 T. water
1 tsp. butter granules
1/4 tsp. cinnamon

Prepare apples and set aside. In a large, heavy-bottomed skillet, put maple syrup, water, butter granules and cinnamon. Bring to boil and add apple rings. Cook, uncovered, over medium heat, until tender. Toss very gently, often. Add additional water if needed, however, water should be absorbed when apples are done.
Yield: 6 servings

Approximate Per Serving:
Calories: 80
Fat: 0.4 g
Cholesterol: 0.0 mg

Carbohydrates: 20.3 g
Protein: 0.0 g
Sodium: 33 mg

Exchanges: 2 fruit

Spray garbage sacks with ammonia to prevent dogs from tearing the bags before they're picked up.

Fresh Fruit Medley

(Recipe contains approximately 2% fat)

2 med. peaches, peeled &
   sliced
1 c. bing cherries, stone
   removed & halved
1 kiwi, peeled & sliced
1 c. fresh strawberries,
   halved
1 banana, sliced

1/3 c. "free" no-fat
   mayonnaise
2 tsp. lemon juice
1 T. honey
Artificial sweetener to =
   1 T. sugar
1/4 tsp. cinnamon

Prepare fruit and put in large mixing bowl. Set aside. In a small bowl, put mayonnaise, lemon juice, honey, sweetener and cinnamon. Blend well. Pour over fruit and toss gently to blend. Chill.
Yield: 8 servings

Approximate Per Serving:
Calories: 75
Fat: 0.2 g
Cholesterol: 0.0 mg

Carbohydrates: 16.5 g
Protein: 3.1 g
Sodium: 114 mg

Exchanges: 2 fruit

Glycerin makes an excellent lubricant for egg beaters or other kitchen utensils that have moving parts. Unlike oil, it will not spoil the taste of food mixed with it by accident. The glycerin may be applied with a medicine dropper.

Fried Apples

(Recipe contains approximately 7% fat)

4 lg. Granny Smith apples,
    cored & sliced 1/4" thick
1/4 c. water
1 tsp. butter granules

1/4 to 1/2 tsp. cinnamon
Artificial sweetener of choice
    to = 1/3 c. sugar

Put water, butter granules and cinnamon in a skillet and bring to boil. Add apples and cook, over medium heat, uncovered, until tender; tossing often. Liquid should be absorbed when apples are done. Remove from heat and sprinkle with artificial sweetener. Toss to blend.
Yield: 6 servings

Approximate Per Serving:
Calories: 62
Fat: 0.5 g
Cholesterol: 0.0 mg

Carbohydrates: 13.8 g
Protein: 0.0 mg
Sodium: 33 mg

Exchanges: 1 1/2 fruit

Fruit in Sour Cream

(Recipe contains approximately 27% fat)

1 (20 oz.) can "light" pineapple
    chunks, drained
2 (11 oz.) cans mandarin
    oranges, drained
1 (16 oz.) can peach slices,
    drained

1 c. "light" sour cream
2 T. milk
1 (8 oz.) pkg. "free" no-fat
    Philadelphia cream cheese
Artificial sweetener of choice
    to = 1/3 c. sugar

Put drained fruit in a mixing bowl and set aside. Blend remaining ingredients until smooth. Pour over fruit and toss gently to blend. Chill several hours before serving.
Yield: 8 servings

Approximate Per Serving:
Calories: 139
Fat: 4.1 g
Cholesterol: 2.5 mg

Carbohydrates: 23.7 g
Protein: 5.9 g
Sodium: 178 mg

Exchanges: 1 1/2 fruit; 1 milk

Melon Compote

(Recipe contains approximately 5% fat)

3 c. watermelon balls or chunks
2 c. cantaloupe balls or chunks
2 c. honeydew balls or chunks
1 c. grapes

1/4 c. orange juice concentrate, thawed
1 T. honey

Prepare fruit and put into a large mixing bowl. Blend orange juice concentrate and honey. Drizzle over fruit, tossing gently until coated.

Yield: 8 servings

Approximate Per Serving:
Calories: 79
Fat: 0.4 g
Cholesterol: 0.0 mg

Carbohydrates: 16.5 g
Protein: 1.1 g
Sodium: 6 mg

Exchanges: 2 fruit

A cheap brand of lawn fertilizer will melt snow and ice just as quickly as salt. It will benefit your lawn instead of killing it.

Orange-Glazed Bananas

(Recipe contains approximately 2% fat)

5 T. water
1 1/2 tsp. butter granules
Artificial brown sugar to =
   1 T. brown sugar
1/4 tsp. cinnamon

1/8 tsp. nutmeg
1/3 c. unsweetened orange juice
2 med. bananas, split lengthwise & halved

Put 1 tablespoon water and 1/2 teaspoon butter granules in small saucepan and heat. Add artificial brown sugar, cinnamon, nutmeg and orange juice. Cook until heated through. Set aside. In a skillet, put 1/4 cup water and 1 teaspoon butter granules. Bring to boil and add banana sticks. Cook, turning often, until moisture has been absorbed. Remove from stove and put bananas on serving plate. Spoon orange sauce over them.
Yield: 4 servings

Approximate Per Serving:
Calories: 51
Fat: 0.1 g
Cholesterol: 0.0 mg

Carbohydrates: 12.3 g
Protein: 0.7 g
Sodium: 53 mg

Exchanges: 1 fruit

*Pop your contact paper in the freezer about an hour before
you use it and it will handle much easier.*

Poached Pears with Orange Sauce

(Recipe contains approximately 13% fat)

6 sm., ripe pears	2 tsp. cornstarch
1 c. unsweetened orange juice	3 T. water
1/2 tsp. grated orange rind	1/4 tsp. cinnamon

With a sharp, thin-bladed knife, peel pears as smooth as possible. Core pears from the bottom of pear, leaving stem and end intact. In a large, shallow saucepan, put orange juice and grated rind. Bring to boil. Place pears in juice, cover and simmer 10 to 15 minutes, or until pears are tender. Remove pears from pan with slotted spoon, and put on serving plates. Add to juice mixture and cook, stirring constantly, until thickened. Pour sauce evenly over pears.

Yield: 6 servings

Approximate Per Serving:

Calories: 68
Fat 1.0 g
Cholesterol: 0.0 mg

Carbohydrates: 16.8 g
Protein: 1.3 g
Sodium: Trace

Exchanges: 1 1/2 fruit

When the tip of a shoestring comes off, dip the end of the lace in clear fingernail polish and let dry. You will have a hard-tipped shoestring again for easier lacing.

Sautéed Bananas
and Pineapple

(Recipe contains approximately 8% fat)

2 T. water
1 tsp. butter granules
2 med. bananas, peeled &
   sliced

1/2 c. pineapple chunks
1/4 tsp. cinnamon
Artificial sweetener to =
   1 T. brown sugar

In a skillet, put water and butter granules and bring to boil. Add bananas and pineapple. Add cinnamon. Cook until heated through, and liquid is absorbed. Sprinkle with sweetener; stir and serve.
Yield: 4 servings

Approximate Per Serving:
Calories: 54
Fat: 0.5 g
Cholesterol: 0.0 mg

Carbohydrates: 13.0 g
Protein: 0.6 g
Sodium: 46 mg

Exchanges: 1 fruit

Put your old rubber bathtub or sink mats in a car trunk or truck. They give good traction on ice when slipped under the tires. Pour some household bleach over your tires, wait 10 minutes and drive off carefully.

Strawberries and Bananas in Almond Cream

(Recipe contains approximately 2% fat)

1 (8 oz.) ctn. "free" no-fat
   Philadelphia cream cheese
2 T. honey
Artificial sweetener of choice
   to = 2 T. sugar

2 T. skim milk
1/2 tsp. almond extract
2 bananas, sliced
2 c. fresh strawberries, halved

Beat first 5 ingredients with an electric mixer until smooth. In a medium mixing bowl, put bananas and strawberries. Add almond cream and toss to blend. Spoon into individual serving dishes or in one serving dish. Chill.
Yield: 8 servings

Approximate Per Serving:
Calories: 77
Fat: 0.2 g
Cholesterol: 5.1 mg

Carbohydrates: 9.3 g
Protein: 9.0 g
Sodium: 173 mg

Exchanges: 1 fruit; 1/2 milk

If you have one of those instant - on T.V. sets, unplug it when not in use. These sets use and waste electricity even when they're turned off.

Winter Fruit Delight

(Recipe contains approximately 1% fat)

3 cans chunky "light" fruit
   cocktail, drained
1 can "light" pineapple
   chunks, drained

1 banana, peeled & sliced
1 T. lemon juice
1 (3 oz.) pkg. sugar-free
   instant vanilla pudding

Put well-drained fruit in a mixing bowl and add banana. Add lemon juice, tossing fruit to distribute. Sprinkle with dry instant pudding and toss gently to blend. Refrigerate several hours before serving.

Yield: 10 servings

Approximate Per Serving:
Calories: 66
Fat: 0.1 g
Cholesterol: 0.0 mg

Carbohydrates: 16.3 g
Protein: 0.7 g
Sodium: 7 mg

Exchanges: 2 fruit

Pasta Side-Dishes

Fried Noodles

(Recipe contains approximately 11% fat)

8 oz. thin eggless noodles,
   cooked
1/4 c. water

1 tsp. butter granules
1/4 tsp. salt
1/4 tsp. pepper

Put water and butter granules in skillet and bring to boil. Add noodles and toss to coat. Add salt and pepper; cook 5 minutes, tossing as noodles cook.

Yield: 8 servings

Approximate Per Serving:
Calories: 111
Fat: 1.3 g
Cholesterol: 0.0 mg

Carbohydrates: 20.3 g
Protein: 5.0 g
Sodium: 99 mg

Exchanges: 1 1/2 bread

Pasta with Vegetables

(Recipe contains approximately 4% fat)

1 c. sm. shell macaroni	1/2 tsp. garlic powder
2 c. frozen California Mix	1/8 tsp. pepper
6-second spray of cooking spray	1/2 tsp. sodium-free seasoned salt
2 tomatoes, seeded & chopped	1 tsp. Italian seasoning
2 green onions, sliced thin (include green)	4 oz. "free" no-fat Philadelphia cream cheese
1 tsp. parsley flakes	2 T. "free" no-fat mayonnaise

Cook macaroni per package directions, omitting salt. Cook California Mix per package directions. Drain macaroni and spray with cooking spray, tossing to coat. Add California Mix, tomato and onion to pasta, and toss. In a small dish, put parsley flakes, garlic salt, pepper and Italian seasoning. Blend. Stir in cream cheese and mayonnaise, stirring until smooth. Blend into pasta. Serve hot. **Yield: 8 servings**

Approximate Per Serving:

Calories: 98	Carbohydrates: 6.2 g
Fat: 0.4 g	Protein: 5.2 g
Cholesterol: 2.5 mg	Sodium: 139 mg

Exchanges: 1 bread; 1 vegetable

Unwrap bar soap before storing. It will harden and last longer besides giving your cupboard a pleasant fragrance.

Sour Cream Noodles Deluxe

(Recipe contains approximately 10% fat)

2 T. water
1/2 tsp. butter granules
1 med. onion, diced
2 c. eggless noodles, cooked
1/4 tsp. sweet basil
1 (8 oz.) pkg. "free" no-fat
   cream cheese

Egg substitute to = 4 eggs
1 recipe of cream soup mix to =
   1 can
1 tsp. sour cream granules
1/4 tsp. oregano
1/2 c. "free" no-fat shredded
   Cheddar cheese

Put water and butter granules in a skillet and bring to boil. Add onions and sauté until tender, and liquid is absorbed. Pour onions into a large mixing bowl and add cooked noodles; stir to blend. Combine remaining ingredients, except shredded cheese. Blend well, then pour over noodle mixture. Pour into a casserole, that has been sprayed with cooking spray. Sprinkle with cheese. Cover and bake in 350° preheated oven for 1 hour.

Yield: 8 servings

Approximate Per Serving:
Calories: 150
Fat: 1.7 g
Cholesterol: 7.5 mg

Carbohydrates: 12.8 g
Protein: 10.6 g
Sodium: 546 mg

Exchanges: 1 bread

Pam (vegetable spray-on product for cooking) sprayed along the metal frames of windows will keep them moving without a battle. Repeat as needed.

Three-Cheese Noodles

(Recipe contains approximately 11% fat)

1 1/2 c. low-fat cottage cheese
1 (8 oz.) ctn. "free" no-fat
  cream cheese
Egg substitute to = 2 eggs
1/3 c. skim milk
2 T. cheese granules

1/2 c. chopped green onions
1/4 tsp. garlic powder
1/4 tsp. pepper
1 (8 oz.) pkg. med. eggless
  noodles, cooked

In a mixing bowl, put cottage cheese, cream cheese, egg substitute, milk and cheese granules. Blend with electric mixer on medium speed until smooth. Add onion, garlic salt and pepper. Stir into cooked noodles. Pour mixture into 9x13-inch baking dish, that has been sprayed with cooking spray. Bake in 350° preheated oven for 20 minutes.
Yield: 8 servings

Approximate Per Serving:
Calories: 201
Fat: 2.4 g
Cholesterol: 8.5 mg

Carbohydrates: 23.9 g
Protein: 16.1 g
Sodium: 352 mg

Exchanges: 1 bread; 2 meat; 1/4 milk

*When hanging pictures, heat the nail with a flame before driving
it into the wall. You won't crack or chip the plaster.*

Noodle-Roni

For an occasional side dish, it's all right to use the boxed side dishes, however, they should be prepared with less margarine, so follow the general directions to make this an acceptable food as far as the fat goes.

General Instructions

When making sauce, use only 1 tablespoon tub margarine and add 1 teaspoon butter granules. Margarine should not contain more than 6 grams of fat per tablespoon. Use skim milk. Follow package directions.

Angel Hair Pasta   Serves 5
(Approximate 22% fat)

Approximately Per Serving:

Follow General				
Follow General	**Calories**	123	**Carbohydrates**	21.1 g
Instructions	**Fat**	3.0 g	**Protein**	4.6 g
	Cholesterol	0.6 mg	**Sodium**	389 mg

Exchanges: 1 bread; 1 fat

Broccoli Au Gratin   Serves 4
(Approximate 23% fat)

Approximately Per Serving:

Follow General	**Calories**	149	**Carbohydrates**	23.0 g
Instructions	**Fat**	3.8 g	**Protein**	6.4 g
	Cholesterol	0.8 mg	**Sodium**	529 mg

Exchanges: 1 1/2 bread; 1 fat

Corkscrew Pasta   Serves 4
(Approximately 24% fat)

Approximately Per Serving:

Follow General	**Calories**	161	**Carbohydrates**	25.0 g
Instructions	**Fat**	4.3 g	**Protein**	6.4 g
	Cholesterol	0.8 mg	**Sodium**	523 mg

Exchanges: 1 1/2 bread; 1 fat

Fettucini Pasta   Serves 4
(Approximate 20% fat)

Approximately Per Serving:

Follow General	**Calories**	153	**Carbohydrates**	25.8 g
Instructions	**Fat**	3.4 g	**Protein**	6.1 g
	Cholesterol	0.5 mg	**Sodium**	638 mg

Exchanges: 1 1/2 bread; 1 fat

Linguini Pasta   Serves 4
(Approximate 11% fat)
                        Approximately Per Serving:
Follow General **Calories**   146   **Carbohydrates**   24.8 g
  Instructions **Fat**   1.8 g   **Protein**   5.5 g
                Cholesterol 0.0 mg   **Sodium**   456 mg
Exchanges: 1 1/2 bread; 1 fat

Oriental Pasta   Serves 6
(Approximate 20% fat)
                        Approximately Per Serving:
Follow General **Calories**   89   **Carbohydrates**   9.6 g
  Instructions **Fat**   2.0 g   **Protein**   2.9 g
                Cholesterol ---   **Sodium**   393 mg
Exchanges: 1 bread; 1/2 fat

Parmesan   Serves 4
(Approximate 22% fat)
                        Approximately Per Serving:
Follow General **Calories**   156   **Carbohydrates**   23.5 g
  Instructions **Fat**   3.8 g   **Protein**   6.1 g
                Cholesterol 0.5 mg   **Sodium**   390 mg
Exchanges: 1 1/2 bread; 1 fat

Tenderthin Pasta   Serves 5
(Approximate 21% fat)
                        Approximately Per Serving:
Follow General **Calories**   126   **Carbohydrates**   20.0 g
  Instructions **Fat**   3.0 g   **Protein**   5.2 g
                Cholesterol 2.4 mg   **Sodium**   383 mg
Exchanges: 1 bread; 1 fat

Rice Side-Dishes

Golden Rice Casserole
(Recipe contains approximately 9% fat)

1/2 c. brown rice, cooked
2 c. shredded carrots
1/4 tsp. salt
1/2 c. skim milk

2 c. low-fat cottage cheese
2 T. finely-chopped onion
Egg substitute to = 2 eggs

Steam carrots until done. Add to cooked rice. Add remaining ingredients. Blend. Pour into baking dish, that has been sprayed with cooking spray. Put dish in shallow baking dish. Place in oven. Pour boiling water into shallow pan so it comes up 1-inch on baking dish. Bake in 350° preheated oven about 50 minutes. Ready when inserted knife comes out clean.
Yield: 8 servings

Approximate Per Serving:
Calories: 133
Fat: 1.4 g
Cholesterol: 5.0 mg

Carbohydrates: 11.6 g
Protein: 7.0 g
Sodium: 182 mg

Exchanges: 1/2 bread; 1/2 vegetable; 1 milk

Organize a toy lending library and swap toys with other mothers in the neighborhood.

Oriental Fried Rice

(Recipe contains approximately 4% fat)

1/4 c. water	3 c. cooked brown rice
2 tsp. butter granules	2 c. sliced, raw mushrooms
1 c. finely-chopped onion	1 c. chopped water chestnuts
1 c. finely-chopped celery	3 T. "light" soy sauce

In a heavy-bottomed skillet, put water and butter granules and bring to boil. Add onions and celery; sauté until almost tender, and most of liquid has been absorbed. Add remaining ingredients and simmer about 10 minutes, stirring several times.
Yield: 8 servings

Approximate Per Serving:
Calories: 115   Carbohydrates: 24.5 g
Fat: 0.5 g   Protein: 3.4 g
Cholesterol: 0.0 mg   Sodium: 441 mg

Exchanges: 1 bread; 1 1/2 vegetable

Peas and Rice

(Recipe contains approximately 4% fat)

1 c. brown rice, cooked	1/4 tsp. salt
1/4 c. water	1/2 tsp. sugar
1 tsp. butter granules	2 1/2 c. shelled, fresh peas
1 onion, sliced thin, separated	(or frozen peas)
into rings	

Put water and butter granules in skillet and bring to boil. Add onions and sauté until tender, and moisture has been absorbed. Put salt, sugar and peas in saucepan and add 1-inch water. Bring to boil and simmer 10 to 12 minutes. Add onions and peas to cooked rice and serve hot.
Yield: 6 servings

Approximate Per Serving:
Calories: 71   Carbohydrates: 14.2 g
Fat: 0.3 g   Protein: 2.5 g
Cholesterol: 0.0 mg   Sodium: 170 mg

Exchanges: 1 bread

Rice with Broccoli

(Recipe contains approximately 3% fat)

1/4 c. water
1 tsp. butter granules
1 tsp. chicken bouillon granules
1 med. onion, chopped
1 lb. chopped broccoli
1 c. brown rice

Cooking spray
1 1/2 c. hot water
2 1/2 T. chopped parsley, or
   1 T. parsley flakes
1 T. cheese granules

Put water and butter granules in a saucepan and bring to boil. Add bouillon and stir until dissolved. Add onion and sauté 5 minutes. Add broccoli and sauté an additional 5 minutes. In a bowl, spray rice with cooking spray and add to saucepan. Add hot water. Cover and cook over low heat 30 to 40 minutes, or until rice is tender. Add more water, if needed. Stir in parsley and cheese granules.
Yield: 8 servings

Approximate Per Serving:
Calories: 104
Fat: 0.3 g
Cholesterol: 0.1 mg

Carbohydrates: 23.4 g
Protein: 4.0 g
Sodium: 166 mg

Exchanges: 1 bread; 1 vegetable

Damp leather shoes can be reconditioned in the following manner: Dry them thoroughly, clean them with saddle soap, and rub them gently with castor oil.

Steamed Rice

(Recipe contains approximately 1% fat)

1 T. salt   2 c. brown rice
1 lg. pan water

Bring water to a boil. Add salt and sprinkle rice into boiling water. Boil 10 minutes. Drain to serve. Rinse rice. Leave rice in sieve and set over a pan of boiling water (sieve should not touch water). Cover with dish towel, then with lid. Cook 25 minutes, or until rice is fluffy.
Yield: 6 cups rice (12 servings)

Approximate Per Serving:
Calories: 112   **Carbohydrates: 24.8 g**
Fat: 0.1 g   **Protein: 2.0 g**
Cholesterol: 0.0 mg   **Sodium: 179 mg**

Exchanges: 1 1/2 bread

If you are painting with an oil-base paint and need to stop for a short time, wrap the brush in aluminum foil and place in the freezer until ready to return to the job. The paint will not harden.

Side Dishes from a Box

We all like an easy side dish. The following chart is for rice side dishes that can be made quickly. However, when serving rice and noodle, don't forget about the Freezer Rice and the Freezer Noodles in the substitute chapter. They are real convenient to have on hand. The main problem with the rice and noodle mixes is the high sodium content. Avoid these if you are on a sodium-restricted diet.

General Instructions

Use only 1 tablespoon tub margarine when browning rice and vermicelli, stirring constantly and browning per package directions. Add 1 teaspoon of butter granules and follow package directions.

Rice-A-Roni

Beef Flavored — Serves 8
(Approximate 15% fat)

Approximately Per Serving:

Follow General Instructions				
Calories	111	**Carbohydrates**	21.6 g
Fat	1.8 g	**Protein**	2.9 g
Cholesterol	0.0 mg	**Sodium**	494 mg

Exchanges: 1 bread; 1 fat

❖

Beef with Mushrooms — Serves 4
(Approximate 18% fat)

Approximately Per Serving:

Follow General Instructions				
Calories	137	**Carbohydrates**	28.5 g
Fat	2.8 g	**Protein**	4.0 g
Cholesterol	0.0 mg	**Sodium**	795 mg

Exchanges: 1 bread; 1 vegetable; 1 fat

❖

Broccoli Au Gratin — Serves 5
(Approximate 21% fat)

Approximately Per Serving:

Follow General Instructions				
Calories	144	**Carbohydrates**	24.9 g
Fat	3.4 g	**Portein**	3.5 g
Cholesterol	0.0 mg	**Sodium**	313 mg

Exchanges: 1 bread; 1 vegetable; 1 fat

❖

Chicken Flavored   Serves 6
(Approximate 12% fat)

Approximately Per Serving:

Follow General	**Calories**	130	**Carbohydrates**	25.8 g
Instructions	**Fat**	1.8 g	**Protein**	3.5 g
	Cholesterol	---	**Sodium**	545 mg

Exchanges: 1 bread; 1/2 vegetable; 1 fat

❖

Chicken and Broccoli   Serves 5
(Approximate 16% fat)

Approximately Per Serving:

Follow General	**Calories**	137	**Carbohydrates**	26.0 g
Instructions	**Fat**	2.5 g	**Protein**	3.5 g
	Cholesterol	---	**Sodium**	743 mg

Exchanges: 1 1/2 bread; 1 fat

❖

Fried Rice   Serves 5
(Approximate 15% fat)

Approximately Per Serving:

Follow General	**Calories**	144	**Carbohydrates**	28.4 g
Instructions	**Fat**	2.4 g	**Protein**	4.0 g
	Cholesterol	---	**Sodium**	858 mg

Exchanges: 1 1/2 bread; 1 fat

❖

Long Grain with Wild Rice   Serves 4
(Approximate 16% fat)

Approximately Per Serving:

Follow General	**Calories**	104	**Carbohydrates**	23.5 g
Instructions	**Fat**	1.8 g	**Protein**	3.0 g
	Cholesterol	---	**Sodium**	693 mg

Exchanges: 1 1/2 bread

❖

Spanish Rice   Serves 7
(Approximate 13% fat)

Approximately Per Serving:

Follow General	**Calories**	104	**Carbohydrates**	20.5 g
Instructions	**Fat**	1.5 g	**Protein**	2.5 g
	Cholesterol	---	**Sodium**	486 mg

Exchanges: 1 bread; 3/4 fat

Grain Side-Dishes

Barley Pilaf

(Recipe contains approximately 9% fat)

2 tsp. canola oil	2 med.-sized onions, chopped
1 3/4 c. pearl barley	1 c. sliced, fresh mushrooms
1/4 c. water	5 c. boiling water
1 tsp. butter granules	2 chicken bouillon cubes

Put oil in a heavy-bottomed skillet. Add barley when oil is hot. Reduce heat and cook over low heat until barley turns golden brown, stirring constantly. Put into a large casserole, that has been sprayed with cooking spray. Put 1/4 cup water and butter granules in skillet and bring to boil. Sauté onions until tender. Add mushrooms and sauté 4 to 5 minutes, stirring often. Add to casserole. Stir in a cup boiling water. Dissolve bouillon in 4 cups boiling water. Add 2 cups of bouillon liquid to casserole. Cover with tight lid and bake in 350° preheated oven for 45 minutes. Add remaining 2 cups bouillon. Stir, and bake, covered, another 45 minutes.
Yield: 10 servings

Approximate Per Serving:
Calories: 148	**Carbohydrates: 30.7 g**
Fat: 1.4 g	**Protein: 3.6 g**
Cholesterol: 0.0 mg	**Sodium: 224 mg**

Exchanges: 1 bread; 1 vegetable; 1 fat

A quick way to shovel the front steps after a snowfall is with a dustpan.
It is quick, easy and efficient. Work from the bottom step up.

Bulgur Pilaf

(Recipe contains approximately 4% fat)

3/4 c. bulgur (cracked wheat)
2 carrots, shredded
3/4 c. frozen peas
2 green onions, chopped
1/2 tsp. parsley flakes
1 1/2 c. boiling water

1 tsp. chicken bouillon
   granules (or 2 cubes)
1 tsp. butter granules
1/2 tsp. garlic powder
1/4 tsp. sodium-free
   seasoned salt

Put all ingredients in a saucepan and bring to boil. Reduce heat. Cover and cook mixture 5 to 10 minutes, or until liquid is absorbed.
Yield: 6 servings

Approximate Per Serving:
Calories: 108
Fat: 0.5 g
Cholesterol: 0.0 mg

Carbohydrates: 20.0 g
Protein: 5.7 g
Sodium: 234 mg

Exchanges: 1 bread; 1 1/2 vegetable

Moving to an apartment or smaller home and need to reduce storage items? Send old photos that you no longer need to those who are in the picture. You have no idea how pleased one will be to get a long forgotten picture.

Tomato-Topped Polenta

(Recipe contains approximately 9% fat)

2 T. water
1/2 tsp. butter granules
1/3 c. chopped onion
1 sm. clove garlic, minced
1/4 lb. sm. mushrooms, sliced
1/4 tsp. sodium-free
    seasoned salt
1/8 tsp. oregano
1 (16 oz.) can tomatoes, drained

1 c. yellow cornmeal
3/4 c. cold water
3 3/4 c. boiling water
3/4 tsp. salt
1/2 c. "free" no-fat shredded
    Cheddar cheese
2 T. grated, fresh Parmesan
    cheese

In a saucepan, put 2 tablespoons water and butter granules and bring to boil. Add onions and garlic; sauté until onions soften. Add mushrooms and sauté until moisture is absorbed. Add 1/2 teaspoon salt and oregano. Add tomatoes and simmer 1 to 1 1/2 hours. If sauce becomes too thick, add a little water or tomato juice.

In a second saucepan, mix together cornmeal and cold water. Gradually stir in boiling water and salt. Cook over medium heat, stirring constantly, until thick and smooth. Reduce heat and cook an additional 10 minutes. Pour into a shallow baking dish, that has been sprayed with cooking spray. Spread out in even layer and top with sauce. Sprinkle with grated Cheddar and Parmesan cheeses.
Yield: 6 servings

Approximate Per Serving:
Calories: 130
Fat: 1.3 g
Cholesterol: 2.8 mg

Carbohydrates: 26.9 g
Protein: 6.0 g
Sodium: 551 mg

Exchanges: 1 bread; 1/2 milk; 1/2 vegetable

Notes &
Recipes

Desserts -
Pies, Cakes, Puddings, Cookies & Desserts

Desserts

Most of us have a sweet tooth and enjoy our desserts. However, it is best to make dessert a treat rather than a daily part of our life. Serve fresh, canned or frozen fruit, or a selection from the fruit side-dishes or gelatin sections.

If you are not a diabetic, there is not a lot wrong with desserts, except for the sugar they contain. Sugar is a simple carbohydrate and contains next to no nutritional value. It is for this reason it is often referred to as the "empty food".

Many of the desserts in this book are sugar-free (using sugar is an option), but desserts usually contain a lot of calories and take up a lot of precious exchanges. This is another reason for using them sparingly—one or two times a week. The required nutritional needs should be met before including a dessert on the menu.

I have attempted to make desserts easier in this book by allowing cake mixes when altered to acceptable fat levels. I realize that I keep the fat in the book very low, but isn't that the name of the game? KEEPING FAT INTAKE AS LOW AS POSSIBLE.

Have all ingredients at room temperature.

Cakes

Sugar-Free Cakes

Basic Sugar-Free Cake
(Recipe contains approximately 22% fat)

1/4 c. tub margarine (do not
  use diet)
1/4 c. unsweetened applesauce
1 tsp. vanilla extract
1 tsp. almond extract (can use
  vanilla)
2 c. whole wheat blend or
  enriched all-purpose flour
1/2 tsp. salt

1 T. baking powder
1/3 c. nonfat dry milk granules
1 c. unsweetened apple juice
  concentrate, thawed
6 egg whites
18 pkt. artificial sweetener of
  choice to = 3/4 c. sugar
1/4 c. boiling water

In a mixing bowl, blend margarine, applesauce, vanilla and almond. Blend until smooth. In a second bowl, blend flour, salt, baking powder and milk granules. Add dry ingredients to first mixture alternately with applesauce concentrate, beginning and ending with flour mixture. Beat until smooth—DO NOT OVERBEAT. Beat egg whites until stiff and gently fold into batter. Pour into two 9-inch cake pans or one 9x13-inch pan, that have been sprayed with cooking spray. Bake in a 350° preheated oven for 30 to 35 minutes, or until cake springs back when touched.

Blend sweetener and boiling water. Poke holes into cake (or cakes) with fork at 1/2-inch intervals, and slowly drizzle sweet liquid over it. Leave in pan 10 minutes, then remove. If using a 9x13-inch pan, leave in pan.
Yield: 10 servings

Approximate Per Serving:
Calories: 209
Fat: 5.0 g
Cholesterol: Trace

Carbohydrates: 33.0 g
Protein: 5.0 g
Sodium: 237 mg

Exchanges: 1 bread; 1/2 milk; 1 fruit; 1 fat

Basic Sugar-Free Chocolate Cake

(Recipe contains approximately 24% fat)

1 basic sugar-free cake (see index)	**1/2 c. cocoa** **1/4 tsp. cinnamon**

Add cocoa and cinnamon to dry ingredients, then prepare cake as directed for Basic Sugar-Free Cake.
Yield: 10 servings

Approximate Per Serving:

Calories: 220 **Carbohydrates: 36.0 mg**
Fat: 5.8 g **Protein: 6.0 g**
Cholesterol: Trace **Sodium: 237 mg**

Exchanges: 1 bread; 1/2 milk; 1 1/2 fruit; 1 fat

Fill cake pans about 2/3 full and spread batter well into corners and to the sides, leaving a slight hollow center.

Low-Sugar Cakes

Angel Layer Cake
(Recipe contains approximately 2% fat)

6 egg whites, room temp.
1/2 tsp. cream of tartar
Dash of salt
1/3 c. sugar
1/4 tsp. vanilla extract

1/4 tsp. almond extract (can
  use vanilla)
1/2 c. sifted flour (sift 4 times,
  then measure)

Beat egg whites in a large mixing bowl until frothy. Add cream of tartar and salt; beat until soft peaks form. Gradually add sugar, no more than 1 tablespoon at a time, beating until stiff. Add vanilla and almond extracts. Beat another 30 seconds. With a metal spoon, gently fold in flour, in three additions. Pour batter into an ungreased 9-inch cake pan. Bake in a 325° preheated oven for 30 minutes. Cool in pan on wire rack for 40 minutes. Remove from pan and finish cooling on wire rack.
Yield: 6 servings

Approximate Per Serving:
Calories: 98
Fat: Trace
Cholesterol: 0.0 mg

Carbohydrates: 20.0 g
Protein: 8.0 g
Sodium: 90 mg

Exchanges: 1 bread; 1/2 milk

The cake is done when it shrinks slightly from the sides of the pan or if it springs back when touched lightly with the finger.

Apple Crisp Cake

(Recipe contains approximately 11% fat)

1/3 c. oatmeal
3 T. brown sugar
1 T. flour
1 T. tub margarine, melted
1/3 c. unsweetened apple juice
   concentrate, thawed

4 c. Granny Smith apples,
   peeled, cored & sliced
1/2 tsp. cinnamon
1/4 tsp. cardamom

In a small bowl, blend oatmeal, sugar and flour. Cut in margarine. Add 1 tablespoon apple juice concentrate, tossing with fork to blend. Set aside. In a second bowl, put sliced apples, cinnamon and cardamom. Blend well. Add remaining apple juice concentrate, blending well. Pour into an 8-inch square baking dish, that has been sprayed with cooking spray. Sprinkle with oatmeal mixture. Bake in 400° preheated oven for 25 to 30 minutes.
Yield: 6 servings

Approximate Per Serving:
Calories: 153
Fat: 1.9 g
Cholesterol: 0.0 mg

Carbohydrates: 34.7 g
Protein: 1.2 g
Sodium: 26 mg

Exchanges: 1 bread; 2 fruit

After a cake comes from the oven, it should be placed on a rack for about 5 minutes. Then the sides should be loosened and the cake turned out onto rack to finish cooling.

Basic Low-Sugar Cake

(Recipe contains approximately 20% fat)

1/4 c. tub margarine	1/2 tsp. salt
1/4 c. sugar	1 T. baking powder
1/4 c. unsweetened applesauce	1/3 c. nonfat dry milk granules
1 tsp. vanilla extract	1 c. apple juice concentrate,
1 tsp. almond extract (or use	thawed
vanilla for almond)	6 egg whites
2 c. flour, whole wheat blend	
or enriched all-purpose	

In a large mixing bowl, beat margarine until fluffy. Add sugar and beat until well blended and smooth. Add applesauce, vanilla and almond extracts. Blend. Combine flour, salt, baking powder and milk granules. Beginning with flour mixture, add to sugar mixture alternately with apple juice concentrate—ending with flour mixture. Beat egg whites until stiff and, with a metal spoon, very gently fold into batter. Divide batter between two 8-inch cake pans or a 9x13-inch cake pan, sprayed with cooking spray. Bake in a 350° preheated oven for 30 to 35 minutes, or until cake is done and springs back when pressed lightly with fingers. Leave in cake pan 10 minutes before removing from pan. Use desired topping.
Yield: 10 servings

Approximate Per Serving:

Calories: 221	**Carbohydrates: 38.0 g**
Fat: 5.0 g	**Protein: 5.0 g**
Cholesterol: Trace	**Sodium: 254 mg**

Exchanges: 1 bread; 1 milk; 1 fruit; 1 fat

Cakes should not be frosted until thoroughly cooled.

Filled Chocolate Cake

(Recipe contains approximately 18% fat)

1 Basic Low-Sugar Cake (see index)	1/4 c. cocoa 2 T. sugar

FILLING:

1 (8 oz.) ctn. "free" no-fat cream cheese	1/4 c. sugar
2 T. tub margarine	2 T. cornstarch
2 T. skim milk	Egg substitute to = 1 egg
	1/2 tsp. vanilla

To dry ingredients of Basic Low-Sugar Cake, add cocoa and sugar. Prepare according to recipe directions. Spray a 9x13-inch baking dish with cooking spray and put half of batter in baking dish. With electric mixer, blend topping ingredients until smooth. Pour evenly over batter. Top with remaining batter. Bake in 350° preheated oven for 45 to 55 minutes, or until done.
Yield: 16 servings

Approximate Per Serving:
Calories: 175   **Carbohydrates: 29.9 g**
Fat: 3.5 g   **Protein: 5.9 g**
Cholesterol: 2.6 g   **Sodium: 248 mg**

Exchanges: 1 bread; 1/2 milk; 1/2 fruit; 1 fat

Roll fruits and raisins in flour before adding them to the cake batter so they will stay distributed throughout the cake.

Low-Sugar
Cinnamon-Apple Cake
(Recipe contains approximately 15% fat)

4 c. peeled, cored & diced
  apples
1 c. cold water
1 c. apple juice concentrate,
  unsweetened
2 tsp. vanilla
1 c. whole wheat blend or
  enriched all-purpose flour

1/4 c. sugar
2 tsp. baking powder
1/2 tsp. salt
1/3 c. diet margarine
1/2 c. skim milk
Egg substitute to = 1 egg

Put apples in a 9x13-inch baking dish, that has been sprayed with cooking spray; spreading out evenly. Blend water, apple juice concentrate and vanilla. Pour over apples. Blend flour, sugar, baking powder, salt and margarine until crumbly. Stir in milk and egg substitute. Drop by tablespoonfuls over apples. Bake in 350° preheated oven 35 to 40 minutes, or until brown and done. Cool.
Yield: 12 servings

Approximate Per Serving:
Calories: 176
Fat: 3.0 g
Cholesterol: 0.8 mg

Carbohydrates: 29.8 g
Protein: 3.2 g
Sodium: 207 mg

Exchanges: 1 bread; 1 fruit; 1/4 milk; 1 fat

When adding dry and wet ingredients, such as flour and milk, begin and end with the dry ingredients, beating well after each addition for a smoother batter.

Self-Filled Cupcakes

(Recipe contains approximately 12% fat—19% sugar-free)

2 pkg. Estee chocolate cake mix, or 1 Betty Crocker SuperMoist chocolate cake mix	1 (8 oz.) ctn. "free" no-fat cream cheese 1/3 c. sugar Dash of salt

Prepare cake mix per chart in book. Line cupcake tins—16 for sugar-free—24 for Betty Crocker mix—and fill 2/3-full. Blend cream cheese and sugar. Add egg substitute and dash of salt. Drop by rounded tablespoonfuls, using a little extra in the sugar-free cupcakes. Bake according to package directions for cupcakes. Cool on rack.

Yield: 16 sugar-free or 24 low-fat cupcakes

Approximate Per Cupcake: (Sugar-Free)
Calories: 139   **Carbohydrates: 25.5 g**
Fat: 3.0 g   **Protein: 3.0 g**
Cholesterol: 2.5 mg   **Sodium: 220 mg**

Exchanges: 1 bread; 1 milk

Approximate Per Cupcake: (Low-Fat)
Calories: 109   **Carbohydrates: 27.0 mg**
Fat: 1.5 g   **Protein: 2.8 g**
Cholesterol: 1.7 mg   **Sodium: 242 mg**

Exchanges: 1 bread; 1/2 milk

Note: As you can see, the sugar-free cupcakes are not low in calories. This is often true of sugar-free mixes. They are not necessarily low in calories.

If eggs are not beaten well or ingredients not thoroughly mixed, a coarse-grained cake will result.

Chocolate Shortcake
with Strawberries
(Recipe contains approximately 6% fat SF; 5% fat regular)

2 c. whole wheat blend, or
   enriched all-purpose flour
1/2 c. unsweetened cocoa
1 tsp. cinnamon
1/3 c. sugar
2 tsp. baking powder
1/2 tsp. baking soda
1/2 tsp. salt
1/4 c. unsweetened applesauce

1 (8 oz.) ctn. plain low-fat
   yogurt
1 tsp. coffee granules
1 T. boiling water
Egg substitute to = 1 egg
4 1/2 c. sliced strawberries
Artificial sweetener to =
   1/2 c. sugar
1 to 2 drops red food coloring

In a mixing bowl, put flour, cocoa, cinnamon, sugar, baking powder, baking soda and salt. Stir in applesauce yogurt and egg substitute, stirring just until moist. Blend coffee granules and boiling water and stir into dough. Turn out onto a lightly-floured surface and knead 6 or 7 times. Press into a 9x9-inch pan, that has been sprayed with cooking spray. Bake in 450° preheated oven for 10 minutes. Cool on rack. Cut into 9 servings. Put sliced strawberries in mixing bowl and mash slightly. Add sweetener or sugar. Add food coloring. Refrigerate until ready to serve. Serve over shortcake.
Yield: 9 servings

Approximate Per Serving: (Sugar-Free)
Calories: 204
Fat: 1.4 g
Cholesterol: 4.4 g
Carbohydrates: 37.9 g
Protein: 7.9 g
Sodium: 232 mg

Exchanges: 2 bread; 1 fruit; 1/2 fat

Approximate Per Serving: (With Sugar in Strawberries)
Calories: 235
Fat: 1.4 g
Cholesterol: 4.4 mg
Carbohydrates: 49.0 g
Protein: 7.9 g
Sodium: 231 mg

Exchanges: 2 bread; 1 fruit; 1 fat

Cake Mixes

I have experimented with cake mixes because I know that every-one likes to whip up a quick cake at times. I tested Estee and Sweet and Low Sugar-Free Cakes, Lovin' Light and Betty Crocker Light cakes and I converted some of the Betty Crocker SuperMoist Cakes. I did not have time to test and calculate breakdowns for all brands so I chose a brand I knew would be available to everyone. This does not mean that it is the best cake brand going and is not an endorse-ment for this brand.

General Instructions for Cake Mixes:

When using a cake mix, substitute unsweetened applesauce for the oil called for on the box. For the eggs called for, substitute 1/4 cup egg substitute for each egg or 2 egg whites for each egg. Add 1/4 teaspoon baking soda when substituting for eggs. If a mix calls for chocolate, use cocoa. With these exceptions, follow package directions.

Estee Devils Food   Serves 8
(Approximate 25% fat)

Approximately Per Serving:

Follow General	**Calories**	110	**Carbohydrates**	21.0 g
Instructions	**Fat**	3.0 g	**Protein**	1.0 g
	Cholesterol	0.0 mg	**Sodium**	135 mg

Exchange: 1 1/2 bread

Estee White Cake   Serves 8
(Approximate 23% fat)

Approximately Per Serving:

Follow General	**Calories**	120	**Carbohydrates**	23.0 g
Instructions	**Fat**	3.0 g	**Protein**	0.0 g
	Cholesterol	0.0 mg	**Sodium**	80 mg

Exchanges: 1 1/2 bread; 1/4 milk

Sweet and Low Chocolate   Serves 6
(Approximate 18% fat)

Approximately Per Serving:

Follow General	**Calories**	150	**Carbohydrates**	30.0 g
Instructions	**Fat**	3.0 g	**Protein**	2.0 g
	Cholesterol	0.0 mg	**Sodium**	30 mg

Exchanges: 1 1/2 bread; 1/2 milk

Sweet and Low White   Serves 6
(Approximate 18% fat)

Approximately Per Serving:

Follow General Instructions				
Calories	150	Carbohydrates	30.0 g
Fat	3.0 g	Protein	2.0 g
Cholesterol	0.0 mg	Sodium	30 mg

Exchanges: 1 1/2 bread; 1/2 milk

Low Fat Cake Mixes

Lovin' Lites Devils Food   Serves 12
(Approximate 20% fat)

Approximately Per Serving:

Follow General Instructions				
Calories	190	Carbohydrates	34.1 g
Fat	4.2 g	Protein	3.0 g
Cholesterol	0.0 mg	Sodium	358 mg

Exchanges: 2 bread; 1/2 milk

❖

Lovin' Lites White Cake   Serves 12
(Approximate 20% fat)

Approximately Per Serving:

Follow General Instructions				
Calories	190	Carbohydrates	35.5 g
Fat	4.3 g	Protein	3.0 g
Cholesterol	0.0 mg	Sodium	303 mg

Exchanges: 2 bread; 1/2 milk

❖

Lovin' Lites Yellow   Serves 8
(Approximate 21% fat)

Approximately Per Serving:

Follow General Instructions				
Calories	188	Carbohydrates	35.1 g
Fat	4.4 g	Protein	3.9 g
Cholesterol	0.0 mg	Sodium	305 mg

Exchanges: 2 bread; 1/2 milk

❖

Betty Crocker SuperMoist Light Devils Food
(Approximate 15% fat)   Serves 12
                          Approximately Per Serving:

Follow General	Calories	180	Carbohydrates	36.0 g
Instructions	Fat	3.0 g	Protein	3.0 g
	Cholesterol	0.0 mg	Sodium	370 mg

Exchanges: 2 bread; 1/2 milk

Betty Crocker SuperMoist Light White Cake
(Approximate 15% fat)   Serves 12
                          Approximately Per Serving:

Follow General	Calories	180	Carbohydrates	37.0 g
Instructions	Fat	3.0 g	Protein	2.0 g
	Cholesterol	0.0 mg	Sodium	330 mg

Exchanges: 2 bread; 1/2 milk

Betty Crocker SuperMoist Light Yellow Cake
(Approximate 12% fat)   Serves 10
                          Approximately Per Serving:

Follow General	Calories	230	Carbohydrates	43.0 g
Instructions	Fat	3.0 g	Protein	2.0 g
	Cholesterol	0.0 mg	Sodium	330 mg

Exchanges: 2 bread; 1/2 milk; 1 fat

Betty Crocker SuperMoist Cake Mixes
Converted To Low-Fat

Carrot Cake   Serves 12
(Approximate 15% fat)
                          Approximately Per Serving:

Follow General	Calories	214	Carbohydrates	37.4 g
Instructions	Fat	3.6 g	Protein	2.6 g
	Cholesterol	0.0 mg	Sodium	163 mg

Exchanges: 1 1/2 bread; 1 milk; 1/2 fat

❖

Chocolate Cake   Serves 12
(Approximate 21% fat)

Approximately Per Serving:

To a yellow	**Calories**	204	**Carbohydrates**	36.1 g
cake mix add	**Fat**	4.7 g	**Protein**	3.2 g
1/3 c. cocoa	**Cholesterol**	0.0 mg	**Sodium**	304 mg

Follow General Instructions

Exchanges: 1 1/2 bread; 1 milk; 1/2 fat

❖

French Vanilla Cake   Serves 12
(Approximate 20% fat)

Approximately Per Serving:

Follow General	**Calories**	197	**Carbohydrates**	35.7 g
Instructions	**Fat**	4.3 g	**Protein**	2.8 g
	Cholesterol	0.0 mg	**Sodium**	303 mg

Exchanges: 1 1/2 bread; 1 milk

❖

Lemon Cake   Serves 12
(Approximate 15% fat)

Approximately Per Serving:

Follow General	**Calories**	214	**Carbohydrates**	36.4 g
Instructions	**Fat**	3.6 g	**Protein**	2.6 g
	Cholesterol	0.0 mg	**Sodium**	266 mg

Exchanges: 1 1/2 bread; 1 milk; 1/2 fat

❖

Party Cake   Serves 12
(Approximate 17% fat)

Approximately Per Serving:

Follow General	**Calories**	197	**Carbohydrates**	35.7 g
Instructions	**Fat**	3.8 g	**Protein**	2.8 g
	Cholesterol	0.0 mg	**Sodium**	273 mg

Exchanges: 1 1/2 bread; 1 milk

❖

White Cake   Serves 12
(Approximate 19% fat)

Approximately Per Serving:

Follow General	**Calories**	186	**Carbohydrates**	34.7 g
Instructions	**Fat**	4.0 g	**Protein**	2.8 g
	Cholesterol	0.0 mg	**Sodium**	303 mg

Exchanges: 1 1/2 bread; 3/4 milk; 1/2 fat

❖

Yellow Cake   Serves 12
(Approximate 20% fat)

Approximately Per Serving:

Follow General	**Calories**	197	**Carbohydrates**	34.7 g
Instructions	**Fat**	4.3 g	**Protein**	2.8 g
	Cholesterol	0.0 mg	**Sodium**	303 mg

Exchanges: 1 1/2 bread; 1 milk

Jiffy Cake Mixes Converted to Low-Fat

Devils Food Cake   Serves 10
(Approximate 17% fat)

Approximately Per Serving:

Follow General	**Calories**	109	**Carbohydrates**	20.7 g
Instructions	**Fat**	2.1 g	**Protein**	1.3 g
	Cholesterol	0.0 mg	**Sodium**	205 mg

Exchanges: 1 1/2 bread

❖

White Cake   Serves 10
(Approximate 17% fat)

Approximately Per Serving:

Follow General	**Calories**	103	**Carbohydrates**	20.1 g
Instructions	**Fat**	2.0 g	**Protein**	1.6 g
	Cholesterol	0.0 mg	**Sodium**	180 mg

Exchanges: 1 1/2 bread

❖

Yellow Cake   Serves 10
(Approximate 18% fat)

Approximately Per Serving:

Follow General	**Calories**	106	**Carbohydrates**	20.0 g
Instructions	**Fat**	2.1 g	**Protein**	1.3 g
	Cholesterol	0.0 mg	**Sodium**	175 mg

Exchanges: 1 1/2 bread

Angel Food Cake Mixes

Betty Crocker Angel Food Cake
(0% fat)   Serves 12

Approximately Per Serving:

Follow Package	**Calories**	140	**Carbohydrates**	32.0 g
Directions	**Fat**	0.0 g	**Protein**	3.0 g
	Cholesterol	0.0 mg	**Sodium**	280 mg

Exchanges: 2 bread

❖

Pillsbury Angel Food Cake   Serves 12
(0% fat)

Approximately Per Serving:

Follow Package	**Calories**	150	**Carbohydrates**	34.0 g
Directions	**Fat**	0.0g	**Protein**	3.0 g
	Cholesterol	0.0 mg	**Sodium**	360 mg

Exchanges: 2 breads

Cake Toppings

Lemon Sauce
(Recipe contains no fat)

1 T. cornstarch
Artificial sweetener to =
   1/3 c. sugar

1 c. boiling water
3 T. lemon juice
1 T. grated lemon rind

If using sugar, mix with cornstarch in small saucepan. If using sweetener, wait and add at end. Add boiling water, whisking until smooth. Cook over medium heat until thick and clear. Add lemon juice and lemon rind. If using sweetener, add at this time. Serve warm, over cake or bread pudding.
Yield: 6 servings

Approximate Per Serving:
Calories: 13
Fat: 0.0 g
Cholesterol: 0.0 mg

Carbohydrates: 2.0 g
Protein: 0.0 g
Sodium: 32 mg

Exchanges: 1 Serving a Free Food

Mandarin Orange Topping
(Recipe contains approximately 1% fat)

1 (3 oz.) pkg. sugar-free instant
   vanilla pudding
2 c. skim milk

1 lg. can quality mandarin
   oranges, drained

Put pudding mix in bowl and add milk. Beat with electric mixer until thick. Stir in oranges. Top cake and chill.
Yield: 8 servings

Approximate Per Serving:
Calories: 67
Fat: 0.1 g
Cholesterol: 1.0 mg

Carbohydrates: 10.0 g
Protein: 2.1 g
Sodium: 34 mg

Exchanges: 1/2 milk; 1/2 fruit

Orange Sauce—Sugar-Free
(Recipe contains approximately 1% fat)

2 T. cornstarch
1/8 tsp. salt
1/4 c. orange juice concentrate, thawed

Artificial sweetener of choice
to = 1/4 c. sugar
1 (11 oz.) can mandarin oranges, drained

In a small saucepan, put cornstarch and salt. Dissolve orange juice concentrate in water and gradually add to cornstarch mixture, stirring until mixture is smooth. Cook over medium heat until mixture has thickened and is transparent. Simmer an additional 2 minutes. Remove from stove and stir in sweetener or sugar. Fold in mandarin oranges. Serve over cake when warm, or over sugar-free frozen yogurt, at room temperature.
Yield: 8 servings

Approximate Per Serving:
Calories: 65
Fat: 0.1 g
Cholesterol: 0.0 mg

Carbohydrates: 9.0 g
Protein: Trace
Sodium: 36 mg

Exchanges: 1 1/2 fruit

Rum Sauce
(Recipe contains approximately 2% fat)

2 T. brown sugar
4 tsp. cornstarch
1 c. skim milk

1/4 T. dark rum or 1/2 tsp. rum extract

In a saucepan, put brown sugar and cornstarch. Slowly whisk in milk, whisking until smooth. Add rum. Cook over medium heat until mixture thickens, stirring constantly. DO NOT BOIL. Serve over cake or bread pudding.
Yield: 6 servings

Approximate Per Serving:
Calories: 40
Fat: 0.1 g
Cholesterol: 0.5 mg

Carbohydrates: 6.0 g
Protein: 1.4 g
Sodium: 18 mg

Exchanges: 1/2 milk

Cream Cheese Vanilla Frosting— Sugar-Free

(Recipe contains approximately 14% fat)

1 (8 oz.) ctn. "free" no-fat
  cream cheese
1 c. "light" Cool Whip

1 pkg. vanilla sugar-free
  instant pudding

Yield: 1 cake (12 servings)

Approximate Per Serving:
Calories: 46
Fat: 0.7 g
Cholesterol: 3.3 mg

Carbohydrates: 2.0 g
Protein: 2.8 g
Sodium: 113 mg

Exchanges: 1/2 milk

CREAM CHEESE CHOCOLATE FROSTING—SUGAR-FREE:
Same as above, except use sugar-free instant chocolate pudding.

CREAM CHEESE PISTACHIO FROSTING—SUGAR-FREE:
Same as above, except use sugar-free pistachio pudding.

CREAM CHEESE BUTTERSCOTCH FROSTING—SUGAR-FREE:
Same as above, except use sugar-free instant butterscotch pudding.

CREAM CHEESE BANANA FROSTING—SUGAR-FREE:
Same as above, except use sugar-free instant banana pudding.

*To keep icings moist and to prevent cracking,
add a pinch of baking soda to the icings.*

Vanilla Fluff Frosting

(Recipe contains approximately 22% fat)

2 c. "light" Cool Whip
  whipped topping

1 pkg. sugar-free instant
  vanilla pudding

Put Cool Whip in bowl and add pudding. Beat with electric beater on medium speed until blended and smooth. Frost cake.
Yield: 12 servings (frost a 9x13-inch cake or 1 layer cake)

BANANA FLUFF FROSTING:
Same, only use banana instant pudding.

BUTTERSCOTCH FLUFF FROSTING:
Same, only use butterscotch instant pudding.

CHOCOLATE FLUFF FROSTING:
Same, only use chocolate instant pudding.

PISTACHIO FLUFF FROSTING:
Same, only use pistachio instant pudding.

Approximate Per Serving:
Calories: 57
Fat: 1.4 g
Cholesterol: 0.7 mg

Carbohydrates: 4.7 g
Protein: 1.3 g
Sodium: 21 mg

Exchanges: 3/4 milk

*For an interesting flavor, add a melted chocolate
mint to chocolate cake batter.*

Cheesecakes

Low-Sugar Lemon Cheesecake

(Recipe contains approximately 5% fat)

1 graham cracker crust
  (see index)
3 (3 oz.) pkg. lemon gelatin
1 c. boiling water
2 c. cold water

2 (8 oz.) pkg. "free" no-fat
  cream cheese
Artificial sweetener of choice
  to = 1 1/2 c. sugar
2/3 c. lemon juice
2 pkg. Dream Whip, prepared

Dissolve gelatin in boiling water. Add cold water and chill until slightly thickened. Beat cream cheese and sweetener (or sugar) until smooth. Add lemon juice and blend. Blend prepared Dream Whip in with cream cheese mixture. Add gelatin and blend well. Pour into crust. Chill at least 3 hours.
Yield: 8 servings

Approximate Per Serving:
Calories: 188
Fat: 1.0 g
Cholesterol: 10 mg

Carbohydrates: 17.7 g
Protein: 12 g
Sodium: 367 mg

Exchanges: 2 milk; 1/2 fat

To keep chocolate cakes brown on the outside, dust the greased pan with cocoa instead of flour.

Mini Cheesecakes

(Recipe contains approximately 10% fat)

12 vanilla wafers	Egg substitute to = 2 eggs
2 (8 oz.) ctn. "free" no-fat	1 tsp. vanilla
cream cheese	4 T. all-fruit jam or jelly
1/4 c. sugar	

Line 12 mini muffin tins with foil liners and place 1 vanilla water in each liner. Blend cream cheese and sugar with electric mixer, at medium speed, until smooth. Add egg substitute, 1/4 cup at a time, blending after each addition. Add vanilla and blend. Pour mixture over wafers, filling 2/3-full. Bake in 325° preheated oven for 25 minutes. Remove from pans and cool on rack. Before serving, add 1 teaspoon all-fruit jam or jelly to the top of each cheesecake.
Yield: 12 cheesecakes

Approximate Per Cheesecake:

Calories: 97	Carbohydrates: 12.4 g
Fat: 1.1 g	Protein: 6.0 g
Cholesterol: 6.7 mg	Sodium: 251 mg

Exchanges: 1/4 bread; 1 milk

If baking in glass dishes, decrease the oven temperature
25° to prevent overbrowning.

Pie Crusts

Graham Cracker Pie Crust
(Recipe contains approximately 19% fat)

1 1/2 c. graham cracker
   crumbs
1/4 tsp. cinnamon

8-second spray of cooking
   spray

Spray a 9-inch pie plate with cooking spray (2-second spray). Put crumbs in a bowl and add cinnamon. Blend well. Tossing with a fork, spray crumbs for 6 seconds. Press crumbs into pie plate and put in freezer for about 1 hour, or until firm. Fill as desired.
Yield: 8 servings

Approximate Per Serving:
Calories: 72
Fat: 1.5 g
Cholesterol: 0.0 mg

Carbohydrates: 12.4 g
Protein: 1.1 g
Sodium: 12 mg

Exchanges: 1 bread

A pie crust will be easier to make if all ingredients are cool.

Margarine Pie Crust

(Recipe contains approximately 42% fat)

1 c. flour	**1/3 c. tub margarine**
1/2 tsp. salt	**2 to 3 T. water**

Put flour and salt in a mixing bowl and blend. Cut in margarine with pastry blender or two knives, until the consistency of coarse meal. Sprinkle with water as you toss with fork, until dough is moist enough to form a ball. Form dough into ball and wrap with wax paper. Chill 15 minutes. Roll out between 2 pieces of lightly-floured wax paper, to 1/4-inch thickness. Put in 9-inch pie plate and flute edges. Prick dough with fork on bottom and sides. Bake in 425° preheated oven for 12 to 15 minutes.
Yield: 8 servings

Approximate Per Serving:
Calories: 104   **Carbohydrates: 11.9 g**
Fat: 4.8 g   **Protein: 1.6 g**
Cholesterol: 0.0 mg   **Sodium: 224 mg**

Exchanges: 1 bread; 1 fat

A teaspoon of vinegar added to pie dough helps make a flaky crust.

Oil Pie Crust

(Recipe contains approximately 54% fat)

1 c. whole wheat blend, or
    enriched all-purpose flour
1/2 tsp. salt

1/4 c. canola oil
2 T. cold water

Put flour and salt in mixing bowl and stir with whisk to blend. Drizzle oil over mixture while tossing with fork. Continue tossing with fork and drizzle water over mixture. Shape dough into a ball and wrap with wax paper. Chill 15 minutes. Roll dough between 2 pieces of wax paper to 1/4-inch thickness. Put in pie plate, flute edges. If baking for 1-crust pie, prick with fork on bottom and sides of crust. Bake in 450° preheated oven 10 to 12 minutes.
Yield: 8 servings

Approximate Per Serving:
Calories: 119
Fat: 7.2 g
Cholesterol: 0.0 mg

Carbohydrates: 11.9 g
Protein: 1.6 g
Sodium: 134 mg

Exchanges: 1 bread; 1 fat

Meringue Pie Topping

(Recipe contains no fat)

3 egg whites
1/4 tsp. cream of tartar

1/2 tsp. vanilla extract
1/3 c. sugar

Put egg whites and cream of tartar in a bowl and beat at high speed until soft peaks form. Gradually add sugar, beating after each addition. Add vanilla and beat until stiff and glossy. Spread on top of pie, seal edges, and brown.
Yield: 8 servings

Approximate Per Serving:
Calories: 38
Fat: 0.0 g
Cholesterol: 0.0 mg

Carbohydrates: 8.2 g
Protein: 1.1 g
Sodium: 19 mg

Exchanges: 1 fruit

Cream Pies

Banana Cream Pie

(Recipe contains approximately 11% fat)

2 sm. pkg. sugar-free banana
   instant pudding
2 c. skim milk
1 banana, sliced

1 c. "light" Cool Whip
1 graham cracker pie crust
   (see index)

Put 1 package pudding mix in bowl and add skim milk. Beat with electric mixer until thick. Put sliced bananas in prepared pie crust and top with pudding. In a mixing bowl, put 1 package pudding mix and add Cool Whip. Beat with an electric mixer until smooth. Pour over pudding. Chill several hours.
Yield: 8 servings

Approximate Per Serving:
Calories: 189
Fat: 2.4 g
Cholesterol: 2.0 mg

Carbohydrates: 40.9 g
Protein: 17.3 g
Sodium: 265 mg

Exchanges: 1 bread; 1 milk; 1/2 fruit; 1/2 fat

In making custard-type pies, bake at a high temperature for about 10 minutes to prevent soggy crust. Then finish baking at a low temperature.

Chocolate Mint Ribbon Pie

(Recipe contains approximately 27% fat)

1 margarine pie crust, baked
1 sm. pkg. sugar-free instant
   chocolate pudding
1 sm. pkg. sugar-free instant
   vanilla pudding
2 c. skim milk
1 (8 oz.) pkg. "free" no-fat
   cream cheese
1 c. "light" Cool Whip
1/2 tsp. mint flavoring
1 to 2 drops green food coloring

Put chocolate pudding and milk in a bowl and beat until thick. Chill in refrigerator until ready to use. Put remaining ingredients in mixing bowl and beat until thick and smooth. Put 1/2 chocolate pudding in pie crust and top with 1/2 cheese mixture. Repeat layers and chill several hours before serving.
Yield: 8 servings

Approximate Per Serving:
Calories: 194
Fat: 5.9 g
Cholesterol: 6.0 mg
Carbohydrates: 17.9 g
Protein: 7.6 g
Sodium: 425 mg

Exchanges: 1 bread; 1 milk; 1 fat

*To prevent crust from becoming soggy with cream pie,
sprinkle crust with powdered sugar.*

Deluxe Neapolitan Pie

(Recipe contains approximately 27% fat)

1 oil pie crust, baked
1 pkg. chocolate sugar-free
  instant pudding
1 pkg. vanilla sugar-free
  instant pudding

3 1/2 c. skim milk
1 1/2 c. all-fruit raspberry
  jam
1 c. "light" Cool Whip

Prepare crust and cool. Put chocolate pudding in bowl with 2 cups milk. Beat until thick. Pour into pie shell. Put vanilla pudding and 1 1/2 cups milk in a bowl and beat until thick. Add raspberry jam and blend. Pour over chocolate pudding. Top with Cool Whip. Chill.
Yield: 8 servings

Approximate Per Serving:
Calories: 280
Fat: 8.4 g
Cholesterol: 2 mg

Carbohydrates: 32.1 g
Protein: 5.1 g
Sodium: 195 mg

Exchanges: 1 bread; 2 milk; 1 fat

Easy Cheesecake Pie

(Recipe contains approximately 15% fat)

1 graham cracker crust
  (see index)
2 c. "light" Cool Whip
1 sm. pkg. vanilla sugar-free
  instant pudding

2 (8 oz.) pkg. "free" no-fat
  cream cheese
1/2 c. all-fruit strawberry jam
  (or flavor of choice)

Prepare crust and put in freezer. Put Cool Whip in mixing bowl and add pudding mix. Beat with electric mixer until smooth. Add cream cheese and beat until smooth. Pour into prepared pie crust. Spread jam over top. Chill.
Yield: 8 servings

Approximate Per Serving:
Calories: 219
Fat: 3.6 g
Cholesterol: 10 mg

Carbohydrates: 31.4 g
Protein: 9.1 g
Sodium: 358 mg

Exchanges: 1 bread; 2 milk

Mandarin Orange Cream Pie

(Recipe contains approximately 24% fat)

1 sm. pkg. sugar-free instant
    vanilla pudding
2 c. skim milk
2 (11 oz.) cans mandarin
    oranges, drained

1 c. "light" Cool Whip
1 c. low-fat cottage cheese
1 pkg. sugar free orange
    gelatin
1 margarine pie crust, baked

Put pudding mix and milk in bowl and beat until thick. Add oranges. Blend and pour into prepared pie crust. Put Cool Whip and cottage cheese in a bowl and blend with whisk. Add gelatin and blend. Pour over pudding layer. Chill.
Yield: 8 servings

Approximate Per Serving:
Calories: 241
Fat: 6.5 g
Cholesterol: 3.4 mg

Carbohydrates: 31.9 g
Protein: 8.8 g
Sodium: 379 mg

Exchanges: 1 bread; 1 milk; 1 fruit; 1 fat

Strawberry Cream Pie

(Recipe contains approximately 17% fat)

1 c. graham cracker crust,
    prepared (see index)
1 sm. pkg. vanilla sugar-free
    instant pudding

2 c. skim milk
2 c. sliced fresh strawberries
1 c. "light" Cool Whip

Put pudding mix and milk in a bowl and beat until thick. Pour 1/2 of pudding into pie crust and top with 1 cup sliced strawberries. Add remaining pudding and top with remaining strawberries. Spread Cool Whip over top and chill.
Yield: 8 servings

Approximate Per Serving:
Calories: 151
Fat: 2.8 g
Cholesterol: 1.0 mg

Carbohydrates: 20.5 g
Protein: 3.4 g
Sodium: 44 mg

Exchanges: 1/2 bread; 1 milk; 1 fruit

Fresh Fruit Pies

Bing Cherry Cream Pie
(Recipe contains approximately 5% fat—7% sugar-free)

1 graham cracker crust
  (see index)
1 c. finely-chopped bing
  cherries
3 c. halved bing cherries
Artificial sweetener of choice
  to = 1 c. sugar (I use 24 pkt.
  Equal)

3 T. cornstarch
1/2 c. water
1 pkg. sugar-free (or regular)
  instant vanilla pudding
2 c. skim milk

Put chopped cherries, cornstarch, water and sugar (if using) in saucepan and blend well. Do not add sweetener now. Cook over medium heat, stirring constantly, until mixture thickens. Remove from stove. Cool 5 minutes and add sweetener, if using. Cool to room temperature and stir in cherries. Pour into crust. Prepare pudding for pie and pour over top. Refrigerate for several hours before serving.
Yield: 8 servings

Approximate Per Serving: (Sugar-Free)
Calories: 244
Fat: 1.9 g
Cholesterol: 1.0 mg

Carbohydrates: 44.4 g
Protein: 4.3 g
Sodium: 45 mg

Exchanges: 2 bread; 1/4 milk; 1 fruit; 1 fat

Approximate Per Serving: (With Sugar and Regular Pudding)
Calories: 349
Fat: 1.9 g
Cholesterol: 1.0 mg

Carbohydrates: 81.2 g
Protein: 4.4 g
Sodium: 148 mg

Exchanges: 2 bread; 1 1/2 milk; 1 fruit; 1 fat

Fresh Peach Pie

(Recipe contains approximately 8% fat—12% sugar-free)

1 graham cracker pie crust
(see index)
1 c. peeled & mashed fresh
peaches
3 c. peeled & sliced peaches

Sweetener of choice to = 1 c.
sugar (I use 24 pkt. Equal)
3 T. cornstarch
1/2 c. water
2 c. "light" Cool Whip

In a saucepan, blend mashed peaches with cornstarch, water, and sugar, if using. Do not add sweetener at this time. Blend well and cook over medium heat, stirring constantly, until mixture thickens. Remove from stove. Cool 10 minutes, then stir in sweetener, if using. Cover and allow mixture to cool to room temperature. Add sliced peaches. Pour into prepared pie crust. Top with Cool Whip and chill several hours before serving.
Yield: 8 servings

Approximate Per Serving: (Sugar-Free)
Calories: 174
Fat: 2.3 g
Cholesterol: 0.0 mg

Carbohydrates: 29.0 g
Protein: 2.1 g
Sodium: 134 mg

Exchanges: 2 bread; 1 fruit

Approximate Per Serving: (With Sugar)
Calories: 259
Fat: 2.3 g
Cholesterol: 0.0 mg

Carbohydrates: 53.9 g
Protein: 2.1 g
Sodium: 134 mg

Exchanges: 2 bread; 1 1/2 fruit; 1 fat

*Folding the top crust over the lower crust before
crimping will keep the juices in the pie.*

Fresh Strawberry Pie

(Recipe contains approximately 12% fat—18% sugar-free)

1 graham cracker pie crust
   (see index)
1 c. mashed fresh strawberries
3 c. sliced fresh strawberries
Artificial sweetener of choice
   to = 1 c. sugar (I use 24 pkt.
   Equal)

3 T. cornstarch
1/2 c. water
1 c. "light" Cool Whip
   whipped topping

In a saucepan, put mashed berries, cornstarch, water, and sugar, if using. Do not add sweetener at this time. Put on stove over medium heat and cook, stirring constantly, until mixture thickens. Remove from stove and cool 10 minutes. Add artificial sweetener, if using. Cover and cool to room temperature. Stir in sliced strawberries. Pour into pie crust and top with dollops of Cool Whip. Chill several hours before serving.
Yield: 8 servings

Approximate Per Serving: (Sugar-Free)
Calories: 142
Fat: 2.9 g
Cholesterol: 0.0 mg

Carbohydrates: 23.3 g
Protein: 1.6 g
Sodium: 13 mg

Exchanges: 1 1/2 bread; 1 fruit

Approximate Per Serving: (With Sugar)
Calories: 226
Fat: 2.9 g
Cholesterol: 0.0 mg

Carbohydrates: 48.1 g
Protein: 1.6 g
Sodium: 13 mg

Exchanges: 2 bread; 1 fruit; 1 fat

If the juice from your apple pie runs over in the oven, shake some salt on it, which causes the juice to burn to a crisp so it can be removed.

Pudding

Layered Banana Pudding
(Recipe contains approximately 17% fat)

8 oz. "free" no-fat cream cheese
2 1/4 c. skim milk
1 sm. pkg. sugar-free instant
   vanilla pudding

24 vanilla wafers
2 bananas, sliced

Combine cream cheese with 1/2 cup milk, blending with electric mixer, at medium speed, until smooth. Add remaining milk and pudding mix and beat at low speed 1 minute. In a 1 1/2-quart serving bowl, put 1/3 of pudding, I sliced banana, and top with 1/2 wafers. Repeat layers and top with pudding. Chill.
Yield: 8 servings

Approximate Per Serving:
Calories: 173
Fat: 3.2 g
Cholesterol: 6.1 mg

Carbohydrates: 19.4 g
Protein: 7.0 g
Sodium: 266 mg

Exchanges: 1 bread; 1 milk; 1/2 fruit

Whipping cream retains its shape if when whipping you add 1/2 to 1 teasooon of light corn syrup per half pint of cream.

Glorified Rice Pudding

(Recipe contains approximately 12% fat)

1/2 c. brown rice
1/2 c. skim milk
Artificial sweetener to =
  1/3 c. sugar

1 c. "light" crushed pineapple, well drained
1 c. "light" Cool Whip

Cook rice per package directions until tender. Add milk and cook over low heat for 15 minutes. Cool. Add sweetener (or sugar) and pineapple. Blend. Cool to room temperature. Fold in Cool Whip.

Yield: 8 servings

Approximate Per Serving:
Calories: 82
Fat: 1.1 g
Cholesterol: 0.3 mg

Carbohydrates: 15.2 g
Protein: 1.3 g
Sodium: 9 mg

Exchanges: 1 bread; 1/2 fruit

Rice Pudding

(Recipe contains approximately 5% fat)

Egg substitute to = 2 eggs
2 c. evaporated skim milk
1/3 c. sugar
1 tsp. vanilla

1 c. cooked brown rice
1/2 c. raisins
1/4 tsp. nutmeg

Blend together all ingredients, except nutmeg. Pour into 1 1/2-quart casserole dish, that has been sprayed with cooking spray. Set in shallow baking dish and set in oven. Pour enough boiling water into shallow dish to make 1-inch water. Bake in 350° preheated oven 55 to 65 minutes, or until an inserted knife comes out clean. Sprinkle with nutmeg. Serve warm or cold.

Yield: 6 servings

Approximate Per Serving:
Calories: 195
Fat: 1.0 g
Cholesterol: 3.0 mg

Carbohydrates: 35.8 g
Protein: 8.6 g
Sodium: 60 mg

Exchanges: 1 bread; 1 milk; 1 fruit; 1/2 fat

Refrigerator Desserts

Low-Cal Jello-Yogurt Dessert
(Recipe contains approximately 20% fat)

2 pkg. sugar-free red gelatin
  (can use any flavor)
2 c. boiling water

2 c. cold water
2 (8 oz.) ctn. plain low-fat
  yogurt

Dissolve gelatin in boiling water. Add cold water. Refrigerate just until gelatin is lightly jiggly. Add yogurt and whip well with an electric mixer. Refrigerate at least 2 hours.
Yield: 8 servings

Approximate Per Serving:
Calories: 44
Fat: 1.0 g
Cholesterol: 3.5 mg

Carbohydrates: 4.0 g
Protein: 5.0 g
Sodium: 48 mg

Exchanges: 1/2 milk

Add confectioners' sugar to whipping cream before beating.
The whipped cream stands up well even if it is not used immediately.

Fresh Peach Trifle

(Recipe contains approximately 19% SF—14% fat regular)

1 Estee white cake mix or
    1 Jiffy white cake mix
1 pkg. sugar-free or regular
    instant vanilla pudding

2 c. skim milk
3 c. peeled & diced fresh
    peaches
1 c. Cool Whip

Prepare cakes per directions on chart in book (see index). Bake in 9-inch cake pan and cool. Cut cake into 1-inch cubes. Divide cubes into thirds and set aside. Prepare pudding with skim milk and set aside. Prepare peaches. In a small, straight-sided, clear bowl, put 1/3 of cake and top with 1/3 of pudding and 1/3 of peaches. Repeat layers twice. Top with Cool Whip and refrigerate several hours before serving.
Yield: 12 servings

Approximate Per Serving: (Sugar-Free)
Calories: 134
Fat: 2.8 g
Cholesterol: 0.7 mg
Carbohydrates: 20.7 g
Protein: 2.3 g
Sodium: 111 mg

Exchanges: 1 bread; 1 fruit; 1/4 milk

Approximate Per Serving: (Regular)
Calories: 154
Fat: 2.4 g
Cholesterol: 0.7 mg
Carbohydrates: 31.4 g
Protein: 2.1 g
Sodium: 304 mg

Exchanges: 1 bread; 1 fruit; 1/2 milk

To make powdered sugar, blend 1 cup granulated sugar and 1 tablespoon cornstarch in the blender at medium speed for 2 minutes.

Frozen Yogurt Dessert

(Recipe contains approximately 11% fat)

2 c. graham cracker crumbs
1/2 gal. vanilla sugar-free
   frozen yogurt
1 c. skim milk

2 sm. pkg. sugar-free instant
   vanilla pudding (can use
   any flavor desired)

Press cracker crumbs in 9x13-inch baking dish that has been sprayed with cooking spray. Put in freezer for 1 hour, or until crust is firm. Put frozen yogurt, milk and pudding mix into a large mixing bowl and beat with electric mixer until smooth. Pour over crumb crust. Cover and freeze. Allow to stand 10 to 15 minutes at room temperature before serving.

Note: This dessert can be cut and wrapped in foil in individual servings to be used as desired.

Yield: 24 servings

Approximate Per Serving:
Calories: 82
Fat 1.0 g
Cholesterol: 1.8 mg

Carbohydrates: 14.0 g
Protein: 1.8 g
Sodium: 31 mg

Exchanges: 1 milk

*Soak peeled apples in cold water to which 1 teaspoon of salt
has been added. They will not discolor.*

Pistachio Dessert
(Recipe contains approximately 12% fat)

1 1/2 c. graham cracker crumbs
6-second spray of cooking
  spray
2 (3 oz.) pkg. sugar-free instant
  pistachio pudding

1 1/2 c. cold milk
1 qt. softened, sugar-free,
  frozen yogurt
1 (8 oz.) ctn. Cool Whip

Put crushed crumbs in a mixing bowl and spray 4 seconds with cooking spray, as you toss crumbs with a fork. Spray a 9x13-inch baking dish with 2-second spray of cooking spray. Press crumbs in bottom of dish and place in the freezer until crust is firm. Blend pudding, milk and frozen yogurt with an electric mixer, at medium speed. Pour over crust. Chill 30 minutes. Spread Cool Whip over top. Chill.
Yield: 16 servings

Approximate Per Serving:
Calories: 116
Fat: 1.5 g
Cholesterol: 2.9 mg

Carbohydrates: 22.7 g
Protein: 5.1 g
Sodium: 99 mg

Exchanges: 1/2 bread; 1 milk

A pinch of salt added to very sour fruits while cooking will greatly reduce the amount of sugar needed.

Cookies

Apple Oatmeal Cookies
(Recipe contains approximately 20% fat)

1 1/2 c. whole wheat blend or enriched all-purpose flour
2 tsp. baking powder
1/2 tsp. salt
1/2 tsp. cinnamon
2 c. old-fashioned oatmeal

1 c. finely-chopped apples
1/4 c. tub margarine
1/4 c. brown sugar
Egg substitute to = 2 eggs
1/4 c. apple juice concentrate, thawed

Blend together flour, baking powder, salt and cinnamon. Stir in oats and apples; set aside. In a large mixing bowl, cream margarine and sugar until fluffy. Add egg substitute, 1/4 cup at a time. Stir into flour mixture alternately with apple juice concentrate. Drop by teaspoon onto a cookie sheet, that has been sprayed with cooking spray. Bake in 375° preheated oven 12 to 15 minutes, or until golden brown. Cool on waxed paper.
Yield: 36 cookies

Approximate Per Serving:
Calories: 60
Fat: 1.3 g
Cholesterol: 0.0 mg

Carbohydrates: 10.6 g
Protein: 1.6 g
Sodium: 49 mg

Exchanges (2 cookies): 1 bread; 1 fat

When using brown sugar in a recipe, always press the brown sugar firmly into the measuring cup.

Low-Sugar Apple-Date Cookies

(Recipe contains approximately 14% fat)

2 T. tub margarine
1/4 c. unsweetened applesauce
1/4 c. firmly-packed brown
    sugar
2 T. honey
Egg substitute to = 1 egg
1 tsp. vanilla extract
1 c. whole wheat blend or
    enriched all-purpose flour

1/4 tsp. salt
1/2 tsp. baking powder
1/2 tsp. cinnamon
1/4 tsp. cardamom (opt.)
3/4 c. old-fashioned oats
1/2 c. grated red Delicious
    apple
1/4 c. chopped dates
Cooking spray

Put margarine in a bowl and add applesauce, brown sugar and honey. Beat with electric mixer to blend well. Add egg substitute and vanilla and blend. Blend flour, salt, baking powder, cinnamon and cardamom; add to applesauce mixture. Stir in oatmeal, apples and dates. Drop by teaspoonful onto baking sheets, that have been sprayed with cooking spray. Bake in 350° preheated oven for 12 to 14 minutes.

Yield: 42 cookies

Approximate Per Serving:
Calories: 33
Fat: 0.5 g
Cholesterol: 0.0 mg

Carbohydrates: 6.0 g
Protein: 0.7 g
Sodium: 22 mg

Exchanges (3 cookies): 1 bread; 1/2 fat

Baked cookies freeze well and can be stored for several months. Pack as airtight as possible. When ready to use, thaw in refrigerator and warm in oven for a few minutes. They will taste fresh-baked.

Low-Sugar Oatmeal Crispies

(Recipe contains approximately 18% fat)

2 T. tub margarine
1/3 c. firmly-packed brown
   sugar
1/4 c. unsweetened applesauce
Egg substitute to = 1 egg
1 tsp. vanilla extract

1/2 c. whole wheat blend or
   enriched all-purpose flour
1/2 c. quick-cooking oatmeal
1/2 tsp. baking powder
3/4 c. crispy rice cereal

Put margarine and brown sugar in a large mixing bowl and cream. Beat in applesauce. Add egg substitute and vanilla and beat. In a small bowl, blend flour, oatmeal and baking powder. Slowly add to creamed mixture, stirring with wooden spoon. Stir in crispy rice cereal. Drop by heaping teaspoonfuls 2 inches apart onto an ungreased baking sheet. Bake in 375° preheated oven 8 to 10 minutes. Cool on racks.
Yield: 32 cookies

Approximate Per Serving:
Calories: 30
Fat: 0.6 g
Cholesterol: 0.0 mg

Carbohydrates: 5.3 g
Protein: 0.6 g
Sodium: 20 mg

Exchanges (3 cookies): 1 bread; 1/2 fat

After melting chocolate over hot water or in microwave --
cool, before adding to batter.

Sugarless Fruit Cookies

(Recipe contains approximately 29% fat)

1 c. whole wheat or enriched
   all-purpose flour
1 c. oatmeal
1 tsp. baking soda
1 tsp. baking powder
1/2 tsp. cinnamon
1/4 tsp. cardamom
1/4 tsp. nutmeg
1/3 c. tub margarine

1/4 c. orange juice concentrate,
   thawed
1/4 c. apple juice concentrate,
   thawed
Egg substitute to = 2 eggs
1 c. raisins
1/2 c. apples, peeled, cored &
   diced
1/2 c. chopped dates

In a large mixing bowl, combine flour, oatmeal, baking soda, baking powder, cinnamon, cardamom and nutmeg. Cut in margarine. Add orange juice concentrate, apple juice concentrate and egg substitute. Stir in raisins, apples and dates. Refrigerate dough 4 hours. Drop by teaspoonfuls onto cookie sheet that has been sprayed with cooking spray. Bake in 350° preheated oven for 10 to 12 minutes. Watch closely, as these burn quickly.
Yield: 48 cookies

Approximate Per Serving:
Calories: 50
Fat: 1.6 g
Cholesterol: 0.0 mg

Carbohydrates: 7.0 g
Protein: 1.0 g
Sodium: 18 mg

Exchanges (2 cookies): 1 bread; 1/2 fruit; 1/4 fat

Heavy, shiny cookie sheets are best for baking. When using lightweight sheets, reduce oven temperature slightly.

Cream Puffs

(Recipe contains approximately 16% fat)

1 c. whole wheat blend or
    enriched all-purpose flour
1/4 tsp. salt
1 c. water
2 T. tub margarine

Egg substitute to = 2 eggs
1 egg white
1 pkg. sugar-free instant
    pudding (flavor of choice)
2 c. skim milk

Combine flour and salt; set aside. Combine water and margarine in a medium saucepan and bring to boil. Turn heat to low and add flour mixture, stirring constantly, until mixture leaves the sides of the pan. Remove from heat and cool 4 minutes. Add egg substitute, 1/4 cup at a time, stirring after each addition until well blended. Add egg white and stir until smooth. Spray a baking sheet with cooking spray and drop dough by teaspoonfuls onto baking sheet. Bake in 400° preheated oven for 25 minutes, or until crisp and nicely browned. Cool on racks. When cool, make slit in side of puff and fill with prepared pudding; or cut off top of puff, clean out, fill and replace top.

Yield: 24 puffs

Approximate Per Serving:
Calories: 63
Fat: 1.1 g
Cholesterol: 0.3 mg

Carbohydrates: 9.0 g
Protein: 46.7 g
Sodium: 95 mg

Exchanges: 1 bread

Notes &
Recipes

Index

A

B

438

440

FROSTING

G

H

I

J

L

M

N

NOODLE-RONI

447

PASTA WITH SAUCE
FROM A JAR

PIE CRUSTS

PIES
CREAM PIES

FRESH FRUIT PIES

PORK

450

452

457

"THE LOW-FAT DOWN HOME COOKBOOK"   ORDER BLANK

NAME_____

ADDRESS _____

CITY & STATE _____ ZIP_____

How many copies?_____ Amount enclosed _____
  Price per book............................ $19.95
  Postage & handling.........................3.00
  Total $22.95
Please make checks payable to:
  STANGL PUBLISHING COMPANY
Mail orders to: Stangl Publishing Company
     808 W. Second St.
     Ottumwa, IA 52501

"THE LOW-FAT DOWN HOME COOKBOOK"   ORDER BLANK

NAME_____

ADDRESS _____

CITY & STATE _____ ZIP_____

How many copies?_____ Amount enclosed _____
  Price per book............................ $19.95
  Postage & handling.........................3.00
  Total $22.95
Please make checks payable to:
  STANGL PUBLISHING COMPANY
Mail orders to: Stangl Publishing Company
     808 W. Second St.
     Ottumwa, IA 52501

"THE LOW-FAT DOWN HOME COOKBOOK"   ORDER BLANK

NAME_____

ADDRESS _____

CITY & STATE _____ ZIP_____

How many copies?_____ Amount enclosed _____
  Price per book............................ $19.95
  Postage & handling.........................3.00
  Total $22.95
Please make checks payable to:
  STANGL PUBLISHING COMPANY
Mail orders to: Stangl Publishing Company
     808 W. Second St.
     Ottumwa, IA 52501